"Kenneth Ngwa's *Let My People Live* is a refreshing academic exercise in reading for liberation. It not only takes African, postcolonial, and liberation biblical hermeneutics to a whole new level of execution but also effortlessly occupies a whole new place in the biblical scholarship: generating new ways of writing, reading, analyzing, seeing, and interpretating. Ngwa thus invites us to a new exodus—a journey to a whole battalion of new ways of reading the narrative of Exodus, a story that has vexed the oppressed, displaced, dispossessed, and liberation questors in claiming the God who sees, knows, hears, and acts on behalf of the oppressed, while at the same time authorizing the erasure of native people. The God we love to hate. Ngwa's *Let My People Live* invites readers to a new exodus—to the *gershomite-ogbanje* postcolonial identity and hermeneutics, in quest of 'the quality of life forged across time and space . . . outside of the constructions of erasure, marginalization, and singularity.'"

—Musa W. Dube, Professor of New Testament, Emory University

"The author ably foregrounds Africana hermeneutics as being about life. Forces of erasure, alienation, and singularization are resisted in favor of liberation for the communal flourishing of the Africana. This book is an invaluable resource for Hebrew Bible scholars and students alike."

—Madipoane Masenya (Ngwan'a Mphahlele), Professor of Old Testament Studies, University of South Africa

"Dr. Ngwa adeptly weaves together the histories and current realities of peoples of African descent on both sides of the Atlantic with the story of the Exodus. Using a nuanced Africana hermeneutic, he develops key insights from the familiar biblical book that can foster the well-being of our communities and the natural environment today. This is such a timely book!"

—Cheryl B. Anderson, Professor of Old Testament, Garrett-Evangelical Theological Seminary

"*Let My People Live* offers an imaginative and interdisciplinary textual study that replaces the idea of leaving with living by exploring Africana categories to discuss erasure, alienation, and singularity, a triple consciousness that rejects imperialism as it was manifested by the slave ship, the slave castle, and the postcolony. The text demonstrates that

Exodus is always a story of strife that is grounded in hope by offering a postcolonial reading of the exodus motifs, exploring afroecology to counter colonial necrology. The hermeneutics at work here is a wonderful testament to the idea that the Africana world can transform the scotched wasteland depicted in the Exodus narrative into a livable space."

—Elias Kifon Bongmba, Chavanne Chair in Christian Theology and Professor of Religion, Rice University

"Kenneth Ngwa provides African biblical studies and theology with a way of returning to the book of Exodus and the motif of exodus anew, more than twenty-five years after African theologies proposed a turn away from the book of Exodus and from the motif of exodus as 'liberation' to the books of Ezra and Nehemiah and the motif of 'reconstruction.' Ngwa poetically and prophetically summons us to an African(a) return to the book of Exodus. He shifts the hermeneutical frame so that we discern exodus' capacity to resist and transform the dominant systems of our entangled African(a) time, systems of 'erasure, alienation, and singularization.' Ngwa understands his exodus work as offering resources for defying these three systems, foregrounding survival, return, and community as forms of resistance, respectively. Exodus, with Ngwa as our guide, yields useful resources for creating 'viable, concrete, and lasting alternative ideologies and structures to these three destructive systems in order to support communal flourishing.'"

—Gerald O. West, Professor Emeritus, School of Religion, Philosophy, and Classics, University of KwaZulu-Natal, South Africa

Let My People Live

Let My People Live

An Africana Reading of Exodus

Kenneth N. Ngwa

© 2022 Kenneth N. Ngwa

First edition
Published by Westminster John Knox Press
Louisville, Kentucky

22 23 24 25 26 27 28 29 30 31—10 9 8 7 6 5 4 3 2 1

All rights reserved. No part of this book may be reproduced or transmitted in any form or by any means, electronic or mechanical, including photocopying, recording, or by any information storage or retrieval system, without permission in writing from the publisher. For information, address Westminster John Knox Press, 100 Witherspoon Street, Louisville, Kentucky 40202-1396. Or contact us online at www.wjkbooks.com.

Unless otherwise indicated, Scripture quotations are from the New Revised Standard Version of the Bible, copyright © 1989 by the Division of Christian Education of the National Council of the Churches of Christ in the U.S.A., and are used by permission.

Photo on page 170 courtesy of Aliou Niang.

Book design by Drew Stevens
Cover design by Marc Whitaker / MTWdesign.net

Library of Congress Cataloging-in-Publication Data

Names: Ngwa, Kenneth Numfor, author.
Title: Let my people live : an Africana reading of Exodus / Kenneth N. Ngwa.
Description: First edition. | Louisville, Kentucky : Westminster John Knox
 Press, [2022] | Includes bibliographical references and index. |
 Summary: "Reengages the narrative of Exodus through a critical,
 life-affirming Africana hermeneutic that seeks to create and sustain a
 vision of not just the survival but the thriving of Black communities"--
 Provided by publisher.
Identifiers: LCCN 2022007999 (print) | LCCN 2022008000 (ebook) | ISBN
 9780664262594 (paperback) | ISBN 9781646982516 (ebook)
Subjects: LCSH: Bible Exodus--Black interpretations.
Classification: LCC BS1245.52 .N495 2022 (print) | LCC BS1245.52 (ebook)
 | DDC 222/.1206--dc23/eng/20220308
LC record available at https://lccn.loc.gov/2022007999
LC ebook record available at https://lccn.loc.gov/2022008000

Most Westminster John Knox Press books are available at special quantity discounts when purchased in bulk by corporations, organizations, and special-interest groups. For more information, please e-mail SpecialSales@wjkbooks.com.

This work is dedicated to my parents,
Mr. John N. Ngwa
and
Mrs. Catherine B. Ngwa

Contents

Acknowledgments	ix
Prologue: When Your Children Ask You	**1**
From Anecdote to Interpretive Metaphor	4
Obama and Africana Exodus Hermeneutics: A Riposte to Erasure, Alienation, and Singularity	9
Exodus and the Interpretive Shawl of Memory and Imagination	11
Introduction: Hermeneutics after Erasure, Alienation, and Singularity	**13**
Exodus: An Interlocuting Story and Motif	13
Meaningful Interlocution: Africana and Clustered Narration	18
Exodus: Movement Motif and Story	22
Back to the Future: Exodus and Ubuntu Hermeneutics	28
1. Tears of Redesign: Birthing Exodus and Badass Womanism	**35**
Exodus and Badass Womanism	38
Exodus as a Badass Womanist Story	47
2. Triple Consciousness and the Exodus Narrative	**55**
Triple Consciousness, Biopolitics, and Scripturalization	58
Triple Objects of Africana Exodus Engagements: Slave Ship, Slave Castle, and Postcolony	62
From "Let My People Go" to "Let My People Live"	78
3. A Postcolonial Africana Reading of Exodus 2	**81**
Introduction	81
Gershomite Identity and Exodus	84
The *Ogbanje*: Gershom's African Kin	88

vii

CONTENTS

Three Scenarios of *Gershomite-Ogbanje* Subjectivity
in Exodus 2 92
Conclusion 108

4. Afroecology and Exodus 111
Introduction 111
Wangari Maathai and the Green Belt Movement 112
Hermeneutical Reflections 115
Exodus Plagues: A Narrative Ecological
"Prelude" to Wilderness 119
Afroecology and Exodus 122
Conclusion 129

5. Miriam: The Water-Woman and Exodus Ecology 133
Introduction 133
Contra Necroecology: Miriam and Exodus 2:1–10 139
The Greening of Miriam in the Wilderness: Numbers 12 ... 143
The Death of Miriam: The Dangers of an
Erased Exodus Future 148
A Poetics of Exodus Environments: Exodus 15:20–27 150
Conclusion 153

6. Facing and Backsiding the Mountain 155
Introduction: Narrativizing the Mountain 155
Africana Framing of the Mountain 157
Facing the Mountain 160
Rupture and Redesign in the Mountain Area 162
Hermeneutics on the Backside: Bonded beyond Lacunae ... 169
The Future of the Past: Body-Carrying Bodies 170
Can Liberation Happen in Egypt and at the Mountainside? 175
Can Liberation Happen through/with the Law? 178
Can Liberation Happen in the Ritual Space? 182
Conclusion 184

Conclusion: Let My People Live 185
Bibliography 193
Index of Scripture 201
Index of Subjects 205

Acknowledgments

This work has many intellectual and communal parents and siblings—forged and nurtured in and around classroom discussions, chapel services, academic conferences, my parents' farming and gardening practices, etc. All these spaces and moments have shaped my thinking on the theoretical, philosophical, and practical work of womanism, Ubuntu, necropolitics, biopolitics, Africana, and scripturalization, and thus they have informed my reading of Exodus as a story but also as an unending motif of resistance against the triple consciousness of erasure, alienation, and singularity.

My profound gratitude goes first to my wife, Jole, and our two sons, Michael and Etin, who often inquired about the work and supported and encouraged me along the way. They helped me see and be reminded again and again that scholarship is never truly done in isolation.

Several colleagues have also been my intellectual companions along the way. The faculty and staff—both current and former—at Drew Theological School has been a tremendous community for me in ways that are hard to fully articulate. I name here only some: Arthur Pressley, Danna Fewell, Ernie Rubinstein, Althea Spencer-Miller, Jesse Mann, Gary Simpson, Chris Boesel, Stephen Moore, Melanie Johnson-DeBaufre, Vanessa Wilson, and Sharon Williams have entertained conversations with me on portions of this manuscript. Their encouragements and feedback—formal and informal—helped to clarify my thinking around many of the ideas developed and expressed in the book. I had the opportunity to present portions of this manuscript at the Bible and Cultures area colloquium at Drew Theological School and at the Old Testament Research Colloquium at Princeton Theological Seminary. Both occasions were joyous ones for me because of the scholarship and community that framed the feedback I received.

My deep appreciation also goes to members and the leadership team of the African biblical hermeneutics section of the SBL. I have been honored to work with such scholars and leaders as Madipoane Masenya, Gerald West, Funlola Olojede, Andrew Mbuvi, Gilbert Ojwang,

Robert Kuloba, Aliou Niang, and Alice Yafeh-Deigh. Their commitment to the work of African biblical hermeneutics has sharpened my focus, expanded my thinking, and deepened my own ethical commitments to this kind of work.

My interest in writing a manuscript on Exodus began some years ago, after a Wabash Center mini research grant. I extend my appreciation to the leadership of the Wabash Center—then and now—for their support. I want to especially thank Tim Lake for his abiding and enduring friendship over the years and for being a brilliant conversation partner as I wrestled with some of the difficult issues in Exodus.

Finally, I am grateful to my two editors during this entire process. First, I extend appreciation to Dr. Bridgett Green, who was the first editor I worked with from Westminster John Knox. Her dedication to the process and her professionalism helped me to navigate the early stages and structure of the manuscript. I also extend deep appreciation to Ms. Julie Mullins, who took over the editorial work and moved the process forward with equal professionalism and grace. Her attention to detail and her probing queries have contributed to this manuscript.

Prologue

When Your Children Ask You

This monograph represents a stirring and a toiling of my interpretive soul—and the interpretive soul that produced me—as I consider the biblical story of Exodus in ways that, in consonance with Africana methods of interpretation, engage the concerns of the ancient Israelites and those of Africana peoples.[1] The work sits at the intersections of narrative, postcolonial, and ideological hermeneutics. There is a long-standing paradox to this interpretive endeavor. On the one hand, the Exodus story is partially located, and begins, in Egypt, which was part of ancient African intellectual, political, and religious innovation.[2] On the other hand, Exodus tells a story in which ancient Egypt was vacated by oppressed Hebrews after a major struggle for liberation.[3] This paradox is not just about historical location and time but also about hermeneutics. It was recognized and narratively engaged by the Jewish community that interpreted Exodus while resident in, and contributing

---

1. Africana biblical hermeneutics is an enormous and growing field of study and scholarship and cannot be fully represented in any single work. For my purposes, I use Africana broadly to refer to intersecting epistemologies, theories and praxis of communal meaning-making, and identify formation by persons of African descent across time and space. A good example of such work is *The Africana Bible* (ed. Hugh Page Jr. et al.), to which I will return later. Throughout this book, I use uppercase *Exodus* to refer to the biblical story and lowercase *exodus* to refer to motifs and themes that animate the story.

2. Hulisani Ramantswana, "'I Shavha i sia muinga i ya fhi?' Decolonial Reflections on African Biblical Hermeneutics," *Stellenbosch Theological Journal* 2, no. 2 (2016): 401–29; F. V. Greifenhagen, *Egypt on the Pentateuch's Ideological Map: Constructing Biblical Israel's Identity* (Sheffield: Sheffield Academic Press, 2002), 1–23.

3. For example, Greifenhagen, *Egypt*, 46–157; Cheikh Anta Diop, *African Origin of Civilization: Myth or Reality* (Chicago: Chicago Review Press, 1989); Flavius Josephus, *Against Apion*, trans. M. G. Barclay (Leiden: Brill, 2007).

to intellectual, economic, and religious life in ancient Alexandria.[4] So the paradox is about the conceptual flow of the story—from Egypt through the wilderness into the mountain area en route to Canaan—and the literary and interpretive flows that have unfolded from generations of engagement with its concerns, aspirations, traumas, and memories. That paradox is expressed in the story as an interpretive question, posed by children to their parents, and narrativized as part of exodus storytelling and its central ritual, the Passover: "And it will be that your children will say to you, 'What does this service mean to you?'" (Exod. 12:26, author's translation). The meaning of Passover merges with the meaning of Exodus discourse and lives beyond the story's original setting and timing (13:14–15).[5]

In line with this framing, my Africana engagement with Exodus is not theorized as disembodied fantasy devoid of historical or geographical specificity;[6] nor as a unitary, stable storage system of subconsciously encoded and retrievable data for recycling identity within and against the vicissitudes and traumas of time and space; nor as singular unilinear reading of history. Rather, I engage the story and its flows as a hermeneutical struggle for meaning that is not only unstable, oftentimes uncertain, dangerous, and austere; but also meaning that is hopeful, generative, and undying. The focus is as much on Exodus' capacity to make something new of the carcass or wreckage of exile and oppression (cf. Isa. 43:18, 19; 65:17; Rev. 21:5) as it is about an exodus community's capacity to summon distinctive memory (Isa. 46:9) for the work of liberation and equity.

Within Exodus' grand narrative struggle against ideologies and structures of oppression stretching across generations and geographical locations, something precise and pernicious happens: encounters with oppressive political, environmental, and religious systems result in three interrelated but distinct experiences. First, erasure or fragmentation in the form of death (physical or social). Second, alienation in the form of marginalization or exile from geographical, social, and ecological home—real or imagined. Third, singularization or isolation in the form of restrictive confinement that chokes out multiplicity. Against these three realities, exodus work foregrounds survival,

---

4. Benjamin G. Wright III, *The Letter of Aristeas: 'Aristeas to Philocrates' or 'On the Translation of the Law of the Jews'* (Berlin: Walter de Gruyter, 2015).

5. Scott M. Langston, *Exodus through the Centuries* (Malden, MA: Blackwell, 2006); Thomas B. Dozeman, Craig A. Evans, and Joel N. Lohr, eds., *The Book of Exodus: Composition, Reception, and Interpretation* (Leiden: Brill, 2014); Joel S. Baden, *The Book of Exodus: A Biography* (Princeton, NJ: Princeton University Press, 2019).

6. On fantasy and memory, see Laura Feldt, "Fantastic Re-Collection: Cultural vs. Autobiographical Memory in the Exodus Narrative," in *Religious Narrative, Cognition and Culture: Image and Word in the Mind of Narrative*, ed. Armin W. Geertz and Jeppe Sinding Jensen (Sheffield: Equinox, 2011), 191–208.

PROLOGUE 3

return/restoration, and community respectively; but it also resources the creation of viable, concrete, and lasting alternative ideologies and structures to these three destructive systems in order to support communal flourishing. Thus understood, the children's question about the meaning of exodus work is embodied and precise: Will the endangered community survive and find freedom? And, if they will, when? Will a displaced community find new space? And if so, where? Will communal voices outlast the power and allure of single-hero narration? And if so, how?

For Africana, this triple consciousness animates Exodus' three prominent material locations—Egypt, the wilderness, and the mountain area—but is also concurrently present in the ideological character of each of those spaces (Egypt, Wilderness, and Mountain). To explore this triple consciousness as intersecting historical, geographical, and ideological forces is to engage the Exodus narrative and exodus work along hermeneutical lines that Gerald West has termed "struggle."[7] Liberation is not just about movement from one place to another, but especially about how Exodus' multiple movements become mechanisms for bringing liberation to the material and ideological structures of oppression in Egypt, the Wilderness, the Mountain, and beyond. The catalyst for exodus liberation movement ("let my people go") serves a larger goal: "let my people live"—the hermeneutical and material transition from erased, marginalized, and singularized existence to creative freedom, wholeness, and community that enshrine the full flourishing of the material and interpretive soul/life. More than a desire to re-tell or exegete an original story, it is this shift that informs my Africana reading, premised on the children's question: "What does this service mean to you?"

One tells the story in order to name and resist the structures of erasure, alienation, and isolation. But one interprets the story *and* the interpretive labor and flow of Exodus' liberation motif as correlative functions of community formation and meaning-making. The bitter lives that Exodus talks about (Exod. 1:13) are genealogical, economic, and political lives under the chokehold of oppression. But such lives are also the catalyst for the interpretive methods of descendants of oppressed, marginalized, and singularized communities. These lives and methods require the turning of bitter oppression into sweet liberating multiplicity ("let my people go"). That communal release and its interpretive flows—the narrative and methodological movements

---

7. Gerald O. West, *The Stolen Bible: From Tool of Imperialism to African Icon* (Leiden: Brill, 2016).

out of the oppressive material realities in Egypt, the wilderness, and the mountain area, and out of the ideological character of Egypt, the Wilderness, and the Mountain—seek to produce life beyond the power and structure of erasure, beyond the processes of marginalization, and beyond the ideology of toxic singularity. This release and interpretive flows constitute the embodiments of "let my people live."

FROM ANECDOTE TO INTERPRETIVE METAPHOR

Indulge me in an anecdote. Several years ago, I went to my then six-year-old son's school for curriculum night. There was a sizable crowd of parents chatting in the gymnasium as children played and enjoyed popsicles. As I walked around, greeting other parents and guardians, I saw an international student who had also accompanied his son to the event. I stayed to chat with him. Suddenly, a gentleman walked up to us and introduced himself before stating that he had spotted us from across the hall and had come to greet us because, as he said, "I can recognize an African from a distance." I assumed that he was speaking of the new African community that was forming in the United States at that time; he was theorizing about the new African diaspora. Though I did not ask how he could make that determination from across the hall, or "from a distance" as he put it, the issue of "African" identity and its associative meanings presented itself—associations that can transcend multiple spaces and yet inhabit one body.[8] As evident in Jideofor Adibe's edited volume, *Who is African?*[9], these issues touch on notions of African identities shaped by historical forces of nationality, culture, travel, and economics, and they constitute part of the theorizing that informs Africana diaspora-home discourses.

What was it that stood out about our bodies to be recognizable as "African"? What are the organizing principles and spaces where African life takes form, faces concrete challenges, and forges new opportunities for survival and transformation? Are these spaces and principles cultural or linguistic or national? After we introduced ourselves, the gentleman surmised, based on our names, that the student with whom I had been speaking was from the same ethnic group as he. And so, standing in

---

8. See J. Lorand Matory, "The Many Who Dance in Me: Afro-Atlantic Ontology and the Problem with 'Transnationalism'" in *Transnational Transcendence: Essays on Religion and Globalization*, ed. Thomas J. Csordas (Berkeley: University of California Press, 2009), 231–62.

9. Jideofor Adibe, ed., *Who is African? Identity, Citizenship and the Making of Africa-Nation* (London: Adonis and Abbey Publishers Ltd, 2009).

PROLOGUE

that international space, they started speaking in Ibo. The complexity of the African body manifested itself anew—seemingly homogenous when viewed from distance but intriguingly complex and diverse up close. Knowing that there is a large Ibo population in postcolonial Cameroon, I tried to recreate a sense of our social interconnection by stating that I was their neighbor.[10] Our new conversation partner and friend, however, thought I was referring to the Yoruba and stated with excitement, "Oh, my wife is Yoruba." Then I said, "No, I mean your national neighbor to the east, Cameroon." Then we all laughed—I'm not sure whether our laughter was at our own internalized assumptions about postcolonial identities or at the absurd follies of colonialism itself, put on display. The interaction nevertheless highlighted the layered consciousness of postcolonial and diasporized subjects, subjectivity, and hermeneutics.[11]

Context matters. There we were, engaged in discussions that impinged on the new African diaspora in the United States. This new diaspora is a community that increased exponentially since the second half of the twentieth century, for a variety of intersecting reasons: the civil rights movement and its impact on United States immigration policy, especially the 1965 immigration act; the lobbying work of Trans-Africa against apartheid in South Africa; and the 1990 immigration laws that created the Diversity Lottery (DV) program. These advocacy movements and policy changes had direct impact on the emergence of the new African diaspora. According to a Pew Research finding, there were 2.1 million new diaspora Africans living in the United States in 2015, up from 881,000 in the year 2000, and substantially up from 80,000 in 1970. Thus, in 2015, foreign born Africans in the United States made up 4.8 percent of the total population, up from 0.8 percent in the 1970s. The top ten sending countries are Nigeria, Ethiopia, Egypt, Ghana, Kenya, South Africa, Somalia, Morocco, Liberia, and Cameroon, in that order.[12] Because these migrants maintain strong religious, cultural, political, and economic bonds with sending countries, they constitute a new and rapidly growing constituency in theorizing African

10. In fact, before independence in 1961, citizens of the then Southern Cameroons were a part of the British colony, managed from Nigeria, for economic reasons. In 1961, part of Southern Cameroons joined the French-speaking La République to create the Federal Republic of Cameroon. A plebiscite in 1972 solidified that union between Southern Cameroons and La République, resulting in the United Republic of Cameroon.

11. Francis B. Nyamnjoh, "Blinded by Sight: Divining the Future of Anthropology in Africa," *Africa Spectrum* 47, nos. 2–3 (2012): 63–92; Gerald O. West, "Do Two Walk Together? Walking with the Other through Contextual Bible Study," *Anglican Theological Review* 93, no. 3 (2011): 431–49.

12. Monica Anderson, "African Immigrant Population in U.S. Steadily Climbs," Pew Research Center, http://www.pewresearch.org/fact-tank/2017/02/14/african-immigrant-population-in-u-s-steadily-climbs/.

diaspora, especially in relation to the historic diaspora that emerged from the transatlantic slave trade. Because of generations and centuries of African American and Pan-African intellectual and political work, Africa's long diasporic journey to the United States of America was taking place in new forms—with different and new colonial histories, memories, and identities.

The week of this meeting turned out to be a remarkable one. Later that week, I picked up my son from school, and, on our way back to our apartment, he asked me whether I had ever been in a class where I was the only Black person. I knew that *something* had happened to him. I knew that he had entered a distinct sphere of consciousness. He had entered a space of social production that compelled him to explore kinship relation building as a response to the solitary status attached, as a social virus, to the natural and cultural texture of his body, a solitary status that isolated, wounded, and ruptured his Blackness. In Black Atlantic parlance and theorizing, he had crossed the proverbial "door of no return,"[13] not in actual body but in psychic and cultural body; and not because he wanted to cross that door, but because a particular mode and reality of history had forced that epistemological journey on him.

For a moment, I recoiled as I tried to recognize, symbolize, and intuitively attach myself to the gravity of the lacuna I feared had—without our permission—opened up in our kinship narrative. Of course, I could mentally scan my own life experiences, looking for data points that would mirror or approximate his experience of solitary Blackness. That sort of memory work—scanning for data points—would be easy and yield an easy answer of yes or no to his question. In narrative terms, I could find experiential data that resonated with his, for intertextual analyses. But such a reading of his question would only be tangentially related to the narrative *release and flow* of exodus work reframed by children (Exod. 12:26–27; 13:8, 14).

My son's narration of the lacuna of singularity and its possible presence in a history of my Blackness necessitated assessments of Africana's capacity for communal embrace of the return of Blackness from exile— the capacity for exodus to happen as part of our shared sense of home and home-making. His exodus-type question was, broadly, a search for

---

13. The door of no return is a physical and ideological door located in slave castles on the coastline of the Atlantic Ocean that embraces continental Africa. It represented the time and place where captured bodies transitioned into a new reality of departure without the seeming possibility of return to the communities they had known, the communities to which they belonged socio-historically, culturally, and politically. For an excellent theorizing of this concept of door of no return, see Dionne Brand, *A Map to the Door of No Return: Notes to Belonging* (Toronto: Vintage Canada, 2001).

something within the history of our kinship that offered a communitarian approach to the possibility of return from the space of Black triple consciousness—its encounters with erasure, alienation, and singularity around the ideological and structural machineries of racism, genocide, slavery, colonialism, postcolonial autocracy, ethno-nationalism, and imperialism. His question struck me to be about the perennial struggle that has attached itself, historically, geographically, and ideologically, to the ontology and subjectivity of Africana: *Blackness as solitariness and scarcity* versus *Blackness as community survival and surplus.*

As we continued our conversation, it occurred to me that his question was *also* about the experience of diaspora attached to a (communal) body; it was about an exilic voice speaking simultaneously to its formative past and to its future. The issue was whether the community to which he sought to return had the cultural repertoire, the imaginative resources, the historical perspective, and the interpretive shawl of memory to anchor his experience of rupture and give him a viable future. Such hermeneutical work would provide *a capacity to exit the experience of endangered self—the capacity to create exodus—without exiting the communal generations that preceded and produced exodus.* That work of Africana exodus is semantic, not episodic. The meaning line stretches beyond re-telling originating stories to transformative storytelling. That is why, for Africana, Exodus is more than about the liberating movement of one generation out of Egypt toward the promised land; it is also about transforming structures of oppression in the multiple locations that the story identifies.

Although my son and I shared genealogical, social, and cultural kinship, I had never been the *only* Black student in a classroom. The nature of that experience was not something that I could claim to have. But that discordant data point of history didn't ultimately matter, because his *question* was paramount as a starting point for repositioning ourselves, and thus our futures. Biological genealogy could not explain the fracturing he had encountered. But his question joined us in ways that historical experiences did not. We now also shared community framed around an unshared experience of a particular mode of isolation. The reason for this discrepancy is not the mystery and happenstance of nature. Instead, it is partly a function of the geographical and demographic context of my upbringing: the reality of my having grown up in a majority Black space in postcolonial Cameroon where other social markers—e.g., language, ethnicity, economic status, religion, culture, gender, etc.—are in greater and more frequent production, circulation, and function as quotidian modifiers for negotiating citizenship in public spaces. Our dissimilar experience was also a function of the fact that the public space he occupied—the Black Atlantic space—and from where he engaged me had its own genealogies, etiologies, and forms of geographical, political, and demographic history in which Blackness as solitariness and unnaturalness is common, routinized, and entrenched in the fabric of nations and their associated political and interpretive privileges around whiteness. The production of *this* Black Atlantic identity may be traced to the slave castle, where Africans of multiple ethnic groups were literally chained into a singularized mass of blackness to suit racist ideological frameworks.

Could our experience in the United States be akin to the distressful subjectivity that characterized Black students' experiences in Paris in the early 1930s that gave rise to the Negritude movement—its trailblazing leaders including Jeanne Nardal, Paulette Nardal, Leopold Senghor, Léon-Gontran Damas, and Aime Cessaire—and to Black struggle in apartheid South Africa? The issue was my son's experience of Blackness as isolation, Blackness that attracted voyeuristic curiosity in the hallowed places of white privilege, without affirmation of the integral role of Blackness in quality knowledge production and interpretation. His phenotypical distinctiveness in the classroom had been subjected to social analyses as atypical, as requiring explanation. The questions posed to him by white classmates were embodied and precisely anatomical: Why did he have brown eyes and kinky hair? Faced with that challenge in that space of social production where brown-eyed-enlightenment was unknown, my genetic and phenotypical kinship with his brown eyes and kinky hair were—understandably—not sufficient remedies to the social perception of Blackness as supposedly abnormal.

Exodus-type hermeneutical heavy lifting was required. We turned to collective memory about Africana. The conversation would require something of a historicized unveiling of the African concept of Ubuntu—life in community, held together not by a singular thread of kinship but by kinships of collective belonging. By removing him from the isolated space in class and placing him within Africana history and creativity—in the space of brown-eyed enlightenment—we (and our conversation) were able to forge a bond around our shared and unshared experiences. We could see dimly individually, but communally we could see multiply and more fully. Our Africana futures started to form, not in unquestioned assumptions of an unfolding promise of security and liberation and independence from colonial mapping and racist demands on the interpretive mind, but in the unrelenting creative work of producing multiplicity that is held together in community. *We* insisted on life beyond the grip of erasure, beyond the apathy of alienation, and beyond the fragility of toxic singularity.

OBAMA AND AFRICANA EXODUS HERMENEUTICS: A RIPOSTE TO ERASURE, ALIENATION, AND SINGULARITY

At the time that my son and I had these conversations, the world was enraptured in the hopeful and hope-filled candidacy and eventual presidency of Barack Obama, whose biographical story touched on Africa in specific ways. Was America ready for the Africa in his African American identity? Would Africa be wrapped up tidily into America's national story of immigration, of rugged individualism and the promise of meritorious achievement? Or would Obama's biographical and political presence on the national and international stage compel renewed reflection on the history of America's commodification and use of Africa's Blackness to subsidize the "nation" since 1619? Obama and his family would soon find out what it means to be the "only" Black persons in the history of the White House. And the nation and world would find out too.[14]

During his tenure as president, specifically on March 23, 2012, Obama reacted to the shooting death of Trayvon Martin, an unarmed Black teenager, and he made what was widely considered to be uncharacteristically personal and intimate reflections on Martin's death:

> Well, I'm the head of the executive branch, and the Attorney General reports to me so I've got to be careful about my statements to make sure that we're not impairing any investigation that's taking place right now.
>
> But obviously, this is a tragedy. I can only imagine what these parents are going through. And when I think about this boy, I think about my own kids. And I think every parent in America should be able to understand why it is absolutely imperative that we investigate every aspect of this, and that everybody pulls together—federal, state and local—to figure out exactly how this tragedy happened. . . .

---

14. That struggle continues with the 2020 election of Kamala Harris as the first Black and Southeast Asian woman to serve as vice president of the United States.

But my main message is to the parents of Trayvon Martin. If I had a son, he'd look like Trayvon. And I think they are right to expect that all of us as Americans are going to take this with the seriousness it deserves, and that we're going to get to the bottom of exactly what happened.[15]

Martin's death was tragic in and of itself, but it was also, tragically, only one of many such deaths. And so, on July 19, 2013, after Martin's killer was found not guilty on all counts, the president, speaking from the Rose Garden, returned to his initial remarks and provided a broader interpretive framing of the perennial problem that haunts Black lives and subjects in America:

You know, when Trayvon Martin was first shot I said that this could have been my son. Another way of saying that is Trayvon Martin could have been me 35 years ago. And when you think about why, in the African American community at least, there's a lot of pain around what happened here, I think it's important to recognize that the African American community is looking at this issue through a set of experiences and a history that doesn't go away.[16]

Much of the media analyses focused, rightfully so, on Obama's outreach to Martin's family: "If I had a son, he'd look like Trayvon." But an equally striking aspect of these words is that they were spoken by the man who, in American political narrative and lingo, held the position of the most powerful man in the world, the presidency. Obama brought the weight of his office to his narrative to fully emphasize the magnitude of the tragedy. The tragedy of Martin's death, Obama's words signified, was for Black America a crisis that reached the most intimate spaces of American political authority, including the White House. After the verdict, he reflected the agony of a Black community burdened by a traumatic history that seems to outlast political achievements and aspirational justice. The president placed this burden at the intersection of history, politics, and identity: "Another way of saying that is Trayvon Martin could have been me 35 years ago."

The president's remarkable juxtaposition of his own Black political power and achievement with the burden of Black vulnerability

---

15. David A. Graham, "Quote of the Day: Obama: 'If I Had a Son, He'd Look like Trayvon,'" *The Atlantic*, March 23, 2021, https://www.theatlantic.com/politics/archive/2012/03/quote-of-the-day-obama-if-i-had-a-son-hed-look-like-trayvon/254971/.

16. James S. Brady, "Remarks by the President on Trayvon Martin," The White House, Office of the Press Secretary, July 19, 2013, https://obamawhitehouse.archives.gov/the-press-office/2013/07/19/remarks-president-trayvon-martin.

crystalizes a fundamental issue at the heart of the history of marginalized subjectivity and the telling of the work and history of liberation. For Obama to fundamentally agree with what would become the rallying cry and movement, Black Lives Matter, is to understand the origins of that movement in historical terms.[17] But most importantly, it is to understand that acts of erasure, experiences of alienation and apathy, and feelings of being singularly targeted all contribute to the hermeneutics of liberation storytelling. It was toward the end of a presidency fueled by enduring tropes of exodus and struggle for freedom that Obama reflected on the death of Trayvon Martin and the depth of anguish that comes with repeated encounters with a history that doesn't go away. Joseph Winters has argued in *Hope Draped in Black* that one must tell liberation stories with hope and determination, as well as with a healthy dose of critical assessments of providential storytelling.[18] Furthermore, as Robert Warrior has taught biblical interpreters, readings of histories—even exodus-induced histories—that assert progress without adequate attention to equally persistent forms of oppression can and do transition into conquest narratives.[19]

EXODUS AND THE INTERPRETIVE SHAWL
OF MEMORY AND IMAGINATION

Africana hermeneutics illumine interpretive work on Exodus in precise ways. On the one hand, there are unrelenting forms of imperial, racist, and colonial devastation that create erasures, dispersals/diasporas, and confinements—along with incentive and providential structures to sustain such manifestations of power and storytelling. The result is the creation and the distressful experience analogous to *conditional* or *contingent citizenship* that Benny Liew has identified and named in Asian American communities.[20] On the other hand, there is Exodus' unrelenting capacity to produce intellectual, cultural, religious, and political resources that inform and propel movements for political liberation,

---

17. For more on the BLM movement and its liberation work, see Keeanga-Yamahtta Taylor, *From #BlackLives-Matter to Black Liberation* (Chicago: Haymarket Books, 2016).

18. Joseph R. Winters, *Hope Draped in Black: Race, Melancholy, and the Agony of Progress* (Durham, NC: Duke University Press, 2016).

19. Robert Warrior, "Canaanites, Cowboys, and Indians," *Union Seminary Quarterly Review* 59, nos. 1–2 (2005): 1–8.

20. Tat-siong Benny Liew, "Militarism, Masculinism, and Martyrdom: Conditional Citizenship for (Asian) Americans," in *Critical Theology against US Militarism in Asia: Decolonization and Deimperialization, New Approaches to Religion and Power*, ed. Nami Kim and Wonhee Anne Joh (New York: Palgrave Macmillan, 2016), 25–52, italics in original.

legal justice, and equity. Exodus provides the impetus for intergenerational re-learning and re-membering, for communal bonding, liberation, and healing. The story summons communal imagination as much as memory. Having been born into a story of endangered genealogies and tenuous claims to the structures of social, political, and ecological formation, Exodus-Israel has the capacity, through cunning, strategic planning, and engagement with memory, to process threats to its communal existence and restructure life beyond the wreckages of erasure, alienation, and singularized existence.[21]

The exodus hermeneutical question, "What does this service mean to you?" represents the way Exodus creates an intergenerational story, which creates an intergenerational community and intergenerational meaning. It is not just distinct communities—tribes—that unfold from this story; what unfolds is also a particular hermeneutic of interrogating and locating meaning in the flows of the story and the communities it produces. In response to the probing question about the meaning of exodus work, the story recounts liberation that shifts the focus from movement out of a place to the work of redeeming life: "When Pharaoh stubbornly refused to let us go, the LORD killed all the firstborn in the land of Egypt, from human firstborn to the firstborn of animals. Therefore, I sacrifice to the LORD every male that first opens the womb, but every firstborn of my sons I redeem" (Exod. 13:15). The story is about brutal interruption, but it is also about forging identity by redeeming (ransoming) the future—the life of the firstborn of the children. Through narration across generations and regions (places), exodus memory is resourced and attached to the mythical genealogical womb, but also to bodies that are killed, or lost, or survive vicariously to become the initiators (the firstborn) of liberation and its future. There is a shift and a thread connecting the flows of histories of liberation ("let my people go") as departures from oppression to understanding such flows as productions of multiple liberating life-forms ("let my people live"). Exodus mobilizes intergenerational and interregional resources to bring liberation to Egypt, the Wilderness, and the Mountain; that is, to resist and transform systems of erasure, alienation, and singularization. The merit of that work lies in its capacity to create and distribute value for the many, not privilege for a few. This is the work of Africana hermeneutics that I pursue in this book.

---

21. I use the phrase "Exodus-Israel" as a literary representation of the distinct material and historical realities that undergirded ancient Israel's struggles for freedom, and the exodus thrust that flows beyond ancient Israel into the modern world. Throughout history and across geographical regions, there are distinct exodus stories, but similar and intersecting exodus motifs. That reality is represented in the nomenclature "Exodus-Israel."

Introduction

Hermeneutics after Erasure, Alienation, and Singularity

EXODUS: AN INTERLOCUTING STORY AND MOTIF

How does one live and interpret after erasure, after alienation, and after singularity? In articulating the hermeneutical rationale for *The Africana Bible*, Hugh Page Jr. describes the book as "an interlocutor with scripture."[1] The *edited volume*, not just the individual authors, is the interlocutor and interlocution. The volume does more than provide traditional commentary on the biblical text; it simultaneously examines how interpretive meaning flows out of and back into the text, as readers engage it. Still speaking of *The Africana Bible*, Page writes:

> One of its major functions is to empower readers to ask questions and to consider further the meaning and implications of the First Testament and cognate writings for communities that revere them, that have been shaped by them, and that—in some instances—have been destabilized by interpretations of them.[2]

Central to my appropriation of this hermeneutic of interlocution is the prioritized attention that the biblical Exodus story *and* Africana exodus theories on identity formation give to forms of power that facilitate and authorize access to, and control of, individual, communal, and cosmic

---

1. Hugh R. Page Jr., et al., eds., *The Africana Bible: Reading Israel's Scriptures from Africa and the African Diaspora* (Minneapolis: Fortress Press, 2010), 4.
2. Page, *The Africana Bible*, 5.

life force, *nephesh*. At the outset of Exodus, we encounter interlocution around Pharaoh's hypothetical but deeply harmful claims about the children of Israel: "Come, let us deal shrewdly with them, or they may increase and, in the event of war, join our enemies and fight against us and escape from the land" (Exod. 1:10). Pharaoh's wartime scenario constitutes the epistemological and policy location for the emergence of triple consciousness in Exodus. First, Pharaoh's scenario ruptures citizenship into binaries that evolve into ethno-nationalist oppression of the Hebrews and his policies of erasure. Second, Pharaoh's scenario links ruptured identity and history to marginalized or alienated subjects, framing these marginalized subjects as enemies. Third, his scenario remaps geopolitical existence and belonging as a form of singularizing move or departure. As the political embodiment and narrative symbol of governing authority, Pharaoh's hypothetical wartime scenario—backed by institutional, discursive, and legislative power—performs political, social, and geographical functions that undermine Exodus and its embodiments in the "children of Israel"—those who, in exilic and postexilic settings, ask the question, "What does this service mean to you?" and thereby push Exodus' meaning beyond the interests of ethno-nationalism, global conflict, or imperialism.

Interlocutions about the "cradle of the nation"—to evoke Julius Wellhausen's phrase—and about Exodus' portrait of Pharaoh, unfold at the intersection of the "war camp" and the "birth stool."[3] David Lamb has shown how taunts, insults, parries, and ripostes functioned in pre- or postwar ideology in ancient Near East and biblical texts.[4] It is not just the jarring nature of erasure, marginalization, and singularity—the "shock and awe" of war, to use a disturbing metaphor popularized at the start of the Iraq war in 2003—that is critical to my interlocuting analyses; it is also that the story of Exodus can be read as a signifier of the triple consciousness that results from colonial, racist, and imperial productions of war camps and birth stools.

In such colonial, racist, and imperial landscapes, Pharaoh's official policy advocating that Hebrew boys be killed in Egypt morphs into

---

3. Julius Wellhausen, *Israelitische und Jüdische Geschichte* (Berlin: Walter de Gruyter, 1958), 24; Claudia D. Bergmann, *Childbirth as a Metaphor for Crisis: Evidence from the Ancient Near East, the Hebrew Bible, and 1QHXI, 1–18* (Berlin: Walter de Gruyter, 2009), 60–71.

4. David T. Lamb, "'I Will Strike You Down and Cut off Your Head' (1 Sam 17:46): Trash Talking, Derogatory Rhetoric, Psychological Warfare in Ancient Israel," in *Warfare, Ritual, and Symbol in Biblical and Modern Contexts*, ed. Brad E. Kelle, Frank Ritchel Ames, and Jacob L. Wright (Atlanta: SBL, 2014), 111–30; Lamb, "Compassion and Wrath as Motivations for Divine Warfare," in *Holy War in the Bible: Christian Morality and an Old Testament Problem*, ed. H. Thomas, J. Evans, and P. Copan (Downers Grove, Ill: InterVarsity Press, 2013), 133–52.

INTRODUCTION   15

threats on the life of the exodus community in the Wilderness, and into the traumas of near extinction in the Mountain, and into the conquest narratives about Canaan, and into foreign wives being sent away in a postexilic space-time. Once produced, the violence of endangered life attaches itself to the flows (the birth stools) of the story. That is how the expulsion of Hagar, the Egyptian slave woman, from Abraham and Sarah's household, her distress in the wilderness, and her and Ishmael's near-death experience also reads, interlocutionally, with the developing national story. As children of Hebrew women faced death in the waters of Egypt, the child of the Egyptian mother faces death in the wilderness. Both stories sit at the intersection of socio-political identity around erasure-survival, both within the nation and beyond the nation.

Second, does alienation within the nation (experienced by Hebrew children) and alienation beyond the nation (experienced by Egyptian children) transition to permanent departure from notions of home and belonging—political, cultural, and geographical? Political/ethnic home (land) intersects with an ecological home (land) in exodus imagination and work. That intersection becomes the avenue for resisting the exploitation of ecosystems or the deployment of ecosystems as subsidies to the story's national political ends. Against exploitation of human and non-human life, the Exodus story's earthly and earthy focus—the rootedness of home in the earth—signifies that political liberation without ecological liberation is not only insufficient but also deficient and ultimately unacceptable.

And third, what risk does a partially displaced (diaspora-home) community and its earthy environments face if identity formation is modeled after the allure of imperial ideology that wrestles communal multiplicity into singularity, evident in Pharaoh's anxieties about the epistemological and demographic multiplicity that made up the exodus community (Exod. 1:7, 9; cf. 12:38)? How does community resist the costly allure of privileged singularized existence? The story of Exodus is not only multilocal, but also polyphonic and perennially communal. No single heroes are allowed and none ultimately survive the robust multiplicity that the story produces. Instead of colonial, patriarchal, and imperial singularity, the story produces an ethos of communal oneness—oneness with the divine, with others, and with the earth itself.

The Exodus story is about liberation's interlocution with a triple experience of *erased, marginalized/alienated, and confined/singularized* existence. This triple experience generates distinct but intersecting phenomena and processes around which the storyteller organizes the narrative: *oppression in Egypt, alienation in the Wilderness, and singularization*

16   LET MY PEOPLE LIVE

in the Mountain. This narrative and spatial structure constitutes part of Exodus' interlocuting range across regions and generations. The narrative flow across regions and generations is also the reason why Exodus is ultimately not about moving a people from one location to another, but about the ability of such movement to bring liberation to Egypt, the Wilderness, and the Mountain, and therefore to the generations that inhabit those narrative spaces and places.

In Egypt, Pharaoh's escalating manifestation of triple distress takes many forms. First, it takes the form of ethnophobic necropolitics—the politics of death attached to a pathologized ethnic body. Pharaoh deploys his governing infrastructure to institutionalize enslavement and economic extraction and also to summon the work of the "Hebrew midwives" (Exod. 1:15) and redeploy its otherwise life-generating power toward implementing conditional existence for a targeted group: "If it is a boy, kill him; but if it is a girl, she shall live" (Exod. 1:16). The history produced by pharaonic thinking and action degenerates to embittered existence and conditional existence. This degenerating history is structured around ethnic and gendered tropes and located at the site of non-pharaonic flow of multiplicity—the birth stool of the *Hebrews*.[5] Pharaoh's rise to power and his form of governance are antithetical to the multiplicity of Hebrew life. And Pharaoh's history is one of introducing and formalizing death at the place of life. In the midst of pharaonic history, routine acts of life (birth, naming ceremonies, eating, drinking, movement) become symbols of the precariousness of conditional existence. This is where the first act of exodus radicalization takes place. The midwives refuse to become agents of death. But more importantly, they move the story beyond the confines of Pharaoh's deadly time zone, saying of the Hebrew women: "they give birth before the midwives arrive" (Exod. 1:19). The midwives decenter Pharaoh's necropolitics because the Hebrew women engender multiplying biopolitics.

But there is more to the story: Pharaoh's erasing action attaches itself to alienation. Pharaoh's decree to kill Hebrew boys compels Hebrew life and culture to go underground and into seclusion, from where they emerge to forge survival, chart paths of self-determination, and struggle against

---

5. Over a third of the uses of *Hebrew* in the Hebrew Bible are found in Exodus: 1:15–16, 19; 2:6–7, 11, 13; 3:18; 5:3; 7:16; 9:1, 13; 10:3; 21:2. Konrad Schmid, *Genesis and the Moses Story: Israel's Dual Origins in the Hebrew Bible,* trans. James D. Nogalski (Winona Lake, IN: Eisenbrauns, 2010), 123 n465. Other occurrences include Gen. 14:13; 39:14, 17; 40:15; 41:12; 43:32; Deut. 15:12; 1 Sam. 4:6, 9; 13:3, 7, 19; 14:11, 21; 29:3; Jer. 34:9, 14; Jon. 1:9. Except for a few instances (Gen. 14:13; Exod. 21:2; Deut. 15:12; Jer. 34:9), the term is usually used in the presence of, or comes from the lips of, someone considered to be foreign. Shammai Engelmayer, "Ivri: Naming Ourselves," *Judaism* 54, nos. 1–2 (2005): 13–26, has argued that the word is used to describe descendants of Eber who adhered to an exclusive belief in God. Thus, although all Hebrews would be Israelites, not all Israelites were Hebrews. Note the distinction between Hebrew and Israelite in 1 Samuel 14:21.

INTRODUCTION 17

the transactional lure and carnival of national, colonial, and imperial patronage. This experience initiates a narrative flow around marginalization: Moses is born precisely at such a time, when Hebrews are not only endangered but also nursed in hiding—that is, denied the right to publicly create identity and use it to authorize communal belonging beyond Pharaoh's ethnocentric ideology of the nation-state. It is in this context of marginalization that the second act of radicalization takes place. Moses' mother and Miriam perform this radical act of placing the child in the public space. It is a move that takes the muffled cries of the marginalized subject to the public space where governing power manifests itself. This move brings the sounds of the marginalized/alienated to the hearing of the Egyptian Princess and, by extension, Pharaoh; and it ultimately brings these cries to Yahweh. A second consciousness is forming.

Third, in the flow of the story, marginalization/alienation attaches itself to singularity. Recognizing that Moses was one of the Hebrew children, and likely understanding his public presence and cry as a response to existing policy, the Egyptian princess adopts Moses after consultation with Miriam. Their dialogue ensures that Moses is placed in Pharaoh's court. The story verges on creating a single hero. Yet, this is where the third form of radicalization takes place. Unlike other exilic Hebrews that inhabit imperial courts as shadowy cupbearers (e.g. Daniel, Joseph), susceptible to imperial patronage and imperial forgetting, the Exodus narrator places Moses in Pharaoh's court as an adopted son—adopted from (but still resourced by) his biological and his ecological mother (he was placed among the reeds by his mother and drawn from the watery Nile). It is a risky move toward the epicenter of erasure. But in that move, in that flow, resourced from the community, access to power and authority is conceived as an acquired socio-genealogical and political right forged by the oppressed and marginalized, not a conferred political gift of the nation or the empire. As Judy Fentress-Williams has argued, Moses' identity is best understood as constructed, resourced, and grounded in community, not singularity, and shaped by the women in the story.[6] Thus resourced, Moses will face the allure of imperial singularity in the Mountain, and he will effectively resist (Exod. 32:10–14).

This triple consciousness informs the interlocuting flows of the Exodus story, which begins as an account of the children of Israel moving into Egypt. Precisely, Exodus opens with a list of names of Jacob's children and their households. This is something of a generational and

6. Judy Fentress-Williams, "Exodus," in Page, *Africana Bible*, 82

intergenerational narrative kin-list on the move toward a place that is not altogether foreign, because, as the narrator indicates and the reader of Genesis knows, Joseph was already in Egypt. The story moves toward history, toward Hebrew life that precedes the rise of Pharaoh and anchors resistance to oppression. Although Pharaoh will attempt to ignore or erase that history, the Exodus community—or its story about exodus—begins as communal work of interrogating and transforming structures and systems that produce erasure, alienation, and singularity. This transformative flow seeks to turn the flow of exile into the flows of exodus. Questions emerge: Did the past produce the present? The note about Joseph's presence in Egypt (Exod. 1:5) functions to narratively preempt, contextualize, and ultimately undermine the otherwise totalizing effects of the collision of the past and the future. The children on the move represent a form of narrative interrogation that assumes familiarity with, and resistance to, erasing authoritarianism; familiarity with, and resistance to, the apathy of diaspora as partial loss and alienation; and familiarity with, and resistance to, the anguishing depths of unshared existence. The children's narrative and interpretive move in and out of the space-time of erasure, alienation, and singularity also signals Exodus' capacity to be multiply resilient in Egypt, the Wilderness, and the Mountain—to forge genealogical and interpretive constituency across time and space, and to assess the deep and broad cultural and environmental impact of a trek that comes to mean more than a journey. The imagined narrative and interpretive land that Exodus creates is "a good and broad land, a land flowing with milk and honey" (Exod. 3:8). As a postexilic story, this land is portrayed as a gift of the liberating deity. Yet, its material and embodied value as a product of exodus work depends on recognizing its ability to generate creative herstories (flows) before the arrival of erasure, alienation, and singularity.

MEANINGFUL INTERLOCUTION: AFRICANA AND CLUSTERED NARRATION

At the turn of the twentieth century, in the midst of what would ironically be known as the war to end all wars, or World War I, W. E. B. Du Bois wrote a short essay examining the cause and impact of war, which he called "our chiefest industry."[7] Bringing history, race, religion, eth-

---

7. W. E. Burghardt Du Bois, "Of the Culture of White Folk," *The Journal of Race Development* 7, no. 4 (1917): 436.

INTRODUCTION   19

nicity, economics, and psychology to bear on his analyses of colonial oppression, du Bois diagnosed the propensity to conquer and dominate others and linked that propensity to an ideological thrust that he called "the world-wide mark of meanness—color."[8] The meaning of the war, Du Bois argued, could not be divorced from the global constructions of meaning along and around color and race.

> This world war is primarily the jealous and avaricious struggle for the largest share in exploiting darker races. As such it is and must be but prelude to the armed and indignant protest of these despised and raped peoples. . . . Is then this the end of war? Can it be so long as its prime cause, the despising and robbery of darker people sits enthroned even in the souls of those who cry peace? So if Europe hugs this delusion then this is not the end of world war—it is the beginning.[9]

This diagnosis of the souls of white folk came just over a decade after Du Bois had diagnosed and talked about the strivings of the souls of Black folk, the hermeneutical overlap between the two diagnoses unfolding around color; the worldwide mark of meanness articulated in 1917 was the latest articulation of "the color line" found in the *Souls of Black Folk*. "The problem of the twentieth century," Du Bois had written, "is the problem of the color-line—the relation of the darker and lighter races of men in Asia and Africa, in America and the Islands of the sea."[10] When Du Bois wrote those words, effective colonialism was in full force, so his 1917 essay and its critique of the search for peace in Europe without attention to Europe's colonizing madness was as much about the hypocrisy of unaccountable meaning-making in Eurocentric discourse about global distributions and regulations of citizenships as it was about the starting point of interpretation and the interlocuting stance that colonized communities adopt by necessity of anticolonial work and by generative posture.

The question, as Brian Blount has diagnosed and posed it in relation to biblical studies, is about the "meaning line"—the tension between standardized meaning and meaning potential, the methodologies that are granted power and prestige, and the troubling of the interpretive soul that reads otherwise. Working from Du Bois's description of the color-line, Blount writes:

8. Du Bois, "White Folk," 439.
9. Du Bois, "White Folk," 444–45.
10. W. E. B. Du Bois, *The Souls of Black Folk* (Champaign, IL: Project Guttenberg, 1996 [1903]), 7.

Instead of a color line, biblical operations proceed about a meaning line. Simplistically put, text meaning is determined through historical and literary engagement that uncovers text intent, or text meaning is ascertained through an engagement between the reader, reading out of her place, and the text as it is engaged in that space. There develops an interpretive veil behind which cultural interpreters are positioned and from which they must operate frequently in the shadows. . . . The meaning line is destructive to readers on both sides of it. All are Othered from each Other by its very existence. It is because interpretive power rests on the historical, literary scientific side that cultural hermeneuts are required to become at the very least bi-cultural, knowing their own space and its influence on text meaning as well as they know the historical and literary principles that allegedly unearth static text meaning. But this prescience comes with a cost. The necessity to acquire it threatens the very soul of the cultural hermeneut, who must occupy and absorb the space of the objective Other without losing hold of the spiritual mooring of his own space. . . . Scores of souls are thereby troubled.

The troubling, though, can also be efficacious. Du Bois recognized that wherever Others operated with sincerity across the color line, particularly when whites engaged empathetically out of the black space, there dawned the potential for just societal transformation. *Reading from an Other's space transforms not only how one reads but how one lives.*[11]

This troubling of the historical and cultural interpretive soul means, in part, that in methodology and subject-matter, biblical hermeneutics travels a richly contested and varied road. Sometimes, it survives improbably, but it always seeks to transition from survival to thriving. In the face of devastating colonial, racist, ethnocentric, ecological, and patriarchal ideologies, practices, and structures, Africana biblical hermeneutics has emerged and forged its identity and subject matter from the margins of interpretive alienation, erasure, and singularization. But it is also taking shape in centers of cosmopolitan and global academic and governing power, as well as in research and teaching centers and institutions on the African continent and in the diaspora.

A key element of this interlocuting hermeneutic is cluster-storytelling. It is a method not unfamiliar in the exodus story, where Moses finds himself face-to-face with the divine in a burning bush. To initiate and structure liberation life after erasure, after alienation, and after

---

11. Brian K. Blount, "The Souls of Biblical Folk and the Potential for Meaning," *Journal of Biblical Literature* 138, no. 1 (2019): 9, emphases in original.

INTRODUCTION

singularity, Yahweh strategizes with Moses and proposes a method of cluster narration that partners with Aaron: "You shall speak to him and put the words in his mouth; and I will be with your mouth and with his mouth and will teach you what you should do. He indeed shall speak for you to the people; he shall serve as a mouth for you" (Exod. 4:15–16). Multiple bodies and stories are linked up together in time and across time and space. Likewise, African/a biblical hermeneutics considers African/a epistemologies—creative theories and histories of religious, cultural, and political discourse—and the conditions and livelihood of African/a people to be invaluable and legitimate contexts and resources in biblical interpretation.[12] The task is enormous, not just because of the deep textures of history and genres of analyses that fall under the rubric of African/a, but also because the methodologies that define African/a biblical hermeneutics often navigate vexing problems of theorizing multiplicity as the starting point of analyses: the African/a interpreter begins with the Bible in its current canonical form but also begins with questions about the Bible's origins and location in the ancient world, with questions about a version of the Bible's reception history, and with the present context of the interpreter. The question of the meaning line is not about a menu of hermeneutical options to choose from; it confronts the hermeneut as inherently clustered. So the interpretive task is not guided and assessed by methods supposedly unencumbered by the subjectivities of contextual specificities and exigencies, or inherently averse to vocalizations put into the mouths of others. In cluster narration, somehow diachronic and synchronic voices and realities co-exist sequentially and concurrently. The meaning waves that emerge from such simultaneity produce interpretations that are both imaginative conjuring and historical analyses.[13]

By no means is this interpretive method unique to African/a readers and interpreters, but its formulation in African/a scholarship emerges, in part, as a riposte to global mappings and oppression of Africa-descended people, and in part in affirmative embrace of African/a identity—real and/or imagined—that is rooted in the narrative, poetic, religious, cultural, and philosophical traditions and creations of persons of African descent. From text-critical and typological analyses to postmodern approaches, African/a interpreters seek to engage texts,

---

12. Madipoane Masenya (Ngwan'a Mphahlele) and Kenneth Ngwa eds., *Navigating African Biblical Hermeneutics: Themes and Trends from Our Pots and Our Calabashes* (Cambridge: Cambridge Scholars Publishing, 2018).

13. See, for example, Andrew Mbuvi's "African Biblical Studies: An Introduction to an Emerging Discipline," *Currents in Biblical Research* 15, no. 2 (2017): 149–78.

textual productions, and the histories that texts co-produce, but also the changing material and ecological resources of African-descended communities and epistemologies. The goal of such hermeneutics is to make interpretation accountable and liberative, not just interesting or novel. The task is to produce interpretation that is answerable to those whose lives and livelihoods are affected by particular methods of reading Bible and history; to excavate and compare source texts and then assess the processes of interlocution within and beyond the text.

David T. Adamo's edited volume *Biblical Interpretation in African Perspective* represents a textual form of communal interpretation, a form of cluster storytelling, that highlights Africana multiplicity.[14] So too is the edited volume by Jione Havea, Margaret Aymer, and Steed Davidson, *Islands, Islanders and the Bible: RumInations,* which explores the possibility of reading biblical texts as islands, in fact, as archipelagic, and thus inviting reflection on hermeneutics as *talanoa,* story that is both fiercely independent and yet interdependent on other stories.[15] These similes between readers and texts and spaces are not simply metaphoric; they have material interpretive significance. Interpretation itself is experienced and performed as "waves"— movements that have direction but also depth, specific story but also generic motif.

EXODUS: MOVEMENT MOTIF AND STORY

The work of interpretive interlocution being pursued here may be viewed in terms of the relation between Exodus as a story and exodus as a motif. As a story, Exodus is a grand narrative about Israel's experience of oppression, departure from Egypt, journey through the wilderness and the mountain, and eventual arrival in the land of promise. This story's divine, human, and non-human characters all contribute to communal experiences around ritual practices, legal disputes and resolutions, economic concerns and remedies, identity crises and covenantal agreements, and creative celebrations of ongoing successes. These experiences give the story its distinctive flavor; they make the historiography of the story relevant to particular peoples, places, and

---

14. David T. Adamo, *Biblical Interpretation in African Perspective* (Lanham, MD: University Press of America, 2006).

15. Jione Havea, Margaret Aymer, and Steed Davidson, eds., *Islands, Islanders and the Bible: RumInations* (Atlanta: Society of Biblical Literature Press, 2015).

INTRODUCTION 23

times. Those details about the story, however, also contain a motif of exodus. This motif attends to the ideological makeup and construct of the story—why the story is necessary in the first place; how the story comes to mean more than a journey; and how the story finds and makes an interpretive home beyond its originating place and time and people. As motifs, the narrative identifiers—Egypt, Wilderness, and Mountain—become ideological realities to engage, rather than simply vacate, in exodus work.

The relation between Exodus as a story and exodus as a motif may be exemplified by reference to Amos 9:7, which states: "Are you not like the Ethiopians to me, O people of Israel? says the LORD. Did I not bring Israel up from the land of Egypt, and the Philistines from Caphtor and the Arameans from Kir?" Israel has an exodus story, but so do other communities. Within Israel's narration itself, a similar interlocution between story and motif is evident in the Mountain when Moses invokes Egyptian storytelling to dissuade Yahweh from destroying the community: "Why should the Egyptians say, 'it was with ill intent that he brought them out, to kill them in the mountains and to wipe them off the face of the earth'"? (Exod. 32:12). Here, Moses appeals to Egyptian storytelling to frame how exodus' motif extends beyond liberation to include ongoing necessity to ensure communal survival from imperial and national threats. Amos refers to Others' exodus stories, and Moses refers to other exodus motifs. There can be one exodus story with multiple motifs (Exod. 32:12) and one exodus motif with multiple stories (Amos 9:7).

This is an important insight for Africana hermeneutics, which recognizes interlocution between the story/stories and motif/motifs within the biblical text but also presses the question of the methodological implications of interpretive flows that enable one exodus story to hold multiple motifs, and one exodus motif to generate multiple stories. Such interrogation sits at the intersection of place, history, and hermeneutics, and it explains how one community's liberation story or struggle for survival becomes an ally story-motif for another community or another generation. That is why a new generation of exodus children pose the interpretive question to a preceding generation: "What does this service mean to you?" How and why does a Black liberation struggle and theology in North America find resonance with Black liberation struggle and theology in South Africa? Why and how does a Black Lives Matter movement resonate with or differ from the civil rights movement in the United States? How do struggles for minority rights by Anglophones in Cameroon resonate with struggles for freedom by Oromo protesters in Ethiopia?[16]

Similarly, Artapanus's *On the Jews*, Ezekiel the Tragedian's *Exagoge*, the Wisdom of Solomon, and Philo's *Life of Moses* all portray Jewish writers' reworking of Exodus-exodus (story-motif) to address the land of Egypt directly—as a specific land and an ideology to be vacated—but also as a place and an ideology to be reimagined and redesigned because of its role in shaping identity. As Nathalie LaCoste argues in regard to those Jewish writings, "the descriptions of Egypt they offer allow us to see changing perceptions of the physical environment in Jewish Literature."[17] In reimagining Egypt for Ptolemaic and Roman-era Jewish communities, these works shaped "a distinct form of Judaism" that continuously reexamined Exodus and expanded on its significance.[18] They could hold onto the meaning of Exodus as a story but also extend its motif beyond exiting Egypt to transforming Egypt.

Centuries before the Ptolemaic and Roman eras, Amos' words about Exodus-exodus elevated an understanding of liberation movements rooted in justice-work that is legal and political. For Hosea (11:1), Exodus-exodus narration was about Israel as a child called out of Egypt: Israel's early self-consciousness was formed around memory of Egypt as simultaneously a place of origin and a place where departure/liberation began. For both Amos and Hosea, the liberation of one community finds affinity with the liberation of another community, not because of social and political happenstance or fortuity, but because each community, while articulating its liberation story, also comes to understand and allow for the inherent capacity of Other communities to do the same. That is what connects the story to the motif in ways that are meaningful and enduring. The capacity to recognize the qualitative and distinct value of Others' exodus stories without devolving into isolationism is the interpretive gift of the biblical prophets. Amos and Hosea help us to see and understand Exodus-exodus kinship in ways that are neither simplistic of original communities nor fantastical in their imagination.

What triggered these Exodus-exodus recollections for the prophets? Did experiences of violence and conquest by eighth century Assyrian

---

16. Siobhán O'Grady, "Divided by Language: Cameroon's Crackdown on Its English-Speaking Minority Is Fueling Support for a Secessionist Movement," *Washington Post*, February 5, 2019, https://www.washingtonpost.com/graphics/2019/world/cameroon-anglophone-crisis/; "Death Toll from Clashes between Ethiopian Amhara, Oromo Groups Rises to 50-Residents," Reuters, April 20, 2021, https://www.reuters.com/world/africa/death-toll-clashes-between-ethiopian-amhara-oromo-groups-rises-50-residents-2021-04-20/.

17. Nathalie LaCoste, *Waters of the Exodus: Jewish Experiences with Water in Ptolemaic and Roman Egypt* (Leiden: Brill, 2018), 16.

18. LaCoste, *Waters of the Exodus*, 1.

INTRODUCTION 25

military forces trigger early memories of an exodus motif as forced displacement, or did appeal to a nationalist exodus story and ideology mobilize and "justify" violence on the Other (a cipher for uncontrolled multiplicity)?[19] Amos' critique of a singularized appropriation of an exodus motif does not mean his rejection of the Exodus story's capacity to produce a just and nonviolent nation. The prophet's call for justice and righteousness to accompany the story is instructive because it gives voice and credibility to the use of the motif of justice (not just liberation) in prophetic literature and beyond.

This expansive prophetic ethos is evident in a narrative analyses of Exodus. Thus, William Propp finds the exodus story to be narratively satisfying in its capacity for resonance with several traditional motifs: (a) heroic tales in traditional folklore: in this formulation, Moses emerges as the main hero character coming to the rescue of a people that do not immediately embrace him; (b) Canaanite mythology about the storm god, Balu, who conquered the mythical sea and established his abode in the mountains. Here, Yahweh is the heroic character that overcomes mythical forces, but also historical and political forces of oppression; and (c) ancient rites of passage or initiation rites that transformed the social identity and function of the initiated. Here, Israel's journey out of Egypt—sometimes portrayed as a pilgrimage—toward the wilderness brought them into a new relationship with Yahweh, into a new space and sense of self-consciousness. Overall, Propp concludes, there is not one hero, but three in Exodus: Moses, Yahweh, and Israel.[20] I argue for an additional heroic character: the earth/land itself, without which there is no complete story and no capacity to nurture the flow of life.[21] In this multiply heroic story, transformation emerges as a function of the exodus community's internal capacities to produce multiply, and the exodus motif's ideological capacity to generate ripostes to recurring threats of erased, displaced, and singularized existence.

The story's quest for life-enhancing existence exceeds embodiment in any single individual or deity or generation. For its part, the motif

19. See Michael Walzer, *In God's Shadow: Politics in the Hebrew Bible* (New Haven, CT: Yale University Press, 2012), 34–49; Jan Assmann, *Moses the Egyptian: The Memory of Egypt in Western Monotheism* (Cambridge, MA: Harvard University Press, 1998); Jan Assmann, *The Price of Monotheism*, trans. Robert Savage (Stanford, CA: Stanford University Press, 2010).

20. William H. Propp, *Exodus 1–18: A New Translation with Introduction and Commentary* (Anchor Bible 2; New York: Doubleday, 1999), 32–36. George Coats has written extensively on Moses as a heroic character. See, for example, *Moses: Heroic Man, Man of God* (Sheffield: JSOT Press, 1987); George Coats, *The Moses Tradition* (Sheffield: JSOT Press, 1993).

21. I am grateful to Ryan Armstrong for suggesting that I consider the phrase "heroic character of the earth" rather than simply identifying the land/earth as another hero in a long list.

produces a "narrative cosmology" of exodus kinship of divine, human, and non-human characters.[22] This narrative cosmology is genealogically thick, spatially elastic, and politically mixed; it extends from Egypt as a site/time of birth as resistance to erasure, into the Wilderness as a site/time of survival as resistance to alienation, and into the Mountain as the site/time of belonging as resistance to singularity. It is the work of community belonging *through kinships of narrative strangers* in which Israel emerges as a mixed multitude (Exod. 12:38).[23] These Exodus-exodus kinship relations develop around specific narrative and social markers that also become a cluster of interpretive tropes.

First, ethnicity functions as a marker of malleable identity in Egypt and Midian, but it also defines the narrative "mixed multitude" of migrants and residents within a geopolitical landscape that stretches from Egypt to Canaan (Exod. 2:6, 19; 3:8, 17; 12:38). This ethnic malleability underlies communal narratives about "ethnic crossings" and anxieties about "mixed identities" in exilic and postexilic biblical texts (cf. the books of Ruth, Ezra, Nehemiah, and Esther). This malleability comes under particular duress during Pharaoh's oppressive regime and later in the Mountain area when faced with imperial power that attempts to restructure the liberated exodus community into the image of a single privileged individual or ideology (Exod. 32). Questions of ethnicity continue to function as socio-political and ideological determinants of the quality of life for a historically marginalized community.

Second, questions about sustainable freedom are particularly acute around women and their mostly male children.[24] At the intersection of gender and ethnicity, notions of singularized patriarchal ubiquity are set against notions of matriarchal multiplicity as resistance to singularity. This is what we find in the ancestral stories about Sarah and Hagar, and their children Isaac and Ishmael. The determining question in those stories of intergenerational, interregional, and interethnic mixing, oppression, expulsion, return, and divine encounter is not "who is the father?" (the question about singularity) but rather, "who

---

22. I borrow the expression "narrative cosmology" from Jeppe Sinding Jensen's essay "Framing Religions Narrative, Cognition and Culture Theoretically," in *Religious Narrative, Cognition and Culture: Image and Word in the Mind of Narrative*, ed. Armin W. Geertz and Jeppe Sinding Jensen (Sheffield: Equinox, 2011), 31–50. The expression refers to the total worldview—cognitive, social, and material—that is navigated, for example, in the Muslim pilgrimage to Mecca, the *Hajj*.

23. Kenneth Ngwa, "The Exodus Story and Its Literary Kinships," in *The Oxford Handbook of Biblical Narrative*, ed. Danna Nolan Fewell (Oxford: Oxford University Press, 2016), 125–36.

24. Danna Nolan Fewell and David M. Gunn, *Gender, Power, and Promise: The Subject of the Bible's First Story* (Nashville: Abingdon Press, 1993).

INTRODUCTION 27

are the mothers?" or, more specifically, "what are the ethnicities of the mothers"? In Exodus, gendered language is mapped onto geographical spaces and subjected to patriarchal futures: Canaan, the land promised to the patriarchs is a "good and spacious land, a land flowing with milk and honey" (Exod. 3:8, 17) but also, ironically, a land that devours its giant inhabitants (Num. 13:32); that is, a land subjected to singularizing ideology. In this gendered rendering of Exodus-exodus, generative motherhood (genealogical and geographical) is subsumed under a future construed as a gift to patriarchy. Exodus names and resists such limiting and gender binary futures by foregrounding the multiplicity of the Hebrew women, the midwives, and the Egyptian princess who are described as producers of demographic, epistemological, and political multiplicity (Exod. 1–2).

Third, politically, identity is intricately linked to violent geopolitical tussles that begin outside of, and then stretch into, the land of promise. As political boundaries emerge or break down; and as people are displaced in the wake of violence, regional identity transitions into transnational or internally displaced identity. This reality produces asylum-seeking Israel in the wilderness, en route to an old-new land (Exod. 6:6–8), a place affiliated with the erasure of other ethnic groups (Exod. 3:1–12; 14–15).[25] These shifting identities undergird multidirectional flows to the story, and frame the repeated back-and-forth between Yahweh and Moses over whose people Exodus-Israel is: Yahweh's or Moses'? A people living in, and coming out of, Egypt, or a people remembering a time when their ancestors lived in, and came out of, Egypt? To recognize these shifting identities is to resist totalizing generalizations about Exodus-Israel and assumptions that Exodus-Israel is an insular community.

Fourth, ecologically, the land of Egypt is subjected to massive exploitation and devastation in the form of plagues. The devastation is enormous and compels people to move into the wilderness, where the water is bitter—as if it had taken on the subjectivity of the bitter experience of political oppression. In that world of eco-political bitterness, the survivability of marginalized communities and of the earth and its species is informed by the story's response to political, theological, and ecological toxicity. To name, probe, and respond to this toxicity of thought, praxis, and space not as a consequence of some inherent inescapable flaw in natural ecosystems but as unethical

---

25. On Israel as asylum seeking, see, Jonathan Burnside, "Exodus and Asylum: Uncovering the Relationship between Biblical Law and Narrative," *Journal for the Study of the Old Testament* 34, no. 3 (2010): 254.

instrumentalizations of human and non-human life is to engage in Exodus-exodus thinking and becoming framed by ecological concerns. Once Pharaoh is removed from the scene, the community turns to the land more intentionally and fully as the primary subject to engage in the work of exodus. The people are described as belonging to the land—they are the people of the land (Exod. 5:4)—just as they are the people of Yahweh or Moses. It is as much a broken relation between humans and the land, as the broken political dynamic, that plagues the story. The emerging community cares as much about its obligations to the land as it does to the deity. Violations of divine precepts results in revulsions of the land (Deut. 27–28).

Fifth, resurgence and ongoing contestations in notions of "traditional" religion, within and beyond the geographical confines of Egypt, connect matriarchal and patriarchal traditions with the exodus deity (Yahweh) who, ironically, is tangentially linked with ancestral traditions (Exod. 3:13–18; 4:1–17; 6:2; cf. Gen. 21:15–21). These religious traditions become the bases for the communal move toward adherence to a deity proclaimed ("hear, O, Israel"—Deut. 6:4), a deity that demands oneness of devotion. The ability to align ancestral worship with exodus devotion is vital to communal survival in the face of a singularizing deity in the Mountain.

Clustered together, these identifiers—ethnic, gendered, geopolitical, ecological, and religious—weave a grand intergenerational and inter-regional narrative that addresses oppression (erasure), expulsion from land (alienation), and isolated (singularized) identity. To survive and eventually thrive, Israel becomes Exodus-Israel and transforms the traumas of oppression and expulsion and isolation into trauma-hopes and acts of liberation, regeneration, and revalorization that connect the story's human and divine residents with the earth/land—locally and globally.[26]

BACK TO THE FUTURE: EXODUS AND UBUNTU HERMENEUTICS

To say that Exodus-exodus has had life altering influence on modern history, religion, global politics, legislation, literature, ecology, war, migration, ethnicity, and race is to venture an understatement. To

---

26. Norman C. Habel, *The Land Is Mine: Six Biblical Land Ideologies* (Minneapolis: Fortress Press, 1995); Walter Brueggemann, *The Land: Place as Gift, Promise, and Challenge in Biblical Faith* (Minneapolis: Fortress Press, 2002); Sarah J. K. Pearce, *Land of the Body: Studies in Philo's Representation of Egypt* (Tübingen: Mohr Siebeck, 2007), 103–27.

INTRODUCTION   29

attempt to plumb the layers of that impressive, overwhelming history and historiography, with its varied attendant geographies, religious belief systems, and economic and political systems is to venture over-achievement. The breadth and depth of Exodus-exodus interpretation renders every interpreter and interpretation subjective, contextual, and limited. Yet, the motif of exodus requires a surpassing of singularized identity, the geopolitics of erasure, and marginalized existence. Such exodus overflow includes hermeneutics. The magnitude of textual anal-yses and reception histories surrounding Exodus accords hermeneutical grandeur to its interpretation, by virtue of the shared and contested meanings that make reception theory as consequential as historical-critical analyses.[27]

Like every interpreter, my interpretation is not that of a disinter-ested reader of the Bible or of Africana history, culture, religion, and politics. Instead, it develops and endorses an activist mode for three reasons. First, it is an interpretive response to a history and an ideology that portrays Africa as a place of incessant death and decay, a recent iteration of which was Donald Trump's reference to African countries as sh*thole countries. Africana hermeneutics is not just about inter-pretive survival and creativity, structured around comparative analyses between the ancient text and modern Africana realities; it is also about hermeneutics as defiance and resistance against erasure—colonial, rac-ist, gendering, ecological, or imperial. Second, Africana hermeneutics is an interpretive act that resists marginalization and creates new forms of being, belonging, and knowing not from methodological leftovers from so-called mainstream epistemologies, but from its own credible constructive resources. Third, Africana hermeneutics positions itself outside of singularizing blind spots of oppressive forms of nation-state, colonial, patriarchal, and imperial manifestations.

Whether Moses the man of Exodus-exodus was himself an Egyptian (as Sigmund Freud theorized in *Moses and Monotheism*) or a black Afri-can (as Zora Neal Hurston theorized in *Moses Man of the Mountain*) is of interpretive importance but is not fully determinant of the impact of thinking about Exodus-exodus in light of Africana experience. Of more importance is how to interpret the divine question to Moses in the burning bush, "What is in your hands?" (Exod. 4:2), and the deployment of that resource for the difficult work of liberation. From Musa Dube's *Postcolonial Feminist Interpretation*, to Nyasha Junior's

---

27. Thomas Dozeman, Craig A. Evans, Joel N. Lohr, eds., *The Book of Exodus: Composition, Reception, and Inter-pretation* (Leiden: Brill, 2014).

30   LET MY PEOPLE LIVE

Reimagining Hagar, to Aliou Niang's *A Poetics of Postcolonial Biblical Criticism,* to Alice Yafeh's *Paul's Sexual and Marital Ethics,* Africana biblical scholars labor in a tradition of interpretation that examines communal productions of meaning, freedom, power, and accountable living as quintessential antipathies of historical modes of dehumanizing confinement (enslavement and colonization and patriarchy) and attendant epistemological erasure, marginalization, and isolation of Africana and Black subjects, cultures, and religious thought.[28] To that end, Africana scholars and religious leaders have found in Exodus-exodus a story-motif of liberation or emancipation and empowerment. Having experienced violent erasure, dispersal, and isolation, African and African American readers turned to the story-motif, seeking an antidote but also, more importantly, seeking a new future. In *The Talking Book,* Allen Dwight Callahan writes about the homeopathic exegetical tradition of African American interpretation:

> African Americans found the Bible to be both healing balm and poison book. They could not lay claim to the balm without braving the poison. The same book was both medicine and malediction. To afford themselves its healing properties, African Americans resolved to treat scripture with scripture, much like a homeopathic remedy. . . . Their cure for the toxicity of pernicious scripture was more scripture. The antidote to hostile texts of the Bible was more Bible, homeopathically administered to counteract the toxins of the text.[29]

This homeopathic hermeneutic of squeezing generative and restorative exodus out of erasing and alienating exile often included the deployment of textual polyphony as a recipe for producing hopeful futures and experiences. As Rhondda Robinson Thomas argues in *Claiming Exodus,* African American appropriations of the biblical story between 1774 and 1903 were marked by remarkable fissures and fragments, pieced together from the Joseph story, the Moses story, and the Joshua story to mirror the complex realities that defined African American struggles for emancipation, justice, and equality. Thus, African Americans

> produced narratives of fragmentation, discontinuity, and instability that reflect the ultimate insufficiency of the Exodus story to help

---

28. Musa Dube, *Postcolonial Feminist Interpretation of the Bible* (Atlanta: SBL Press, 2000); Nyasha Junior, *Reimagining Hagar: Blackness and the Bible* (Oxford: Oxford University Press, 2019); Aliou Niang, *A Poetics of Postcolonial Biblical Criticism: God, Human-Nature Relationship, and Negritude* (Eugene, OR: Cascade Books, 2019); Alice Yafeh, *Paul's Sexual and Marital Ethics in 1 Corinthians 7: An African-Cameroonian Perspective* (New York: Peter Lang, 2015).

29. Allen Dwight Callahan, *The Talking Book: African Americans and the Bible* (New Haven, CT: Yale University Press, 2006), 40.

Afro-Atlantic peoples *fully* achieve their goals of freedom, equality, and opportunity. As they invoked the Exodus narrative, no Moses appeared to unite slaves and free blacks and demand that British kings and American presidents outlaw slavery and lift slaves from degradation. And no promised land loomed on the horizon where former black peoples and their brethren could permanently enjoy freedom and equality.[30]

Instead of relying on a single heroic character, readers and interpreters turned to multiple texts, piecing together portions of the biblical text of Exodus, supplementing those stories with other biblical texts as well as episodes of secular history "to share their experiences and delineate their demands" for a more just society.[31]

In South Africa, one of the earliest proponents of Black Theology, Itumeleng Mosala, brought together analyses of the Bible and analyses of the land:

> The task now facing a black theology of liberation is to enable black people to use the Bible to get the land back and to get the land back without losing the Bible . . . Black theology must employ the progressive aspects of black history and culture to liberate the Bible so that the Bible may liberate black people.[32]

Attuned to cultural analyses animating religious communities in Cameroon, Jean-Marc Éla sounded a similar alarm against distancing biblical interpretation from the history and context of the interpreter: "for millions of Africans, the signs of a world in quest for freedom and justice are too evident not to attract the attention of churches that boast the Judaeo-Christian revelation or claim that the message of the exodus occupies a central place."[33] Éla's work, published two years after a violent, failed coup d'état in Cameroon, signaled how liberation from colonialism and authoritarianism had stalled in Cameroon and indeed come to a violent halt. Independence ceased to be an ongoing work of liberation and instead became a political trophy, ritualized in highly militarized annual ceremonies. In the face of postcolonial necropolitics, Éla argued that the African church needed to renew its purpose, confront "today's Pharaohs," and prioritize the "new aspirations of all

---

30. Rhondda Robinson Thomas, *Claiming Exodus: A Cultural History of Afro-Atlantic Identity, 1774–1903* (Waco, TX: Baylor University Press, 2013), 7, italics in original.
31. Thomas, *Claiming Exodus*, 7.
32. Itumeleng J. Mosala, *Biblical Hermeneutics and Black Theology in South Africa* (Grand Rapids: Eerdmans, 1989), 153.
33. Jean-Marc Éla, *The African Cry*, trans. Robert R. Barr (New York: Orbis, 1986), 36.

the disinherited by bringing problems of women and men crushed by injustice into religious education, religious formation, and prayer."[34] Biblical and political interpretation and power again converged around issues of life.

The applicability of these modes and methods of interpretation to the Exodus-exodus is multiple. In this book, I focus on the notion that Africana biblical interpretation routinely examines the deployment of power in the production and concrete distribution of freedom, not solely through liberation historiography, or solely through homeopathic attempts to turn exile into Exodus-exodus, but also through robust re-articulations that put the motif *before* the story in a hermeneutical form of exodus-Exodus. In this mode, the decolonial exodus movement, "let my people go," is preceded by the precolonial exodus form, "let my people live." From anticolonial movements across the African continent to movements against apartheid in South Africa to resistance movements against slavery, Jim Crow, and segregation in the United States, Africana subjects have understood and appropriated Exodus as a story that compels the transformation of ideologies and systems where Black people live (pre-, during, and post-oppression), rather than solely a call to move from one land to another. The story thus calls for a redesign of Egypt, the Wilderness, and the Mountain, which represent systemic structures where the Hebrew people lived and suffered but also where they worked to bring liberation. In these distinct places, the exodus community cobbles together new ideas to generate life and meaning that is enduring.

The philosophical and hermeneutical concept I will use to explore these issues is Ubuntu, the complex Bantu-derived concept of political, social, psychological, and spiritual communal belonging most famously popularized and enacted by Desmond Tutu during the Truth and Reconciliation Commission's work in post-apartheid South Africa.[35] My use of Ubuntu as an epistemological and hermeneutical concept for reading Exodus is based on three framing issues. First, Ubuntu resources resistance against erasure. Communal interconnectedness enables an oppressed community to do the difficult work of forging geopolitical survival-liberation where the (former) oppressed and (former) oppressors share the same living space—a

---

34. Éla, *African Cry*, 38.
35. Desmond Tutu, *No Future without Forgiveness* (New York: Image Books, 1999); Michael Battle, *Ubuntu: I in You and You in Me* (New York: Seabury Books, 2009).

INTRODUCTION   33

space where institutional identity still bears memories and forms of erasure. In this scenario where Exodus and erasure coexist, Ubuntu fosters a hermeneutic of trauma-hope. By foregrounding communal interconnectedness, exodus-Exodus as Ubuntu can address the legacies of oppression in their structured manifestations. The erased self returns, not as an imperial presence but as a rebirth, a transformation of death into life. Second, the concept of Ubuntu as personhood in community illumines a healthy response to alienation, the partial loss of self, and even the sense of disposal associated with displacement. Here, Ubuntu fosters communal memory as an act of repositioning that seeks to reclaim communal wholeness. The marginalized self can return to the future because the communal body remembers and re-members its displaced kin. Third, Ubuntu hermeneutics illumines a reading of Exodus-exodus as a story-motif where liberation is enhanced as the act of departure from singularized subjectivity. Communal well-being is approximated and created when the singularized body—divine or human—responds to the beckoning voice of community and embarks on a risky journey and process of hermeneutical repositioning.

Through these multiple techniques, I intend to move the meaning line in biblical studies articulated by Brian Blount by switching the hermeneutical frame from Exodus-exodus (story-motif) to exodus-Exodus (motif-story). The motif is not just a concept, it is a genre; it foregrounds a communally endangered body, examines and listens to its articulations of survival in between fractured histories and narrative lacunae, and persists to ensure that the story birthed from this motif is qualitatively different from the story to which the motif responds. That is, the switch from "let my people go" to "let my people live" means that liberation is more than a response to oppression. Africana life and hermeneutics include a response to oppression, and so accord with the epistemological and hermeneutical force of "let my people go." The power and future of liberation—the power to transform unformed futures into formed futures—depends on making sure that those narrative lacunae speak, and that they speak not so much as perfectly designed stories with only occasional detours but as resilient voices that regenerate and produce new life and life-forms. In addition, Africana life and hermeneutics moves the meaning line by insisting that the qualitative value of its hermeneutical priorities and approaches to the biblical text exceed a response mechanism to systems of oppression and the centering of colonialism, racism, patriarchy, and imperialism.

"Let my people live" shifts the paradigm because conquest and oppression and racism are not only avoidable evils, they also are unnecessary. That is what makes structural redesign imaginable, conceivable, and possible in exodus-Exodus interlocution.

1

Tears of Redesign

Birthing Exodus and Badass Womanism

> Have mercy! Lord, have mercy on my poor soul! Women gave birth and whispered cries like this in caves and out-of-the-way places that humans didn't usually use for birthplaces. Moses hadn't come yet, and these were the years when Israel first made tears.[1]

These opening words from Zora Neale Hurston's now classic novel, *Moses, Man of the Mountain*, represent an enduring hermeneutical entry point into exodus storytelling for endangered and marginalized communities. Hurston's words represent and interpret exodus as life formed and nurtured through immense tears and grit and anguish, in dark places and darkened modes of being, tethered to a future yet unformed and a past/present mired in trauma. Hurston's formulations constitute part of a larger project of Africa-related cultural and historical criticisms and interpretations of the Bible that emerged during the interwar period—the period when official colonization and exploitation of the majority world by Europe came under new and renewed critical assault. If the First World War shattered faulty notions of historical objectivity under the control of colonizing and imperial powers and their embodiments of toxic singularity, the interwar period opened up the space for a theoretical alternative: the application of rigorous political critique of colonialism and the emergence of new beginnings to enhance the value and importance of marginalized voices in shaping discourse about the production of global space sharing and meaning making. It was the early stages of anticolonial movements taking official narrative stage and eventually taking over official governing infrastructure. According to

---

1. Zora Neale Hurston, *Moses, Man of the Mountain* (New York: Harper Perennial, 1991), 1

Hurston, Moses the liberator had not been born; but there were many cries around the world, and anticolonial movements were gathering real and lasting momentum that would usher in the official demise of colonialism. Discourse about the future—about the postcolonial space and time—was etched into assessments of the impact of unaccountable power on marginalized and minoritized communities. Such analyses unfolded as much in the fields of political theory as in the fields of economic, psychological, cultural, literary, and religious analyses. Examples included Akiki Nyabongo's *The Story of an African Chief*, Samir Amin's *Re-reading the Postwar Period*, Alan Paton's *Cry, the Beloved Country*, Ferdinand Oyono's *Houseboy*, and Buchi Emecheta's *The Joys of Motherhood*, to name a few.[2]

These cultural-historical formulations were developed for the interpretive purposes of probing how meaning takes shape and form in culture broadly and in popular culture in particular, but they were also vital to creating the parameters for the emergence of African biblical hermeneutics from the margins after World War I.[3] In responding to the histories and ideologies of colonialism and the anticipated dawn of its official end, such cultural-historical analyses explored notions of beginnings as simultaneous manifestations of novelty and continuity, located at the liquid time-space of transition from death to life, from marginalized to recognized existence, and from isolation/singularity to community. The novelty of historical and interpretive beginnings may be sourced into the past, or in darkened places and historical lacunae of marginalization, but novelty and originality are not permanently lodged in the past; the novelty of beginnings is canonical in the sense that it is able to travel into the future and, in fact, to produce a future that is like the creative past but also—and this is crucial for hermeneutics from the margins—unlike the oppressive past. To invoke and paraphrase a quote attributed, with uncertainty, to Mark Twain: "History doesn't repeat itself but it often rhymes." Well, so does the flow of literature and interpretation. Assessments of the non-repetitive but

---

2. Akiki Nyabongo, *The Story of an African Chief* (New York: C. Scribner, 1935); Samir Amin, *Re-reading the Postwar Period: An Intellectual Itinerary*, trans. Michael Wolfers (New York: Monthly Review, 1994); Alan Paton, *Cry, the Beloved Country* (New York: C. Scribner's Sons, 1948); Ferdinand Oyono, *Houseboy*, trans. John Reed (Long Grove, IL: Waveland Press, 1966); Buchi Emecheta, *The Joys of Motherhood* (London: Heinemann, 1994).

3. Joseph J. Williams, *Hebrewisms of West Africa: From the Nile to Niger with the Jews* (Baltimore: Black Classic Press, 1999). See also Timothy Beal, "Cultural-Historical Criticism of the Bible," in *New Meanings for Ancient Texts: Recent Approaches to Biblical Criticism and Their Approaches*, ed. Steven L. Mckenzie and John Kaltner (Louisville, KY: Westminster John Knox Press, 2013), 1.

rhyming character of history and literature are possible and meaningful because memory, or rememory, as Toni Morrison has taught us, is coded not just in textual details and facts of history and literature themselves but also in their flows—in the discordant and convergent material human and cultural bodies that have shaped and been shaped by that history and literature. The interpreting subject cannot meaningfully live without engaging history—its reality and artifacts and flows. And the survivor of a brutal flow of history and interpretation cannot live meaningfully without rememory—the capacity and necessity to interpret history—its erasures, its tears, hopes, whispering, and/or soaring rhetoric—for the purposes of giving creative and transformative structure to current identity and to a healthy future for community.

Like Hurston's marginalized community, exodus-Exodus begins with the motif-story of the children of Israel journeying into a future that is yet unborn/unformed but that somehow contains the burdens and groans of the past and present. The children are in fact en route to a place where Joseph was already (Exod. 1:5)! It is a journey down a dreaded path already trod. For this moving community, exile is intimate and experienced not simply in terms of geographical displacement but also in terms of anxieties about the infrastructure and the functioning of the nation (or empire) toward which one journeys. Is this journey toward the empire already doomed? It certainly is a journey of trauma-hope, represented by Joseph's experience portrayed in Genesis—his encounter with, and dreams of, empire and the anxieties and conflicts that such dreams caused him and his brothers; his capture and sale into slavery; his experience of sexual harassment and imprisonment; his skills in mantic and experiential wisdom; his release from prison; his rise to political prominence; and his referential role in the narrative imagination of Exodus and its narrator (Gen. 37–50). Thus framed, the first narrative lacuna, the first release of communal tears, in this storied journey is that the oppressive Pharaoh did not know Joseph (Exod. 1:8). What it is about Joseph that this Pharaoh—only the latest in a succession of pharaohs within the political institution—did not know is unclear and unstated. But Pharaoh's epistemological amnesia screams for narrative and interpretive attention. His amnesia is corrosive to the communal and interpretive existence of the Hebrews. And it is from that abyss that exodus-motif begins to birth Exodus-story.

EXODUS AND BADASS WOMANISM

Like the writers of Genesis 1 and of Exodus (1–2), Hurston begins her narrative in a watery and mythical geopolitical space-time of the womb and of tears. It is both a probing and a telling of herstory through embodied mythic memory, including memory that is projected into the future (Moses had not been born) because it lives as yet in flowing watery spaces and in the literary imaginations of its incubators and ancestors. The motif thus vocally embodies and represents its muted productions of liberation life, even as it also shifts those beginnings away from anxieties about imperial and patriarchal power of death to possibilities of futures detached from forces of marginalization, erasure, and singularity. The exodus-motif begins to produce an Exodus-story flow of resistance by portraying the Israelites as "fruitful and prolific" (Exod. 1:7) and describing the Hebrew women as "vigorous" (Exod. 1:19). Pharaoh's amnesia—as consequential as it is—is nevertheless relativized by the antecedent fruitful and prolific work of the Hebrew women and by the subsequent vigorous work of the community.

What kind of life work might one discern at the birthplaces of the story? What I would call badass womanist work! Badass womanism is an epistemological, embodied, and strategic hermeneutical approach that, as I frame here as an iteration of womanism, recognizes, resists, and ultimately overcomes the triple consciousness and experiences of erasure, alienation, and singularity.

Womanism is the theoretical and interpretive gift from Alice Walker and many Black women to all—but especially to women of color. In the preface to her work *In Search of Our Mothers*, Walker provides a four-part definition of womanist. The first part includes the following: "usually referring to outrageous, audacious, courageous or willful behavior. Wanting to know more and in greater depth than is considered 'good' for one."[4] As a self-redeeming and self-asserting posture, ethos and process of restorative and expansive dignity and creativity, womanism represents forms of subjectivity and belonging that examine deep textures of life in the shadow of oppression and the vibrant textures of generative belonging in epistemological, sociocultural, economic, and political production. As Monica Coleman's edited volume, *Ain't I a Womanist, Too?* shows, womanism's engagement with

---

4. Alice Walker, *In Search of Our Mothers' Gardens: Womanist Prose* (San Diego: Harcourt Brace Jovanovich, 1983), xi.

religious experience, culture, and politics requires as much historical depth as theoretical breadth. The metaphor of "waves" is deployed to sequence and herstoricize the intellectual movements and disciplinary methodologies of inquiry associated with womanism and to explore its layered textures of being and belonging.[5]

Womanism's impact on biblical interpretation, in general, and the exodus in particular is well established.[6] Delores Williams's *Sisters in the Wilderness* was an important intervention in liberation theological discourse, in general, and in Black liberation theology in particular. The book's title foregrounds two important voices in exodus discourse: first, womanist formulations about dimensions of oppression that are inherent and routinized in the story, and the epistemology of sisterhood necessary to enhance full liberation; and second, Wilderness that functions less as a transitional space-time in the Exodus and more as the place where Black women's creativity and subjectivity unfolds beyond nationalistic, patriarchal, and androcentric vectors. To be sisters in the Wilderness, to embody the temporal and spatial location of wilderness as central to Exodus interpretation, is to resist the tendency to engage non-male and non-androcentric readings of the story as either afterthoughts or secondary. What unfolds among these sisters and this sisterhood epistemology is more than an addition of meaning to a story whose parameters are already set and more than a corrective measure to an established trajectory gone awry. What unfolds is a reformulation of the story's basic structures and goals. From the Wilderness emerges a new and distinct exodus-Exodus, tethered not to national identity to be reclaimed in the future, but to a future that is still unformed, a future still being born and still gathering its promissory character. This womanist exodus community is not completely shackled (though it is burdened) by the routines of established oppressive national and patriarchal practices seeking to stop new births, nor is it interested in reproducing disparities in privilege in national and patriarchal formulations.

Williams's work did more than expand the interpretive space and vernacular of liberation; she also made a hermeneutical and ethical claim: that Wilderness religious experience, more than Black male

---

5. Monica Coleman, ed., *Ain't I a Womanist, Too?: Third-Wave Womanist Religious Thought* (Minneapolis: Fortress Press, 2013).

6. Renita J. Weems, *Just a Sister Away: A Womanist Vision of Women's Relationships in the Bible* (San Diego: LuraMedia, 1988); Madipoane J. Masenya, *How Worthy Is the Woman of Worth?: Rereading Proverbs 31:10–31 in African South-Africa* (New York: Peter Lang, 2004); Wilda C. Gafney, *Womanist Midrash: A Re-introduction to the Women of the Torah and the Throne* (Louisville, KY: Westminster John Knox Press, 2017).

experience, is appropriate for describing African American women's experience in North America. It was an interpretive and theoretical move that distinguished womanism from the concerns of white women and the concerns of Black men; the experience of Black women needed to be studied in its own right. Williams provided six reasons to support her claim: (1) wilderness experience includes female-male-family structures, rather than just male-female formulations, and is more expansive than racial parameters; (2) wilderness experience, more than Black male experience, speaks to human initiative in creating community; (3) wilderness experience signals resistance to binary constructions of religious and secular experience; (4) moving beyond negative portrayals of Black experience of oppression, wilderness offers possibilities for reflecting on Black ingenuity and intelligence for the creation of cultures of resistance; (5) wilderness experience enhances and supports the building of leadership roles for women and mothers; and (6) wilderness experience is the space for engagement and discourse between Black liberation theologians, feminist theologians, and womanist theologians.[7] All of these points are summed up in a rationale about the significance of the wilderness as critically important "not only because Hagar's black women's and black people's experiences with God gained dimension in the wilderness, but because the biblical wilderness tradition also emphasizes survival, quality of life formation with God's direction, and the work of building a peoplehood and a community."[8]

Williams's pan-African view of womanism is evident in her alignment with the work of African women that was already formalizing around the Circle of Concerned African Women Theologians, simply known as the Circle.[9] Launched in 1989, the Circle itself—the brainchild of Ghanaian theologian Mercy Amba Oduyoye—was at once a response to the movement of cultural retrieval that had animated and informed much of African male theologies since the early 1950s and a desire to articulate an alternative theoretical anchoring space that recognized the inherent ingenuity of African women and their determination—and divine invitation—to rise. For Oduyoye and other members of the Circle, the critical thrust for Circle framing and analyses comes from Mark 5:21–43 and is encapsulated in the phrase *Talitha Cum*—"Little girl, I say wake up." The Circle's first two publications would

---

7. Delores Williams, *Sisters in the Wilderness: The Challenge of Womanist God-Talk* (New York: Orbis Books, 1993), 141–42.

8. Williams, *Sisters*, 142.

9. Williams, *Sisters*, xiv.

TEARS OF REDESIGN

directly appeal to this powerful image of life overcoming death.[10] Like Alice Walker's womanist thrust, *Talitha Cum* is based on authentic self-knowing and resourcing, and the ability to transgress any and all boundaries of restriction, including intellectual and material isolation, alienation, and death.

If womanism as defined by Walker was "wanting to know more and in greater depth than is considered 'good' for one," then that embodied epistemological and socio-political posture might well be called badass womanism. Badass womanism is an embodied, epistemological, and hermeneutical rising against patriarchal and colonial triads of toxic masculine singularity, disempowering alienation, and traumatizing erasure. To that end, badass womanism multiply produces modes of resistance and being that parallel and exceed the theoretical insights of feminism.[11] But it is also the courage to narrativize such resistance as invaluable to full appreciation of the concrete times and spaces that create and sustain holistic liberation. In this sense, the metaphor of Circle is hermeneutically and metaphorically pertinent because it intentionally produces multiplicity that privileges non-hierarchical formulations and structures of power and knowledge production.

A few years after the work of the Circle was launched, Oduyoye published *Daughters of Anowa*, one of her most theorized and piercing critiques of African and colonial patriarchy and its impact on African women.[12] The brilliant irony in Oduyoye's title is that Anowa—the protagonist in Ama Ata Aidoo's 1970 play by the same title—has no biological children and finds herself agonizing and struggling under the cultural burdens of patriarchal expectations about her need to bear children. The framing and subjugation of the African woman's body to biological functions of childbearing and the patriarchal freak-out when her body refuses to fill that defined and constraining role are two recurrent themes that Oduyoye explores in her reading of African narrative and material cultures.

If Hurston began her work on *Moses* around the racial tears of life-giving Hebrew (and African American) women, Oduyoye began her rereading of Anowa at another place of tears—in colonial and

---

10. Mercy Amba Oduyoye and Musimbi R. A. Kanyoro, eds., *The Will to Arise: Women, Tradition, and the Church in Africa* (Maryknoll, NY: Orbis Books, 1992); Mercy Amba Oduyoye, *Talitha Qumi!: Proceedings of the Convocation of African Women Theologians, Trinity College Legon-Accra, September 24–October 2, 1989* (Accra, Ghana: Daystar Press, 1990).

11. Sarah Shahan, "Alice Walker and Her Badass Women: How Womanism Is Stronger than Feminism and Why It Pertains to the African American Woman Experience," Odyssey, https://www.theodysseyonline.com/alice-walker-badass-women.

12. Mercy Amba Oduyoye, *Daughters of Anowa: African Women and Patriarchy* (New York: Orbis Books, 1995).

postcolonial economic and cultural kitchens in Africa: "For the vast majority of African women there is no food without fire. I mean *firewood* fire, producing smoke that stings your eyes and makes you cry. One ought really to say there is no life without smoke in Africa."[13] In the end—or in the midst of colonial, postcolonial, and patriarchal fires that African women endured and released in tears—Oduyoye reclaims Anowa and gives her epistemological children, precisely where patriarchy refused, failed, or could not. Through the Circle, African women continue to develop their voices, creativity, and tears, and they contribute to the theory and work of liberation, which Oduyoye variously describes as "eruption," as "boiling lava beneath the patriarchal clan," and as "a multi-vocal theme song."[14]

Oduyoye's diagnoses of the patriarchal response to women's movements such as the Circle is both sarcastic and incisive. Portrayed as preening about how well-behaved, docile, and content African women were, African (Akan) men who invested in patriarchy's ideology and structure would describe the unfolding work of African women as, in Oduyoye's description, "a few *bad* eggs under the influence of decadent women of the West."[15] *Bad* eggs. Through her rereading of intersecting patriarchal, cultural, and colonial oppressions, Oduyoye turns this characterization of trouble-making women around, describing what I call *badass womanism*:

> Faced with the increasing social pressure on women to return to tradition, it is of the most importance that women join together to define what tradition they are being asked to return to, and whether it is advisable for women to *return* while men *move on* into the [future]. We should take another look at the model of the traditional West African market woman. . . . If women are to make an impact on public policy, we must look seriously at how our solidarity at the local level can be brought to bear upon national legislation. And we must do this now, refusing to let seemingly trivial issues—such as our naming by Madam, Mrs., or Ms.—overshadow questions of real autonomy, the naming and defining of who we are.[16]

In their framing of the Circle's work, Oduyoye and Kanyoro present the issue in stark terms of life and death: "African women theologians have come to realize that as long as men and foreign researchers remain

---

13. Oduyoye, *Daughters*, 1, italics in original.
14. Oduyoye, *Daughters*, 1.
15. Oduyoye, *Daughters*, 3, italics added.
16. Oduyoye, *Daughters*, 108, italics in original.

the authorities on culture, rituals, and religion, African women will continue to be spoken of as if they were dead."[17] Teasing out the implications of being treated as if dead, or as if one lived in the dead zone of necropolitics, Oduyoye and Kanyoro talk about the ethical costs of the truth about African women's experiences remaining hidden. The interpretive work of the Circle includes a "compelling and compulsory" sense of engaging biblical interpretation in a way that addresses the realities of life: "controversial elements of life in Africa, such as culture, sexuality, rituals, and rites of passage. These elements of life are part of their religion."[18]

The work of the Circle has significant methodological impact for biblical interpretation. The hermeneutical line between biblical interpretation and lived experience is that "biblical history continues in the lives of God's people."[19] The methodological and theoretical parameters of this interpretive through-line in biblical studies is now a well-recognized subject of scholarship. To that endeavor, badass womanism contributes by shaping the theoretical and hermeneutical praxis of liberative triple consciousness.

The work of the Circle resists toxic singularity, which prioritizes and incentivizes single (male) heroes. This resistance is evidenced, for example, in Musa Dube's edited volume *Other Ways of Reading*, where she identifies two methodological insights for biblical interpretation.[20] The Circle's intentional description of its meetings as "consultation" translates into hermeneutics as *storytelling* and as *divination*. Storytelling, Dube points out, is a female gendered role in African traditional cultures, even though substantial numbers of African stories themselves are gender neutral. The story world, its characters, and the storyteller become the space for exploring philosophies of survival and processes of negotiation and dexterity that make "storytelling itself (and the story itself) a moment of community writing or interpretation of life, rather than an activity of the teller or author."[21] Here is a distinctive decentering and distancing of biblical interpretation from the privilege of so-called omniscient narrator(s). Here is also a mode of centering the transformative work of storytelling that can only be more fully done by and in community: "the teller or writer thus does not own the story or

---

17. Oduyoye and Kanyoro, eds., *The Will*, 1.
18. Oduyoye and Kanyoro, *The Will*, 1.
19. Oduyoye and Kanyoro, *The Will*, 5.
20. Musa Dube, ed., *Other Ways of Reading: African Women and the Bible* (Atlanta: Society of Biblical Literature, 2001).
21. Dube, *Other Ways*, 3.

have the last word, but rather the story is never finished: it is a page of the community's fresh and continuous reflection."[22] Through badass womanist storytelling work, the interpretive and liberating meaning line is moved beyond the privileges of single individuals, or one-directional narrative movement.

Alongside storytelling, *Other Ways of Reading* also examines divination as a method of biblical interpretation. Dube sets the premise of divination as

> reading an authoritative book of social life. Diviner-healers read divining sets to diagnose problems and to offer solutions to consulting (nonprofessional) readers. Divining sets, which could be composed of carved bones, beans, beads, coins, and so on, are not fixed or closed canons or stories. Rather, each consulting reader . . . writes and reads her/his own story with the diviner-healer in the reading session.[23]

Conceptualized as a distinct interpretive approach, Dube associates divination—"a practice that is tantamount to reading an authoritative social book"—with the womanhood (*bosadi*) hermeneutics of Madipoane Masenya and womanist hermeneutic of Sarojini Nadar.[24] Hermeneutics as a form of divination is thoroughly communal. In that socially constructed epistemological space, the expertise of the specialist meets the routineness of the consultant to produce and deploy social meaning. The Bible is understood as a "talking book" much like divining sets. Divination is a method of knowledge production "that demands ethical commitment from all participating readers. It involves the realization that one is socially connected and has a responsibility to create and maintain healthy relationships, as well as to *avoid those that negate life*."[25] By placing the diviner, the consultant, and the religious objects in a multimodal relation of simultaneous and dynamic creativity, divination reads and interprets more than an isolated text; it reads and enhances communal life.

Womanism as embodied and represented in the Circle also resists interpretive and spatial alienation. In *Daughters of Dignity*, LaVerne McCain Gill poses provocative, existential, and vitally critical hermeneutical questions that frame and contribute to Africana hermeneutics:

22. Dube, *Other Ways*, 3.
23. Dube, *Other Ways*, 181.
24. Dube, *Other Ways*, 10–11.
25. Dube, *Other Ways*, 184, emphasis added.

How did African women transform themselves into today's African American women? What was the process that they used to envision their lives as women of God and not slaves of men? How did they move from the mantle of oppression to the altar of praise; from the bottom of the slave ship to the halls of Congress? What is their link to the stories of African women in the Bible?[26]

Gill's questions weave a thread of meaning across spatial range and depth—stretching from Africa to the Americas. This interpretive thread across space and time is significant, not because it aggregates a variety of subjects and subject-matters pertinent to the character, process, and manifestations of womanist modes of liberation, but because it examines the historical emergence of identity as an outcome of intentional strategic improvisation and creativity. Creativity unfolds as resistance to being marginalized/alienated or used as subsidies in global productions of masculine narratives, biblical and otherwise. African American herstories are as canonical as biblical stories, and they function as cultural and hermeneutical modes and sites of resistance and creativity inside and outside of the biblical text. In the unfolding praxis of herstoriography and its envisioning of futures populated by African-turned-African American women, Gill argues that African American women "forged an ethic of black womanhood that defined the manner in which they would survive in an alien and strange land—America."[27] Gill's work focuses on five biblical characters—Hagar, Zipporah, Rahab, the Queen of Sheba, and the Samaritan woman at the well—as embodying the virtues of justice, love, faith, wisdom, and perseverance respectively. For Gill, these stories contribute to a "justice reading strategy."[28] Resistance against alienation manifests in the form of justice work.

Third, to draw from badass womanism is to resist erasure; it is to turn the tears of racism and patriarchy that Hurston and Oduyoye speak about into theories about the erupting and creative waters of the Harlem Renaissance and the Negritude movement and the Circle—spaces where new futures are formed and new life-forms unfold. In that sense, badass womanism is akin to the theoretical and praxis mode of communal existence, survival, and creativity conveyed in

---

26. LaVerne McCain Gill, *Daughters of Dignity: African Women in the Bible and the Virtues of Black Womanhood* (Cleveland, OH: The Pilgrim Press, 2000), xiv.

27. Gill, *Daughters of Dignity*, xiv–xv. Gill's words about an alien and strange land evoke memories of Moses' experience in Midian, where he said, "I have become an alien in a strange land" (Exod. 2:22). I will return to this story in chapter three, to demonstrate its significance in the emergence of Exodus intergenerational identity and hermeneutics.

28. Gill, *Daughters of Dignity*, xv.

the concept of *kanju* that the Nigerian American journalist, Dayo Olopade, describes in *The Bright Continent*. *Kanju*, writes Olopade, is "the specific creativity born from African difficulty. As it turns out, uncertain electricity, clogged roads, and non existent social protections can make life tough, but they also produce an extraordinary capacity for making do."[29] Drawn from Yoruba language, *kanju* literally means "to rush" or "to make haste." This would translate as "hustle" or "strive" and such wisdom-related concepts as "know-how" or "make do."[30]

The capacity for creative improvisation is part of a cultural approach that is "less about subjective beauty than about practical solutions, and doing much more with far less. In fact, the most important thing about *kanju* is that it is born out of everything outsiders pity in Africa."[31] The things that "outsiders pity in Africa" are the things that would make Africa supposedly erasable. *Kanju* is a riposte to stifling conditions of marginality and austerity that haunt and plague distressed communities. But more importantly, *kanju* is the ability to create life out of the death of culture, religion, politics, and economics, and therefore to create new identity. As an epistemological concept, *kanju* is analogous to what Mitzi Smith has described as "womanist sass."[32] Grounded in womanism, which Smith rightly identifies as feminism's sister, not its child, the concept of sass, used interchangeably with talk-back, is a

> means of agency, of being heard and of combating an other-imposed invisibility; it is resistance language that women, children, people of color, and black women in particular, speak and embody, inside and outside black communities and institutions. Sass is often defined as mouthing off, talking back, back talking, attitude, a woman not backing down to a man, or a child determined to have the final word in response to a real or perceived injustice or wrong.[33]

Such persistent work of righting the wrongs of injustice produces life and then makes life itself the preexisting social and theoretical determinant of hermeneutics. As Teresa Okure puts it, "life as the starting point and abiding context of hermeneutics is not only important; it is a

---

29. Dayo Olopade, *The Bright Continent: Breaking Rules and Making Change in Modern Africa* (New York: Houghton Mifflin Harcourt Publishing Co., 2014), 20.

30. Olopade, *The Bright Continent*, 21.

31. Olopade, *The Bright Continent*, 22.

32. Mitzi J. Smith, *Womanist Sass and Talk Back: Social (In)Justice, Intersectionality, and Biblical Interpretation* (Eugene, OR: Cascade Books, 2018).

33. Smith, *Womanist Sass*, 30.

reality that imposes itself."[34] To read with life imposing itself is to read against Pharaoh's work; it is to insist on biopolitics imposing itself in the space of necropolitics.

EXODUS AS A BADASS WOMANIST STORY

Exodus is a story in which endangered (erased), alienated, and singularized bodies are placed inside crumbling ethnocentric political systems that they work to transform; a story in which ravaged ecosystems compel people to move and adjust; and a story in which death and erasure threaten to saturate political and religious life. Political outcry against the structures of erasure, alienation, and singularity stretches from birth stools to the banks of the Nile to Pharaoh's court, and it fuels the political, social, and religious movements/flows that produce exodus as freedom. This unrelenting, multimodal, and multispatial outcry summons the imagination and expressions of the story's primary key leaders and characters: the midwives, the Egyptian princess, Moses, Aaron, Miriam, Jochebed, Jethro, his daughters (and perhaps their unnamed mother), the earth/land, the waters, and the pillars of cloud and fire. All of these characters are mobilized to resist erasure, alienation, and singularity, not just in episodic forms in Egypt or the Wilderness or the Mountain area but also in their structured and institutional forms. This means that the work of exodus is not just about movement from one place to another, but about bringing liberation to those places. I have named this form of exodus work badass womanist work.

In her introduction to the *Women's Hebrew Bible*, Susanne Scholz asks: "Why did I not ask about Miriam when I was a child?" The question—which identifies what she calls the omnipresence of androcentric biases in theological education—is part of her reflection on the early stages of her theological curiosity, when she had asked her parents, "Who is Moses?"[35] What does badass womanist hermeneutic do with this question ("Who is Moses?"), or with its prioritization? I would suggest that badass womanism does not stop asking that question; rather, it stops asking it as if it were the only or the first question. If Micah

---

34. Teresa Okure, "First Was the Life, Not the Book," in *To Cast Fire upon the Earth: Bible and Mission Collaborating in Today's Multicultural Global Context: A Project of BISAM, and Interest Group of IAMS*, ed. Teresa Okure, SHCJ (Pietermaritzburg: Cluster Publications, 2000), 209.

35. Susanne Scholz, *Introducing the Women's Hebrew Bible: Feminist, Gender Justice, and the Study of the Old Testament* (London: Bloomsbury T&T Clark, 2017), 1, 3.

6:4 is read from a womanist perspective, then the narrative sequencing of Moses, Aaron, and Miriam as genealogical ancestors of exodus may reflect less of the prioritization of Moses and more of a communal crescendo effect of cluster hermeneutics. Such hermeneutic puts Miriam at a premium without simply reversing the pyramid. Badass womanism resists and rejects the singularization of community and narration. One reads toward the communal premium, not the singular hero.

In Hurston's *Moses*, the plenitude of exodus work required and produced multiple myths about Moses, evident in multiple liberation stories around the world. The work of producing these kinds of Moses meant, inter alia, exploring the implications of communal voices that articulated genealogical and political kinships forged in resistance to global violence, kinships that challenged global politics of colonialism and segregation. In her diagnoses of political struggles for liberation, Hurston highlighted a tragic paradox at the intersection of gender and power. She portrayed Moses as a character that continuously held Miriam at bay. In the end, as if to signify the tragic erasure of the female body in the process of the constructions of nationalist movements in the 1930s and into the 1950s, Hurston's Miriam asks to be released from Moses' shadow so that she can die; that is, Miriam, in badass womanist mode of hermeneutics, demanded and worked for liberation that was not tethered to androcentric infrastructure and power. Release from such structures might be costly, even deadly, but in fact functions as the necessary and ultimate expression of life. Hurston's work thus suggests a mode and method of probing Exodus that examines what happens when death oversaturates a liberation struggle and overwrites its discourse and its utopias; and it also examines what kinds of politics and life-forms ought to unfold, become thinkable, doable, and privileged in the face of such realities.

For the form of Africana exodus hermeneutic explored here, badass womanism insists that one understands the words of the midwives to Pharaoh as Miriamic talkback—discourse as narrative resistance and redesign, in the epistemological and embodied style of Miriam. Hermeneutic unfolds as an expansive and a creative manifestation of the power of social and political badass womanist discourse. Its capacity to situate itself and its generative life *prior to* the arrival of disposability, outside totalizing power to control, enables it to resist and ultimately outlive disposability: "'Because the Hebrew women are not like the Egyptian women; for they are vigorous and give birth before the midwife comes to them'" (Exod. 1:19, emphasis added). This is not simply an anecdotal story of trickery by marginalized persons and their narrators—a story that assumes and then uses Pharaoh's ethnic stereotyping to outmaneuver him. Rather, it is a story that gestures toward a truth claim, uttered as a riposte to the Pharaoh, by the Hebrew women—a truth claim that narrativizes beginnings and insists on the primordiality and the sovereignty of life, not death. These are the words of badass womanism—the interpretive capacity, linked with an ideological and interpretive predisposition, to expand the narrative framework beyond its experience of geopolitical, gendered, ethnic, racial, and religious confinement, alienation, and singularity. In the face of oppression and targeted destruction of marginalized communities, one tells the Exodus story to ensure that memory of disposable life is accountable, not just sacred; and that the future life of the marginalized and endangered community is imaginable, fashionable, and expansive, rather than obscure, elusive, and restricting.

How does such a community perform its work as midwives and sustain its exodus ethos to survive and live—produce, nurture, interpret, transmit and assess its values, mourn its tragic losses, and recreate its futures—when life-making develops in the shadows of state-sanctioned death and is continuously hampered by legacies, rhymes, and structures of patriarchal and colonial definitions?[36] *And* how does the exodus community do its work in the face of legacies of displacement and its corruption and blotting out of futures? *And* how does the community thrive in the face of ongoing manifestations of postcolonial distress, political apathy and malaise, and continuing economic and environmental erasure? The issue may be stated otherwise: What happens when life becomes disposable, not by natural causes but by deliberate violation? What does it mean to inhabit, to somehow survive, and ultimately to demand release from the places of disposable life: the space-time of colonial necropolitics that Achille Mbembe theorizes in *On the Postcolony*, the space-time of postcolonial trauma that Emmanuel Katongole explores in *The Sacrifice of Africa*, or the space-time of enslavement and its "after lives" that Christina Sharpe excavates in *In the Wake*?[37] And, once inhabited, how does one recover from that social, environmental, and historical space-time and its ideological force? Does one rise, as the poet Maya Angelou defiantly proclaimed?[38]

---

36. On the role of the midwives, see L. Juliana M. Claassens, *Mourner, Mother, Midwife: Reimagining God's Delivering Presence in the Old Testament* (Louisville, KY: Westminster John Knox Press, 2012).

37. Achille Mbembe, *On the Postcolony* (Berkeley: University of California Press, 2001); Emmanuel Katongole, *The Sacrifice of Africa: A Political Theology for Africa* (Grand Rapids, MI: W. B. Eerdmans Publishing, 2011); Christina Sharpe, *In the Wake: On Blackness and Being* (Durham, NC: Duke University Press, 2016).

38. Maya Angelou, *And Still I Rise* (London: Virago Press, 1978).

50   LET MY PEOPLE LIVE

Does one sink to the bottom of the material and ideological sea/ocean, offering down one's blood to its saltiness, and living on in that cycle—a cycle that could last over 260 million years?

> The amount of time it takes for a substance to enter the ocean and then leave the ocean is called residence time. Human blood is salty, and sodium . . . has a residence time of 260 million years. And what happens to the energy that is produced in the waters? It continues cycling like atoms in residence time. We, Black people, exist in the residence time of the wake.[39]

Does one fly away like the fluttering spirit/wind of creation-world (Gen. 1:3); or hover over the watery face of the broken community (in the creation story, the divine hovers over the face of the water [Gen. 1:2]); or rise and settle like a pillar of cloud (Exod. 13:21; 16:10; 40:34–38); or participate in the aerodynamic subjectivity of endangered persons attached to the wings of an eagle (Exod. 19:4)?

If the Hebrew women are not like Egyptian women in that they give birth before the arrival of disposability, and thus engender a narrative discourse that is not saturated by the masculinized and singularized power of death ("if it is a boy, you shall kill him"), then the endangered-but-creative body lives not just as a posthumous being (the ghost or the reclaimed body of the colonized or enslaved self) but also as the primal subject, creator, and custodian of non-disposability. The postcolony must not allow its primary identity to be saturated with the legacy of colonial death; nor should the postcolony simply develop as escape from death. Its future lies in its ability to foreground life now, and in its capacity to narrativize and institutionalize the sovereignty and transcendence of life. Its future lies in its capacity and necessity to produce value for the multiple, not privilege for the few. This means that the preexisting historical time-space claimed by exodus narration is not ontologically or politically singular; rather, it is strategic, multiple, and multiplying. Beyond the political constructions of disposability as a form of pharaonic national formation, exodus life-forms as imagined and narrated by the Hebrew women through the midwives are taken up as tropes of redesigned futures. Such redesign work is picked up by the migrant or displaced and war-weary community in the wilderness— a community re/assessing how the causes and the effects of displacements are gathered up into unbound departures. Finally, prioritizing

---

39. Sharpe, *In the Wake*, 41.

the primordiality of lively beginnings informs the epistemological redesign of permanent escape and residence in the mountain area. Without this foregrounding of life and its inherent values, exodus from Egypt becomes problematic because it runs the risk of being permanently attached to the narrative of disposability, alienation, and singularity produced by colonial and imperial powers and structured around Pharaoh, the wilderness, the mountain area, and beyond. Without a narrative protest return—redesign of oppressive temporalities, spaces, and structures—by the Hebrew women and the midwives, there is no departure from singularizing confinement, only cosmic dispersal; no communal liberation from structured death, only select survival stories; and no transformative hospitality, only accommodation of the marginalized.

Badass womanist epistemological self-positioning challenges the austerity mindset of autocratic regimes that consolidate power and resources for themselves and compel their citizens to have to move (become internally displaced) and/or scavenge under the burdens of strictly regularized existence (Exod. 5:6–18). When such burdensome life is attached to ethnic profiling and enslavement, the wild and explosive generative force of protest emerges as a groan and expression of life force beyond the grip of necropolitics (Exod. 2:24; 6:5). The people vocally release non-disposable hermeneutics in their crying out, and that release summons human and divine attention.[40] When the postcolony is subjected to wartime devastation and surveillance in Egypt, people ritually embody and enact survival spaces in the Passover (Exod. 12); and when enemies drown in the sea, the community re-narrates the seaside rescue and bears witness to its devastation (Exod. 14–15).

Having encountered and overcome such patronizing and fragile patriarchy and autocracy, the wilderness community—birthed by the Hebrew women and nursed by the midwives—appropriately speaks back to that system. For example, to consider the problems of food insecurity associated with the wilderness story (of manna, Exod. 16), coming as it does on the heels of ecological and environmental destruction (Exod. 7–11), is to explore manna as the quest for food justice and food security; manna sits at the intersection of food insecurity and eco-fragility. Badass womanist return/redesign narratives ensure that the community, deprived of land and a good political structure, is not

---

40. The Hebrew word *nā'aq* used to describe the Israelite groaning is also used in association with a wounded person, presumably a bleeding person. Yahweh promises to fatally wound Pharaoh with the sword of the Babylonian king and cause Pharaoh to groan (Ezek. 30:24).

simply displaced and lost in the wilderness. A future is yet possible for this community because that future is sourced from the generative plenitude of its midwifery, epistemologically and hermeneutically unattached to, and thus untainted by, pharaonic time, structure, and epistemology of austerity.

In the Mountain—the mythological apex of governance and legislative accomplishment—Exodus confronts new forms of erasure, alienation, and singularity. It is the problem of the communal exodus birth stool subjected to imperial gaze and structure, as Moses is summoned to the mountain top and the people are left at the bottom. That spatial arrangement provokes anxieties for a community whose identity is tied to its ability and need to rise from the bottom. The mountainside narrative of the golden calf demonstrates that exodus becomes problematic if, having emerged from the intersections of memory loss and erasure, having developed the capacity and necessity for critical response/redesign to marginalizing hierarchical structures, and having insisted on replacing single-hero narration with communal narration, a mode of imperial scripted or scripturalized return sets in and seeks to re-institutionalize and regularize erasure, alienation, and singularity (Exod. 32–33). When kin perish in tribal conflict in the mountain area, fueled by the toxic allure of singular narration, the story expands its canonical vocalization to secure communal survival. Survivors renegotiate their covenantal, ritual, and legislative codes (Exod. 34–35) but also their relation to the land, its ecology, and the divine (Exod. 40).

The exodus-Exodus work of redesign concludes by narratively bringing the reader back to the beginning and redesigning its time and spatial zones: the story that begins with the Israelites entering (*bô'*) Egypt and filling (*mālā'*) the land now concludes with Moses not being able to enter (*bô'*) the Tent of Meeting because a cloud has settled on it and the divine *kabôd* (weightiness) has filled (*mālā'*) the Tabernacle. In this full redesign, God is neighbor to the community and to its ecology, and Moses recedes from his privileged position into the community that formed him. The story narratively and imaginatively returns to its beginnings, not to affect liberation as extraterritorial displacement or utopia but to embark on the work of transforming the political, environmental, and religious mechanisms that govern un/shared spaces and histories. The fruitful and multiplying life force that the story identified and named at the beginning (Exod. 1:1–6) is being accessed and activated again, to nurture new futures. For this unfolding future, the cloud and the fire, alongside the divine Being, become interpretive signposts for a story of staged journeying (Exod. 40:34–38; cf. Exod. 17:1). The search for life in its fullness is unrelenting. It is, after all, a story of the unending midwifery of badass womanism.

2

Triple Consciousness and the Exodus Narrative

Exodus is a narrative response to profound fractures, shifts, and transformations in communal identities—historical, cultural, political, gendered, ethnic, religious, and regional. Among Africana scholars and interpreters, responses to these shifts unfold around critical interrogation of colonial, postcolonial, and imperial theories and structures and their impact on marginalized communities; but also around creative literary, cultural, and embodied portraits of children, mothers, poets, prophets, midwives, ancestors, ecologies, health systems, and religions. The continuous endangerment that threatens Africana life is perhaps best defined in forms of power that Achille Mbembe calls *necropolitics*: "the power and the capacity to dictate who may live and who must die"[1] (cf. Exod. 1:15–22; 4:21–26; 12:26; 13:8, 14–15; 32–33). Identity and hermeneutics developed in relation to the necropolitics of Exodus are informed by an ideological triple consciousness that I define through the concepts of erasure, alienation, and singularity.

First, for Africana and the Exodus story, consciousness is developed and sustained as an overarching ideological and narrative construct about how to survive erasure, by necessity rather than by choice. This consciousness develops in the *wake* (wake as narrative sequence and/or postmortem subjectivity) of Yahweh's ideological and geopolitical war with Pharaoh; but it begins with nonviolent resistance by the midwives

---

1. Achille Mbembe, "Necropolitics," trans. Libby Meintjes, *Public Culture* 15, no. 1 (2003): 11.

55

(Exod. 1:15–22). This consciousness also develops in the *wake* (wake as crack of dawn) of Israel's political liberation (Exod. 14–15). The force of this consciousness—and its meaning line—is the flow, the thin line, between the necropolitics of the story and its biopolitics. That is, how death and life are mobilized in the story to create identity and communal values; more precisely, how life emerges in a place saturated by death. In framing this consciousness, the narrator signals, almost parenthetically, that Pharaoh's anxieties and governing ideology were rooted in a lack of historical understanding of Hebrew identity and lived experience. Pharaoh "did not know Joseph" (Exod. 1:8). The rise of a new Pharaoh is the emergence of a form of erasure as a founding premise that undergirds oppression; to not know Joseph is to discount the history of the community to which Joseph belongs and its troubling and traumatizing encounters with empire. Pharaoh's governance represents political oppression for a generation of Hebrews, but it also represents the production of Hebrew identity *through* and *out of* erasure. That reality and its consciousness are a hermeneutical fault line in Exodus narration. To interpret that fault line is to develop hermeneutics as an ethical and moral commitment to forge identity beyond the fault—identity that develops in resistance to erasure.

Concurrent with surviving erasure or infusing life into the mortal space-time of erasure, a second consciousness develops around the experience of displacement and rescue: consciousness of rescue (Exod. 2:1–10; 14–15) is also consciousness of displacement. Displacement as a form of conditional existence is folded into Exodus' perennial questions about political, cultural, and legal processes that resist, and sometimes avert, internal and external displacement (Exod. 4–5). Geopolitical alienation emerges around economic infrastructures where the labor and cultural achievements of an oppressed group in Egypt become synonymous with, and symptomatic of, structural disenfranchisement and dislocation. Hebrew labor and work ethic (e.g., the building of the Ramses and Pithom) in the land is slave labor—undignified and undignifying work that embodies dehumanized existence, the short circuiting of opportunities to fully self-determine. In the face of such political, religious, cultural, and economic extraction and alienation, a sense of apathy and self-loathing begins to set in among the Hebrews, not as a character flaw (as ethnocentric pharaonic thinking would suggest—Exod. 5:5–9) but as a manifestation of a political flaw: the flaw and purpose of Pharaoh's amnesia is that it produces systemic disempowerment of the oppressed group and prevents the latter from holding the governing system accountable (cf. Exod. 6:9). Geopolitical deprivation is so intrinsic that the people are internally displaced and must scavenge for straw to meet their obligations to the state (Exod. 5:6–18). Fragile systems and ideologies have a way of producing fragile minds and mindsets that rely on marginalizing others. The appropriate response to this reality is ultimately not to switch residential zip codes but to change governing ideology. That is why the story of Exodus comes to mean more than a journey. To shift location from Egypt to Canaan, without changing the underlying social, political, and ideological determinants of marginalization, is to transfer the problem rather than resolve it.

Narrative episodes of being simultaneously subjected to erasure and/or alienation unfold into a third consciousness—singularity. It is consciousness experienced as imperialism's or patriarchy's ability and tendency to coerce global and gendered multiplicity into monologic modes of being and belonging that manifest as homogenizing enclave mentalities and spaces—colonies, plantations, slave ships, diamond fields, birth stools—that subsidize the empire's claims to totalizing supremacy. Pharaoh's oppression is also genocidal in its singularizing focus on eliminating specific ethnic and gendered identities: the bearers of Hebrew identity (primarily Hebrew mothers) are profiled, and their male children are targeted to be killed at birth or thrown into the Nile. Their deaths are instrumentalized to construct privileged and unaccountable forms of national identity. In this geopolitical mythology of erasure and alienation, the waters of the ethnic and racial womb are linked to the waters of the Nile and the Red Sea, both of which are bodies and sites where death-dealing governance manifests its toxic singularity and sovereignty.[2] Ethnocentric oppression is naturalized through analogous thinking that consigns endangered and marginalized communities to the realm of subhuman instinct, devoid of internal ideological variety and structural coherence and accountability. Resistance to such productions of singularity may manifest with a Hebrew man's challenge to Moses (Exod. 2:13–14), but it begins and sustains itself with the narrator's portrayal of the Israelites as producing multiply: "the more they were oppressed, the more they multiplied and spread" (Exod. 1:12).

---

2. On the importance of the Nile, particularly its annual rise (floods) and fall, for ancient Egyptian economy and political identity, see Daniel Hillel, *The Natural History of the Bible: An Environmental Exploration of the Hebrew Scriptures* (New York: Columbia University Press, 2006), 87–117. In the biblical narrative, the presence of children in the Nile is not portrayed as a consequence of natural disasters such as a flood; instead, it is presented as a political act, precisely a function of wartime legislation.

The cumulative effect of these projections and the resulting governing attempts to control the natural and political rhythms, bodies, and processes of Hebrew identity formation is that the quality of life for the *endangered, marginalized, and singularized* community is embittered. Egypt as a geopolitical space becomes a structure and an infrastructure of slavery, the ideological house of erasure, alienation, and singularity.

These three layers of consciousness fold and unfold into three modes of subjectivity in response to national (Egypt), global (Wilderness), and imperial (Mountainside) logics and rubrics in the Exodus narrative. The critical issue evoked by Pharaoh's wartime ethnocentric ideology (Exod. 1:10) against the Hebrews for supposedly undermining the nation in a time of war is not just the effect of war and violence on identity formation and survival, but also how violence becomes integral to an ideological narrative of self-identity and definition beyond Egypt. Furthermore, the spectacular violence of the new Pharaoh that haunts the oppressed aligns with correlative and attritional violence of long-term, gradual erasure, which haunts the narrative. The spectacular violence of oppressive nation-state regimes merges with metamorphic and metastatic forms of oppression that touch on planetary existence.

Egypt is both the house of slavery and the land experiencing environmental devastation in the form of plagues. The Wilderness is a place without good water/food, and it is also a place where new modes of sustainable ecological identities emerge. The Mountain is the place of supreme legislative achievement and also the place that threatens to reinstate single-hero narration. To these realities and triple consciousness, exodus-Exodus responds with new possibilities and realities.

TRIPLE CONSCIOUSNESS, BIOPOLITICS, AND SCRIPTURALIZATION

Michel Foucault theorized two spheres of biopolitical development in the seventeenth century: the first around deploying the body as a machine—"its disciplining, the optimization of its capabilities, the extortion of its forces, the parallel increase of its usefulness and its docility, its integration into systems of efficient and economic control . . . an *anatomo-politics of the human body.*" This body, I associate with alienation or marginalization. The second focused on the "species body," that is, "the body imbued with the mechanics of life and serving as the basis of the biological processes: propagation, births and mortality, the level of health, life expectancy and longevity, with all the conditions that can cause these to vary. Their supervision was effected through an entire system of interventions and *regulatory controls: a bio-politics of the population.*"[3] This body I associate with the diminishment of life, or erasure. In addition to conceptualizing the body as a machine and as species, there is a third component of biopolitical work that has informed and animated Africana engagements with Exodus. That is the biopolitical work around navigating a singularized body propagated and distributed by empire, in conjunction with the alienated body (Foucault's machines) and the erased body (Foucault's species).

In his reflections on biopolitics, Roberto Esposito writes,

> It is all too evident that politics enters fully into the immune paradigm the moment life becomes the immediate content of its action. . . . Whether an individual life or the life of the species is involved, life itself is what politics is called upon to make safe, precisely by immunizing it from the dangers of extinction threatening it.[4]

This most fundamental task of biopolitics, nevertheless, must also be viewed from another angle, where the focus is "not just on the object of biopolitics, but also on the way that object is grasped: to be able to save life from its tendency toward self-dissolution, politics has to lead life back to the realm of the body." Accordingly, "what appeared to be a relation between two terms—politics and life—must instead be interpreted as a more complex game that includes a third term upon which it depends: the bodily dimension is where life lends itself to be preserved as such by political immunization."[5] The body becomes simultaneously the privileged locus where the work of immunization—the ethic to protect life—takes place and where the opposite—death—is most evidently manifested. This "constitutive binarism" makes such a biopolitical body a liminal body/space where the battle between life and death takes place, and where the work of political immunization unfolds, either as an attempt to delay as much as possible the passage of the body from life to death or as an attempt to "drive death to the farthest point from the presentness of life."[6]

---

3. Michel Foucault, "Right of Life and Power over Death," in *Biopolitics: A Reader*, ed. Timothy Campbell and Adam Sitze (Durham, NC: Duke University Press, 2013), 44, emphasis in original.
4. Roberto Esposito, "Biopolitics," in *Biopolitics: A Reader*, ed. Timothy Campbell and Adam Sitze (Durham, NC: Duke University Press, 2013), 317.
5. Esposito, "Biopolitics," 317.
6. Esposito, "Biopolitics," 318.

60   LET MY PEOPLE LIVE

I want to briefly examine these concepts in relation to three major infrastructures of power that have impacted Africana: the slave ship, the slave castle, and the postcolony. I will proceed under the general interpretive rubric of scripturalization. In his essay titled "It's Scripturalization, Colleagues!"[7] Vincent Wimbush continues to develop and expound a theoretical approach to religious studies and biblical interpretation that he articulated in *White Men's Magic*.[8] As with all theoretical work, scripturalization defines itself (or is defined) both in terms of what it is not and what it is. First, what it is not: "It's *not* the text, *not* the text's soaring rhetoric, *not* the claims about the universal truths it represents, not the proclamations about it as culturalist achievement, and so forth. Nor is it about . . . benign local and regional minority-culturalist textured engagements of the text. It is not about such things apart from some important critical challenges,"[9] says Wimbush. Therefore, if scripturalization is not textual criticism, nor narrative criticism, nor universalizing truth claims, "apart from some important critical challenges," then what is it? For Wimbush, whose seminal project on scripturalization focuses on the encounter between Europe and Africa (as represented in the life of Olaudah Equiano, the abolitionist writer who was captured and taken as a slave from Benin), scripturalization gestures toward the challenge of race or the "race-ing" of Others as a tool for containment and dominance.[10] Because this theory is not about the invention of Scriptures but the exploration of the kind of work that "we make scriptures do for us," a major focus of the theory is "coming to understand how peoples—across societies and time—read, interpret, construct, and communicate meanings about themselves and the world."[11]

White Men's Magic was an intellectual autobiography (a "historicized and theorized self") that allowed Wimbush to expand his study of the Bible beyond its ancient Mediterranean (con)text and thus to explore not just the meaning of texts, but also "the meaning of conditions" that produced the interpreting self: "I can no longer merely *exegete* (the text), I must now *excavate* (the historical self)."[12] This self-reflexive approach to scholarship in general and biblical scholarship in particular

---

7. Vincent L. Wimbush, "It's Scripturalization, Colleagues!" *Journal of Africana Religions* 3, no. 2 (2015): 193–200.

8. Vincent L. Wimbush, *White Men's Magic: Scripturalization as Slavery* (Oxford: Oxford University Press, 2012).

9. Wimbush, "It's Scripturalization," 194, emphases in original.

10. Wimbush, "It's Scripturalization," 195.

11. Wimbush, "It's Scripturalization," 197.

12. Wimbush, *White Men's Magic*, 8.

requires more than a chronicling of history and the production of knowledge; it also requires understanding and responding to the systems and structures of power that produce and regulate knowledge and meaning. With regard to Equiano, Wimbush found a subject-character with whom to examine Scripture as part of a complex phenomenon, "an analytical wedge that created identity-forming beginnings between Europe and Africa, and that developed into scripturalization." Equiano's use of Scripture, Wimbush argues, reveals the ex-slave's understanding of the eighteenth century British world as a construct and his attempts to form a bridge into that world. Seen in relation to biopolitics, the work of scripturalization examines how "the ideology and power dynamics and social and cultural practices built around texts" informs the life and death consequences of the Black subject's encounter with the biblical text.[13] This kind of work—critical history—about the production and regulation of Black subject as a machine, a species, and a singularized being also provokes a response around interpreting the intersections between textual and human lacunas, and doing so in creative and meaningful processes of building hopeful futures.

When he addressed the Society of Biblical Literature in 2011, Wimbush made a bold challenge: "there can be no critical interpretation worthy of the name, without coming to terms with the first contact—between the West and the rest, the West and the Others—and its perduring toxic and blinding effects and consequences."[14] Wimbush used Frederick Douglass's writing[15] to think about consciousness and persons differently situated in this contact between the West and the Others as the enslaving, the enslaved, and the runagate—all of whom exist in a complexly intertwined network of history but whose existential realities still require specific analyses. Wimbush then mapped three categories of interpreters: First, the enslavers who exist and operate under a Manichean psychology of black and white, with a hardened essentialization of the parts. This psychology results in a traumatic splitting of the soul.[16] Second, the enslaved who were not completely prevented from developing thoughts and speech but were rather restricted in their circle of communication, because those not enslaved could not and would not listen to or hear what the enslaved said. The burden was not

---

13. Wimbush, *White Men's Magic*, 87.
14. Vincent L. Wimbush, "Interpreters—Enslaving/Enslaved/Runagate," *Journal of Biblical Literature* 130, no. 1 (2011): 9.
15. Frederick Douglass, *Narrative of the Life of Frederick Douglass, and American Slave, Written by Himself* (New York: Oxford University Press, 1996).
16. Wimbush, "Interpreters," 11–15.

62 LET MY PEOPLE LIVE

so much the physical oppression of enslavement, demeaning though that was, but rather not being seen or heard "in broad terms befitting the dignity of humanity."[17] Third, the runagate, whose condition signals more than physical flight but reaches for a kind of epistemological and material escape or self-extraction from slavery and its institution, a "marronage, running away with an attitude and a plan" or a "psychosocial and discursive marronage" that allowed Douglass to navigate the worlds of the enslaved and the free.[18]

These three forms of consciousness, Wimbush concludes, point to new and different ways of reading Scriptures and operating outside of the circle of dominance, of not just reading Scripture but signifying on Scriptures. I will now examine how these forms of signifying on Scripture are related to the triple consciousness of erasure, alienation, and singularity that I have identified around an Africana hermeneutic and its engagement with Exodus.

TRIPLE OBJECTS OF AFRICANA EXODUS ENGAGEMENTS: SLAVE SHIP, SLAVE CASTLE, AND POSTCOLONY

The Slave Ship

Through the historic transatlantic slave trade, Africa was compelled not only to travel outside of itself but also to experience that travel as erasure, as alienation, and as singularity. That triadic consciousness becomes a historic and hermeneutical fault line around the work of estrangement and becoming that occupies Africana political history and its social and psychic worlds. When the slave ship returned (or made its latest stop) along the west African coast of the Atlantic Ocean, in the centuries-long project of global capture and circulation of commerce and Africans, a kind of unaccountable return—a biopolitical trilogy of producing and circulating African bodies as machines, species, and singularized—was created and recreated: the return of the ideology of enslavement and its material object (the ship), but not the return of the enslaved people. That exile reproduced and solidified horror in the colonized mind, body, and space. For, when the loaded ship moved on, when it continued on its circular exilic motion bearing more captured, erased, and traumatized bodies, it left, in its wake, a drastically altered

---

17. Wimbush, "Interpreters," 17. The crisis is not systemic oppression but systemic refusal to be recognized.
18. Wimbush, "Interpreters," 17–20.

society, system of governance, and ecology. The circular return of the ship is not the return that endangered people seek, for it is a return of "a history that doesn't go away,"[19] the return of a false narrative that ongoing imperialism is a consequence of the failure or incompetence of local systems of government. Attached to this faulty ideological logic, the captured body is launched into a motion of perpetual diaspora toward unformed futures and larger structures of supposedly civilizing governance, headquartered in primarily, if not exclusively, extraterritorial lands—that is, in extremely isolated spaces, created and sustained for the privileged few.

What processes, if any, are set in place to interpret and redress this major fault line and its circulation of political power premised on the disposability of "Othered" life? Is the postslavery and postcolony Africana subject a perennial diasporic subject? Can she ever return? In her captivating book *A Map to the Door of No Return*, Dionne Brand remembers, as a thirteen-year-old with Caribbean roots, trying to help her grandfather remember "what people we came from." They worked through a few possible African ethnic names but settled on none. That unresolved search and conversation, on the Caribbean side of the Atlantic, opened a small space in Brand and, over time, came to "reveal a tear in the world." Brand writes,

> I would have proceeded happily with a simple name. I may have played with it for a few days and then stored it away. Forgotten. But the rupture this exchange with my grandfather revealed was greater than the need for familial bonds. It was a rupture in history, a rupture in the quality of being. It was also a physical rupture, a rupture of geography.[20]

More than physical spaces across several countries along the African coast of the Atlantic Ocean, the doors of no return have become a powerful symbol of ruptured identity in African Diasporic studies, not just for those who were forcefully removed from their homes and placed on slave ships, but also for those who remained—for whom the doors they never physically entered nevertheless remain in the slave castles and represent a gateway to unclaimed and unclaimable loss of familial kin and community, captured and taken. Identity is forever fractured. And the fracturing is coded in bodies and stories—official and unofficial—but also in the structures that hold these doors. Africana hermeneutics

---

19. The phrase is borrowed from the former president of the United States, Barack Obama.
20. Dionne Brand, *A Map to the Door of No Return: Notes to Belonging* (Toronto: Vintage Canada, 2001), 4–5.

64 LET MY PEOPLE LIVE

is transgressive hermeneutics across colonial and imperial "doors of no return."

One of the most impressive explorations of scripturalization has been Gerald West's *The Stolen Bible*[21]—a richly layered analysis of the multidimensional mechanisms and processes affiliated with the arrival of the Bible in Africa, and the long, tortured, but also creative, multiple functions of the Bible in Africa. As West argues, following interpreters like Justin Ukpong and Itumeleng Mosala, the history of African biblical interpretation has moved from a bi-polar comparative analysis between the Bible and the African context to a tri-polar frame that includes ideo-theological axis; that is, the methodological approaches that Africans deploy to engage and appropriate the biblical text.[22]

West opens his book with a brief narrative that captures the textures, gestures, and power dynamics of the Bible as a literary product/object around which communal identity is formed; the Bible's interpretive presence in Africa, first as an inaccessible document and then as a tool of liberation; and the hermeneutical work that Africans do with the text, to demystify and make it accountable.

> In a sermon preached in a rural community in the KwaZulu-Natal region of South Africa in 1933, Isaiah Shembe, an illiterate and itinerant preacher, healer, baptizer, prophet, messiah to some, and founder of a flourishing African Initiated Church, tells the story of how he and his conquered people stole the Bible from the conqueror and used it to restore their community.[23]

The interpretive interlocution here unfolds around three poles: First, the nebulous presence of the Bible in the colonized space. As a cypher for the empire and its power, the Bible is at once present as a secretive powerful object in the hands of the missionary but also unavailable to the conquered community. In this discursive and political sphere, the marginalized subject has no direct access to the new constellation of power and its deployment; she only has indirect access. If she is going to claim her interpretive agency, she must transgress the empire's hermeneutical hiding of the Bible and commit the "illegal" act of accessing

---

21. Gerald O. West, *The Stolen Bible: From Tool of Imperialism to African Icon* (Leiden: Brill, 2016). In a private correspondence, West agreed that *Stolen Bible* is a "kin-project" of scripturalization, with specific African realities at the center.

22. Gerald O. West, "African Biblical Scholarship as Post-Colonial, Tri-Polar, and a Site-of-Struggle," in *Present and Future of Biblical Studies: Celebrating 25 Years of Brill's Biblical Interpretation*, ed. Tat-siong Benny Liew (Leiden: Brill, 2018), 240–73, especially 247–54.

23. West, *Stolen Bible*, 1.

the source of power. But once the marginalized subject makes self-initiating contact with the source of discursive power, a new form of social and hermeneutical consciousness unfolds; there is a crack in the otherwise secretive and hitherto unaccountable code of restrictive and sovereign power. It is not the beginning of polyphony in the colonized spaces; it is the beginning of the deployment of polyphony to demystify sovereignty premised on, and guarded by, exclusivity.

The second pole of meaning in this anecdote is the social legitimation of power around literacy and illiteracy. The anxieties of colonial il/literacy are confronted in the characterization of Shembe's transgressive act of stealing the object of power (the Bible), an act that departs from the moralizing ideology of the colonial project. But the issue is more than a moralizing one; it is strategic. In an act of epistemological and political resistance, Shembe situates himself outside of the credentialing structure of colonialism's supposedly civilizing project and thus anticipates the political and epistemological pitfalls of petit bourgeoisies in postcolonial administration. The postcolonial problem evoked in Shembe's action is this: To what extent does the survival of the liberated community depend on its ability to competently operate the colonial machinery? And given the utility of colonialism as a machinery of erasure, why would the postcolonial subject need to competently operate that machinery, without simply extending and further legitimizing its erasing function? Shembe's narrative signals that one can share the same space with the colonial regime without sharing in its epistemological priorities and futures.

The third pole is the project of restoration. It is an aggregative project that moves the deconstructive work of anticolonial marronage toward communal healing. The marginalized community moves from survival to restoration. It is here that the Bible—or more precisely, Africana modes of interpretation of the Bible—becomes iconic and deployed for new futures.

As European traders, merchants, explorers, and missionaries traveled further inland from the coastlands of Africa in the 1700s and 1800s, they encountered communities firmly under the control of Africans. This encounter created what West calls "a 'pre-colonial' moment, with 'colonialism' emerging in the Colony close by."[24] This moment of proximate colonialism, which eventually became effective colonialism, unfolded in a series of dialogues between the arriving

---

24. West, *Stolen Bible*, 85.

missionaries, explorers, and local peoples. West uses the example of a local tribe (BaTlhaping) to illustrate this development. The gun, the primary and ultimate object of conquest and erasure in the coastal plains, became an object of curiosity and desire for the local authorities farther inland. The trauma of direct colonial rule was linked to the trauma of indirect colonial rule: alongside the Bible, the gun emerged as an object of discourse about political power linking local leaders (consumers) to European nations and leaders (suppliers). In this mode of commercial exchange, timely deliverability of the gun to local leaders began to test the unfolding relationship between European explorers, missionaries, and the local king. The presence of the gun (as an advanced technology of death) in the local space—its integration into the governing machinery of the king—functioned as a catalyst for local political mobilization, struggle, and communal remapping. Once thus mobilized, local citizens were also made available to missionaries.[25]

It is not only historically accurate but also methodologically strategic that West situates and begins his enormous work around the coastal plains under the grip of colonial power, and then moves eastward, inland to the African interior where communities were initially free from the everyday machinations of colonial power and governance. The enormity of the African space-time and the preexisting multiplicity of its cultural, linguistic, and political variety functioned as mitigating factors against the totalizing project of colonial erasure and replacement. Alongside a synchronic analysis of the Bible's presence and increasing gradual penetration into the African heartland, West also provides a diachronic historical assessment of the processes by which Africans, over several centuries, encountered the Bible as an imperial document and, over time—through various stages of interpretation, contestation, and embodiment—appropriated the Bible as a central document in their lives, indeed, as an African icon. This synchronic and diachronic analysis of the Bible's problematic presence in Africa "invites both an academic and an activist engagement,"[26] which coheres with Wimbush's invitation to do critical history. In fact, West does more than analyze the critical history of the work that the Bible has been made to do in (South) Africa; he also does critical engagement of geography, linked around an African concept of entangled or elastic time-space.

---

25. West, *Stolen Bible*, 90, 136–37.
26. West, *Stolen Bible*, 5.

TRIPLE CONSCIOUSNESS AND THE EXODUS NARRATIVE

Colonial projects redesigned both the histories of local communities and their geographies.[27]

In a chapter on "The Contested Bible," West repeatedly cites an anecdote that functions as a proverbial commentary on biblical interpretation in Africa:

> When the white man came to our country he had the Bible and we [Blacks] had the land. The white man said to us, "let us pray." After the prayer, the white man had the land and we [Blacks] had the Bible.[28]

Another version of this anecdote uses *missionary* instead of *white man*, evoking how race and religion intersect in this encounter around land and Bible.

> When the missionaries came to Africa they had the Bible and we had the land. They said, "let us pray." We closed our eyes. When we opened them, we had the Bible and they had the land.[29]

As West points out, "African land and the Bible are integrally related in Africa, with the contours of their relationship following a similar pattern across the continent."[30] The intersections of race and religion have shaped what it means for a dispossessed and "landless" people to "have the Bible" as a substitute for "having the land." Without a land on which to grow crops, to build houses, to play games, and to build healthy communities, the deterritorialized and dispossessed reader/ perpetual migrant is unable to fully dream up utopias, or to translate those utopias into material manifestations within specific herstories/ histories and territories.

The anecdotes indicate how the opening of eyes—the act of self-re/orientation in the newly constituted structure of social existence— inaugurates a hermeneutic of posttraumatic wake/waking that also has a nagging transactional element to its manifestation and its symbols. The trauma of the loss of the darkened (Black) self and material ecology is narratively linked to the afterlives of opened eyes and the object to which the surviving and displaced self is now attached: the Bible. Communal survival is a form of awakening or, better yet, a form of wake work, to use Christina Sharpe's insightful metaphor: "to be *in* the

---

27. West, *Stolen Bible*, 9–84.
28. West, *Stolen Bible*, 318.
29. West, *Stolen Bible*, 326.
30. West, *Stolen Bible*, 319.

wake is to occupy and to be occupied by the continuous and changing present of slavery's as yet unresolved unfolding."[31] What are the implications of this unresolved unfolding of a trauma? Sharpe argues that "rather than seeking a resolution to blackness's ongoing and irresolvable abjection, one might approach Black being in the wake as a form of *consciousness*." Such consciousness performs "wake work" that does not "seek to explain or resolve the question of this exclusion in terms of assimilation, inclusion, or civil or human rights, but rather depicts aesthetically the impossibility of such resolutions by representing the paradoxes of blackness within and after the legacies of slavery's denial of Black humanity."[32] The waking is the birth of a survivor in the midst of exilic trauma-on-the-move. The hermeneutical wake work, however, is also the creation and the quest for new forms of life that divest exile and exilic structures and symbols of their propensity to fragment, alienate, and singularize.

The Slave Castle

The mobile ship, the quintessential object of trans-Atlantic diaspora, leaves behind something—a critical piece of the colonial and imperial ecosystem—that it expects to find the next time it returns in its circular and global production of disposable Blackness. That something is the slave castle. It is the object—the infrastructure of ideology—that holds the door of no return, the door that opened to the ocean and seemingly foreclosed any hope of return for captured Africans. The door is the symbolic and material gateway to exile, a symbol of irredeemable rupture, the final pathway onto the mobile ship. But the castle is the object that first manufactures disposable Blackness. In the slave castle, captives from diverse ethnic and linguistic groups, and persons who were products and producers of, and heirs to, centuries-old complex religious and political systems, were chained and confined in extremely narrow spaces. The capture and the chains represent the production of colonial Blackness as a singularized subhuman category, removed from history and historical development, and deprived of sovereignty.

Attached to phenotype, the racist production of Black bodies and spaces as disposable, erasable, or replaceable identities begins with

---

31. Christina Sharpe, *In the Wake: On Blackness and Being* (Durham, NC: Duke University Press, 2016), 13–14, emphasis in original.

32. Sharpe, *In the Wake*, 14.

TRIPLE CONSCIOUSNESS AND THE EXODUS NARRATIVE

holding posts in the African interior and ultimately in the unmoving castle. This form of racist production of Blackness is grounded in depth of erasure and alienation, not in distance, as evident in the slave castle's architecture, which performs the ideology of Black production through its layers of nightmare premised on political, religious, and racial patronage: the governor's residence at the very top, a chapel at the middle level, and the slave dungeons at the bottom, all designed to compel the captured and chained mind and body to bend and even break (cf. Exod. 6:9).

Louis P. Nelson's excellent study of the architectures of slavery in West Africa "situates the historical narratives of the slave trade not in buildings but in spaces, some permanent, some temporary, some floating, and some created by implements of bondage."[33] Nelson proposes multiple meanings of space, following Henri LeFebvre, as constitutive of physical, socially constructed, and imagined spaces. For Nelson, the most important meaning of architecture (and I would add, of monuments) is to be found in various "human networks—social, economic, political—that tied those spaces one to the next."[34] The slave castle is the monumental text by which colonial slave trade, having committed the initial act of violent invasion in the local space, begins to justify its continued violent existence under the premise of self-defense. The military cannons on top of the ideological and physical castle point toward the ocean and inland.

In *Black Atlantic Writers of the Eighteenth Century*, Adam Potkay and Sandra Burr reflect on the fact that eighteenth century Black writers did not spend much time describing the horrors of enslavement. Whether this refrain was a function of a particular form of eighteenth century politics of representation that labored under the pressures, and in the shadows, of enlightenment literary patrons is difficult to definitively ascertain. What is clear from these writings, according to Potkay and Burr, is that "the very descent into the hell of colonial slave life appears but an episode in the epic series of open air adventure, professions, and avocations that the eighteenth-century black writers recount."[35] To situate the horrors of slavery within the literary genre of these writers' time is not to minimize consciousness of the traumatic depth of enslavement—which these writers did not overlook—but

33. Louis P. Nelson, "Architectures of West African Enslavement," *Buildings and Landscapes: Journal of the Vernacular Architecture Forum* 21, no. 1 (2014): 88.
34. Nelson, "Architectures," 89.
35. Adam Potkay and Sandra Burr, eds., *Black Atlantic Writers of the Eighteenth Century: Living the New Exodus in England and the Americas* (New York: St. Martin's Press, 1995), 2.

rather to historicize the nuances and depths of Africana storytelling about its endangered, diasporized, and singularized selves within the larger global framework of colonial "epic series of open air adventure" that defined much of the political and spiritual approach of Europe to the majority world, and then to respond.

The dominant literary trope that emerges from these Black Atlantic writers, as Henry Gates Jr. has argued, is that of the Talking Book, first articulated in the 1770s in the work of Ukawsaw Gronniosaw (also known as James Albert)—an enslaved man from present-day Nigeria, and later publisher in Britain—and then in the literary work of the next generation up to the 1815s. For Gates, the trope of the Talking Book is the "ur-trope of the Anglo-African tradition" that makes "the white written text speak with a black voice."[36] The importance of voice, of black voicing of a white written text, Gates argues, was critical to the political life of enslaved Africans in England because the literary voice allowed these Africans to demonstrate their humanity and then critique their exploitation within the ideology of enlightenment Europe and its colonial manifestations. In the trope of the Talking Book, one sees Black writers literarily and "literally writing themselves into being through carefully crafted representations in language of the black self."[37] These "carefully crafted representations" of the black self reckoned with Europe as an imperializing body, a boundary-making body, an ideological construct wielding a particular form of global supremacy and toxic singularity subsidized by Black bodies and Black labor—that is, Black breath/life. These writers began to reform and even radicalize the religious and political landscape from "within" and, in their writings, produce a form of intellectual and literary maroonage—analogous to the maroonage and uprisings that characterized slave colonies—that accentuated the dignity of the Black self as a creative and resistant presence against global constructions of colonies and the colonial servitude that subsidized the racial and racist hierarchies of enlightenment.[38] Political advocacy merged with the narrative genre of allegory, which these writers applied to the story of Exodus as a form of spiritual freedom.[39]

In the 1770s, Ukawsaw Gronniosaw's narrative opens with a description

---

36. Henry Louis Gates Jr., *The Signifying Monkey: A Theory of Afro-American Literary Criticism* (New York: Oxford University Press, 1988), 147.

37. Gates, *Signifying Monkey*, 148. See also, Emerson B. Powery and Rodney S. Sadler Jr., *The Genesis of Liberation: Biblical Interpretation in the Antebellum Narratives of the Enslaved* (Louisville, KY: Westminster John Knox Press, 2016), 52–61.

38. See Michèle Duchet, *Anthropologie et histoire au siècle des lumières* (Paris: Francois Maspero, 1971).

39. Potkay and Burr, *Black Atlantic Writers*, 7–16.

TRIPLE CONSCIOUSNESS AND THE EXODUS NARRATIVE

of his state of distress in the face of what he could not quite understand—how to deal with "the MAN of POWER" who ruled over everything. In the context of anxieties about religious and political identity, belonging, ongoing ethnic conflict, and the Slave trade, Gronniosaw's conversations, as a child, with his mother touched on big questions of creation, the mythologies of "national" or "country" origins, and how those mythologies were being redefined by the man of power. Failing to fully understand this power, he was left "dejected and melancholy."[40] That melancholy reflected communal fragility and fragmentation in the face of a global politic of nationalism and imperialism, subsidized by broken bodies and communities. The dejection and melancholy that infused Gronniosaw's life began to develop a permanent character when he left his family on a journey with a merchant from Gold Coast, a merchant who promised him two things: first, to let him see "houses with wings to them walk upon the water" and "white folks"; and second, to "bring me safe back again soon." The first promise became a reality, but the second did not. That promise of reassemblage with his family was the falsehood of colonial global travel, the psychic and political wound that afflicted colonized selves: unlike white travelers, colonized persons could not be brought back safe. And so, for Gronniosaw, the grief of initial communal separation would be surpassed only by knowledge of journey as (forced) departure without the possibility or reality of return: "If I could have known when I left my friends and country that I should never return to them again my misery on that occasion would have been inexpressible."[41]

The journey itself was long—about one thousand miles—and Gronniosaw was accompanied by his mother for part (three hundred miles) of the trek. Gronniosaw's journey was infused with discussions about his potential death (being thrown into a deep pit or into a river) and, upon arrival at the Gold Coast, about being killed on suspicion of being a political spy in the context of warfare.[42] Although he was not killed, the decision to preserve his life and sell him as a slave took place "the morning I was to die." Spiritual/social death and physical death converged around the sale of the Black self. Assailed by the sense of mortal danger and the instrumentalization of his survival, Gronniosaw continued down the path of effective slow death. The loss of his mother's accompanying presence signaled more than the beginning of

---

40. Potkay and Burr, *Black Atlantic Writers*, 30.
41. Potkay and Burr, *Black Atlantic Writers*, 31.
42. Potkay and Burr, *Black Atlantic Writers*, 32, 33.

identity around isolation; it also removed any lingering hope of return and thus deprived him of a history of creativity. Diaspora was not just spatial; it was also social and historiographical. Conditions were set for him to desperately if "voluntarily" offer himself to a Dutch merchant who did not understand his language, in the hopes of avoiding mistreatment or immediate death: "father save me" is the cry of desperation but also the cry of submission to colonial patronage. The tragic and traumatic transfer of self, the manifestation of colonial disassemblage, was culminating in a form of patriarchal/imperial patronage. He was now fully under the control of that mighty power he had tried to understand as a child back in Bornu, his birth place; the power that impacted all things but seemed accountable to no one. He was in the dungeon of white men with houses that moved on the water—the early stages of transformation in identity.

The brief narrative of progressive loss of community, deeply entangled in colonial and native patriarchies, eventually brought Gronniosaw into contact with the Bible, in this case one owned by the merchant who purchased him. Gronniosaw's encounter with the book provoked the most powerful expression of the loss of self, and the codification of that loss in Blackness. Gronniosaw describes watching the merchant read from the Bible:

> When first I saw him read, I was never so surprised in my whole life as when I saw the book talk to my master; for I thought it did, as I observed him to look upon it, and move his lips. I wished it would do so to me. As soon as my master had done reading I follow'd him to the place where he put the book, being mightily delighted with it, and when no body saw me, I open'd it and put my ear down close upon it, in great hope that it would say something to me; but was very sorry and greatly disappointed when I found it would not speak, this thought immediately presented itself to me, that every body and every thing despised me because I was black.[43]

This narrative scene, which Gates interprets as the inaugural moment of the trope of the Talking Book in Black English literature, is compelling as a literary scene.

> For Gronniosaw, the book—or, perhaps I should say the very concept of "Book"—constituted a primary silent text, a text, however, in which the black man found no echo of his own voice. The silent

43. Potkay and Burr, *Black Atlantic Writers*, 34.

book did not reflect or acknowledge the black presence before it. The book's rather deafening silence renames the received tradition in European letters that the mask of blackness worn by Gronniosaw and his countrymen was a trope of absence.[44]

The trope of absence—Black absence from European letters and Gronniosaw's absence from Africa—also constitutes the time and space where Black reinterpretation as homeopathic work happens. The vivid scene in Gronniosaw's experience is compelling because of its geographical location; it is spatially located not in England, where enlightenment epistemology, fueled by the technology of the printing press, had made writing the epitome of moral self and expression of humanity itself. As a writer of the Black self, Gronniosaw placed the trope of the Talking Book on the edge of the African Atlantic coastland—precisely, around the slave castle and ship, the geographical and architectural place of permanent ruptures and transfers of self—religious, spatial, political, cultural, and literary selves. In this narrative scene, the diasporized self returns to the edge of the continent, where the absurdity of writing as the epitome of European self-production and its deployment in colonizing work is exhibited as narrative failure: writing (a book) that failed to *speak life to* anyone other than its (European) author. And even when a distressed and melancholic subject clutches the book close in an effort to infuse humanity into it, that effort unfolds as a void of invisibility and unspeakable silence. The unspeakable silence of the book is only the latest form of the erasure, alienation, and singularity that Gronniosaw was subjected to.

In this cosmopolitan space structured around the intersection of trade, race, Bible, and gender, freedom is portrayed as an individually purchasable commodity. Thus, instead of communally reading and questioning the signs of the sovereign power within the ecological, natural, and political environments that produced his "country," he now singularly looks for, and engages, that power in the talking silence of the book. Its refusal to speak to Gronniosaw—or Gronniosaw's experience of the book's silence toward him—represents a degenerative thought process of colonial toxic singularity imposed on the enslaved: "this thought immediately presented itself to me, that everybody and everything despised me because I was black." Blackness unfolds as historical awareness or consciousness of not being recognized. It is singularized existence in the shadows of imperial erasure.

44. Gates, *Signifying Monkey*, 152.

74 LET MY PEOPLE LIVE

That this awareness and consciousness emerged around Gronniosaw's interaction with the biblical text is critical to Africana biblical hermeneutics; it is the experience of textual lacuna as more than a literary discrepancy or narrative gap in biblical interpretation. The awareness is also Gronniosaw's experience of the colonizing text (the Bible) as a document that refused to meaningfully and creatively engage anything outside of itself, or outside its use in the colonial project, an apparent refusal to respond to the summons of the world it was producing. That experience of interpretation as alienated and disempowered for Black and other marginalized readers unfolds from a colonial hermeneutical pretense or assumption that the biblical text is primarily a text to be read and interpreted in "face-to-face" contact with its author, as opposed to being also a text that reads—a text that lives and travels as much on the wings of slave ships and colonial ideologies as in its literary words. The Black reader, upon experiencing the wounding silence of a colonial model of engaging the text and its identity-conferring power, may walk away with heightened and acute awareness of socially produced identity (Blackness) that mimics the texture of one's skin and functions as a semiotic symbol for the production of invisibility, of interpreting Blackly. Gronniosaw's realization of the book's utility in the epistemological and structural custody of the merchant in a colonial project resulted in interpretive apathy that correlated with displacement; it produced a consciousness of alienation. Another layer of consciousness occurred—that of a Black self produced at the interface of the colonizing voice and its simultaneous silence in the face of demands by the colonized body.

The Postcolony

After the official end of the Cold War and the advent of heightened discourse about political liberalism, Achille Mbembe started theorizing on the political, epistemological, and cultural constructions and manifestations of governance in the postcolony.[45] Mbembe began formulating his theories at a time of deadly crackdown on political dissidents in Cameroon, crystallized in violent clashes between law enforcement and

45. See, for example, Achille Mbembe, *On the Postcolony* (Stanford, CA: Stanford University Press, 2001); "On the Postcolony: A Brief Response to Critics" *Qui Parle*, 15, no. 2 (2005): 1–49; "On Politics as a Form of Expenditure," in *Law and Disorder in the Postcolony*, ed. Jean Comaroff and John Comaroff (Chicago: University of Chicago Press, 2006), 299–335.

citizens, after the launch of a major political opposition party in 1990. The political climate was defined by massive popular demands for multiparty democracy, antigovernment sit-ins, protests, and stay-at-home boycotts of public activity and business (government or private). These boycotts were popularly known as "ghost towns"—an apt, yet dreadful, haunting metaphor for sensibilities about postcolonial subjectivity plagued by endangered existence and profound alienation from official governance.

Mbembe theorizes necropolitics in relation to the power and technology of life and death. He explores a sense of "intimate tyranny" between the ruled and the rulers. For Mbembe, the story of Cameroon is the story of a colony and postcolony produced through a mix of fantastic ideology and violent mapping and remapping of national identity between 1884 and the 1990s, and embroidered in postcolonial violence under a so-called state of emergencies. Often referred to as "Africa in miniature" on account of its vast and diverse geographical landscapes, Cameroon's political history also proved a useful test case for a theory of power and sovereignty. Mbembe argues that "to exercise sovereignty is to exercise control over mortality and to define life as the deployment and manifestation of power." Moving away from questions of ontology (personal, institutional, and national) to questions of praxis, Mbembe asks, "under what practical conditions is the right to kill, to allow to live, or to expose to death exercised? Who is the subject of this right? What does the implementation of such a right tell us about the person who is thus put to death and about the relation of enmity that sets that person against his or her murderer?"[46]

Colonial sovereignty, Mbembe argues, rests on three sorts of violence: (1) founding violence, which underpins the right to conquest and the prerogatives flowing from that right and creates "the space over which it is exercised; one might say it presupposed its own existence," regarding itself as "the sole power to judge its laws"; (2) legitimizing violence, which functions to give the founding order meaning, to justify the "universalizing mission" of the colonial enterprise, and to convert "founding violence into authorizing authority"; and (3) a third form of violence that falls short of what is properly called war and that seeks to ensure the "maintenance, spread, and permanence" of legitimizing authority.[47] Mbembe then concludes:

---

46. Achille Mbembe, "Provisional Notes on the Postcolony," *Africa: Journal of the International African Institute* 62, no. 1 (1992): 12.

47. Mbembe, *On the Postcolony*, 25, italics in original.

> Colonial sovereignty only existed in areas where these three forms of violence were deployed, forming a seamless web. This violence was of a very particular sort, immediately tangible, and it gave natives a clear notion of themselves in proportion to the power that they had lost. Its distinctive feature was to act as both authority and morality. . . . Thus, in regard to colonial sovereignty, right was on *one* side. . . . Anything that did not recognize this violence as authority, that contested its protocols, was savage and outlaw.[48]

As with the slave ship and the slave castle, the colony and postcolony also constitute sites where Africana subjectivity and creativity identifies and responds to the triple consciousness of erasure, alienation, and singularity. The founding violence of colonial ideology and governance is the violence of erasure. It signifies that the colonizing state exists as a consequence of its ability to erase the colonized—body, culture, history, religion, etc. The second form of violence—the legitimizing violence—presents itself as civilizing violence, but it in fact compels the colony to be alienated from self-authenticating values and systems of accountability and to seek meaningful becoming outside of itself. The third form of violence seeks to protect the singular state and to infuse singularity into the political and epistemological infrastructure. When fully developed, this singularity manifests itself as the postcolonial strongman—the dictatorial regime.

Held together in the colony and postcolony, these three manifestations of violence create a scenario in which "we can come to understand that the postcolonial relationship to power is not primarily a relationship of resistance or collaboration but can best be characterized as illicit cohabitation, a relationship made fraught by the very fact of the *commandement* and its subjects having to share the same living space."[49] In these intimate settings, daily routines of life and death—eating, working, drinking, dancing, sleeping, procreating, clothing, singing, farming, funerals, etc.—take on biological, cultural, and political meanings. The work of liberation becomes as much a work of hermeneutics as that of socio-political praxis. How ought one to define and/or understand the use of power in the postcolony? Are there alternative ways of mobilizing and using power in creative rather than erasing (destructive) ways, to enhance community rather than to alienate, and to foster the well-being of the many rather than the safety of a few (or the sole monarch)?

---

48. Mbembe, *On the Postcolony*, 26, italics in original.
49. Mbembe, "Provisional Notes," 4, italics in original.

These concerns took global center stage in 1994 twin events that, by virtue of their temporal proximity and qualitative dissimilarity, constituted a jarring contrast of lived experiences, and, for many an observer, raised questions about narrativizing events that, by definition and character, present themselves as profound disjunctures from expected norms in the postcolony. I am here speaking of the twin events of the Rwanda genocide and the nonviolent transition to post-apartheid South Africa. Mahmood Mamdani's analyses of the events are hermeneutically incisive:

> If Rwanda was the genocide that happened, then South Africa was the genocide that didn't. The contrast was marked by two defining events in the first half of 1994: just as a tidal wave of genocidal violence engulfed Rwanda, South Africa held elections marking the transition to a postapartheid era. More than any other, these twin developments marked the end of innocence for the African intelligentsia. For if some seer had told us in the late 1980s that there would be a genocide in one of these two places, I wonder how many among us would have managed to identify correctly its location. Yet, this failure would also be testimony to the creative—and not just the destructive—side of politics.[50]

As part of a description of the histories and geographies of colonial and postcolonial Rwanda and South Africa, Mamdani's analyses situate this seminal period within a larger context of knowledge production, political history, and memory in Africa. And it is not the political identity of the nation-state (the poster child of colonialism), important as that is, that constitutes the most incisive vector in this experience of destruction, trauma, and trauma survived; rather it is the failure of predictive imagination of the intelligentsia in appropriately and accurately diagnosing and anticipating this turn of events. This loss of innocence, coupled with accompanying feelings of anguish and euphoria associated with the two events, compels a particular form of memory assessment in which the destructive and creative sides of politics (and, I will add, of social existence) are now twin events, a kinship of coexistent insiders. In this historical moment and in these geographical locations and histories distinctively and collectively defined by the creative and destructive sides of politics, accountable memory—memory that responsibly connects events to the systems and structures that produced

---

50. Mahmood Mamdani, *When Victims Become Killers: Colonialism, Nativism, and the Genocide in Rwanda* (Princeton, NJ: Princeton University Press, 2001), 184.

them—functions as a necessary corrective to the failures of predictive imagination and progress.

As the quintessential site for power struggle, the colonial and post-colonial political infrastructure may mimic the architecture of the slave castle, with its hierarchical structure and production of privilege for a few rather than value for the many. The postcolony may also become the place where marginalized and oppressed people navigate, negotiate, and survive official oppression and then continuously create sacred worldviews—what Kä Mana calls *imaginaire*[51]—out of violently wrecked and discarded histories, bodies, and places. This sacred world-view emerges in the wake of historical oppression, but its intergenerational character is hinged on the surviving community's ability to return to, and reclaim, the repressed, to look at the nation-state from the backside or the underside—to face its traumatic genealogy.

Mamdani's linking of two events—liberative and traumatic—and his framing of the failure of predictive imagination as simultaneous testimony to the creative and destructive sides of politics, signals a particular form of Africana hermeneutics about layers of (un)consciousness and identity formation that do not easily or completely succumb to singular or linear modes of liberation, historical narration, or geographical specificity. This methodological linking of the creative and destructive sides of politics—the hermeneutical linking of wombs to tombs—has both political and psychological significance in assessing the importance of history and geography in identity formation and meaning-making. For the postcolony engaged in exodus liberation hermeneutics, geography is as much a custodian and generator of intergenerational memory and redesign of the future as is history; place is as much an instigator of imagination as is time; form of governance (democratic or dictatorial) is as much a symbol of power as policy about racism and xenophobia; and the genre of communal anticolonial storytelling is as vital as the content of democratic principles.

FROM "LET MY PEOPLE GO" TO "LET MY PEOPLE LIVE"

In Africana exodus epistemology, I have argued, triple traumas of erasure, alienation, and singularity are symbolized in the objects of the slave ship, the slave castle, and the postcolony. These traumas require

---

51. Valentin Dedji, "The Ethical Redemption of African Imaginaire: Kä Mana's Theology of Reconstruction," *Journal of Religion in Africa* 31, no. 3 (2001): 254–74, italics in original.

TRIPLE CONSCIOUSNESS AND THE EXODUS NARRATIVE

deep conversations across their doors of no return—their seeming declarative claims that the endangered, marginalized, and singularized community cannot return (undo the damage of racism, patriarchy, colonialism, and imperialism). The urgent depiction of exodus as departure from an oppressive nation-state house and machinery is formulated and encapsulated in Moses' divinely inspired clarion call: "let my people go." But that call is more than an episodic manifestation of negotiation between Yahweh and Pharaoh. The call signifies an equally perennial and persistent call, ushered through voices from below, a call better represented by the words "let my people live." To insist on the primordial imperative of life is to resist Pharaoh's institution of conditional existence ("if it is a boy, he shall live") and to accelerate the production of multiple mechanisms and strategies of communal existence that enhance the vibrancy of life in its multiply gendered, national and transnational manifestations—the character and quality of life that existed prior to Pharaoh's ethnocentric and monogendered governance. In responding to these crises, and in creating foundational epistemologies for its myths of origins and futures, the Exodus story foregrounds resistance to the erasure of life, creates bridges that span the chasms of alienation, and exemplifies insider-outsider endeavors as counteractive to singularized existence. In locating its myths of origins and futures in the creative abilities of a marginalized group, the Exodus story narratively institutionalizes their hermeneutical capacities in ways that exceed ideologies and structures of erasure, alienation, and isolation—in Egypt, in the Wilderness, in the Mountain, and beyond.

Exodus is the loss of Egypt, but not because Egypt alone is oppressive or without promise. Therefore, Exodus is certainly not the loss of all of Egypt, but only of the Egypt that is unable or unwilling to reform, to creatively respond to internal criticism, and to be radically hospitable in ways that enshrine healthy living for its people and the future. Deprived of such work of internal innovation and development, Egypt must be rejected. How that loss or rejection is interpreted is both the work of historical narration as well as of memory and imagination. In the canonical movement of the Exodus story, this work travels from Egypt into the Wilderness and to the Mountain (Sinai). The postcolonial land, the promised land, may be imagined as unlike the colonial/colonized land, but it is constructed and partially populated by bodies from the abandoned land. If Exodus is to become the riposte of exile, such must be the case. Although the exodus community is shaped by Moses, whose association with Pharaoh's court is processed through adoption rather than through the cupbearer motif that placed Joseph there, the future of the story of liberation resides in the community, not in the hands of a singular figure in Pharaoh's court. The Exodus community inescapably brings with it some of the markers of Egypt. But the story has a credible future because, and only if, it reimagines those markers for the thriving of the whole—the human, environmental, and divine communities.

3
A Postcolonial Africana Reading of Exodus 2

INTRODUCTION

In *Critique of Black Reason*, Achille Mbembe theorizes on African nationalisms as a product of conflict between dreams and nightmares:

> Does not the colony produce in the colonized a dreamworld that turns rapidly into a nightmare? The dialectic of a dream that is always on the verge of becoming a nightmare is one of the driving forces behind the potentate. But it is also its Achilles' heel. In many ways African nationalisms are the product of the conflict between dreams and the frustration borne of the impossibility of truly satisfying them.[1]

Colonialism produces desires that are unmet because it is a system and an ideology of deficiency imposed on the Other, even when those desires masquerade as a "civilizing" project available to those who climb the ladder of colonial patronage and privilege. Those unmet desires get attached to the colonized subject, who translates them into a cause for liberation. In that sense, liberation is always a response to a structural deficiency, and thus always a second act—an action in opposition—to the act of erasure, alienation, singularity. Colonialism's response to its generated unmet desires can take a variety of forms: It can take

---

1. Achille Mbembe, *Critique of Black Reason*, trans. Laurent Dubois (Durham, NC: Duke University Press, 2017), 119.

the form of gifts bestowed on the colonized, to remedy their supposed inherent deficiency or as loans to subsidize access to privileged places of colonial power. The result is a particular kind of postcolonial text:

> In the Black text, the memory of the colony necessarily takes two forms. The first consists in inscribing the colony within a mythology of indebtedness by emphasizing what Africa lost through the encounter. The debt itself has two dimensions. On the one hand is the debt of procreation (development), and on the other, the debt of hospitality (immigration). In both instances the goal of the discourse of loss and debt is to incite guilt. The African world, born of the colony, is a world of loss—a loss occasioned by crime. The perpetrator of that crime is not only guilty but also indebted to those whose natural rights were violated.[2]

In a story where violence and debt and loss are part of the postcolonial Black text, "memory of the colony becomes a kind of *psychic work* that seeks to cure."[3] That is, the work of memory about the colony seeks not just to treat the wounds—the traumas—of colonialism but also to "cure" those who have been subjected to its brutality. I have argued that such work requires and involves triple consciousness. First, it involves the ability to structurally hide from colonial violence, that is, to embark on decolonial work that fundamentally and structurally resists erasure. The postcolonial self is not just a self that has survived; it is also a self that is committed to embodying the refusal to die. This refusal of death stands as a commitment to principles of democracy and justice that are not subject to the whims and caprices of the colonial potentate or the postcolonial strongman. The nightmare is that the surviving self must continually survive because it somehow shares the same living space as the colonizing infrastructure. Therefore, the work of cure must include the ability of the colonized/decolonized to create structural and epistemological detours from colonial infrastructures of erasure. The second unmet desire is that departure from the system of erasure may in fact turn into a nightmare of exile, of permanent alienation—because the colonial and imperial project hardly knows anything outside of itself. To avoid this nightmare, the displaced subject must mobilize the next generation into embracing departure (rather than exile) as its epistemological grounding. With departure, the experience of displacement can be recast as a journey, a perpetual pathway toward home-making.

2. Mbembe, *Critique*, 119–20.
3. Mbembe, *Critique*, 120.

A third unmet desire revolves around colonialism's deficient incentive structure that rewards the singular. Although life is fully lived in community, the colonial structure compels its subject to be "exceptional" and to consider exceptionality as a rare achievement or virtue, not easily available to the masses. The nightmare unfolds when the ideals of liberation and justice are available to a few, while the masses continue to languish under unjust practices within the same nation-state. The decolonized self works for epistemological, material, and hermeneutical abundance; it embraces difference, celebrates multiplicity, and foregrounds communal life.

Colonial governance and postcolonial dictatorships have some things in common: to ensure their institutional and ideological survival, they generate policies of erasure and put those into circulation; they create and maintain a profound sense of alienation (and apathy) among the colonized, depriving them of the capacity to hold power to account; and finally, they impose toxic singularity on the multiplicity of the colonized. I want to suggest that these three modes of colonial governance and postcolonial dictatorships are mirrored and rejected in the exodus-Exodus motif-story. Attention to these narrative details allows one to read the Exodus story in ways that do not have to end with the postcolonial community reproducing—as if by necessity or some inherent flaw—the actions and methods of a conquest narrative. I want to further argue that exodus-Exodus work illumines survivors, exiles, returnees, and *remainees* hard at work to form a narrative community, across time and space, that challenges erasure, alienation, and singularity.

From an African postcolonial perspective, I will name this hypothetical community, *gershomite*—in honor of Moses and Zipporah's first born son and the circumstances (Moses escaping violence in Egypt, becoming an alien, and being integrated into a community in Midian) that led to his identification as such (Exod. 2:22), and in honor of the Wilderness community that embraced and embodied this identity. *Gershomite* is also an interpretive process of engaging conditions that make Gershom and his story necessary and meaningful (Exod. 22:21; 23:9). To further anchor this framing, I will present an epistemological kin of *gershomite* identity by examining the literary and embodied character of changelings (*ogbanje*) in Chinua Achebe's *Things Fall Apart*. Depicted as slightly mysterious children who die soon after birth and then return in the form of another child, through the body of the mother, *ogbanje* embody and represent communal experiences with death and survival, alienation and return, singularity and multiplicity. *Gershomite-ogbanje* represents communal endeavors to turn postcolonial nightmares back into dreams. *Gershomite-ogbanje* is therefore a mode of postcolonial identity and hermeneutics. It depicts the fragility of life in the colonial space, and the capacity to survive and to live on in the body of another; that is, to survive in and as a communal body. The decisive meaning line in *gershomite-ogbanje* hermeneutics is the quality of life forged across time and space, and ultimately the need to situate this life-giving hermeneutic outside of the constructions of erasure, marginalization, and singularity.

GERSHOMITE IDENTITY AND EXODUS

"I have been an alien residing in a foreign land" (Exod. 2:22). As an endangered and displaced Hebrew-Egyptian, these are Moses' first articulations of self-definition, though not his first identity-forming moments, in Exodus. Coming at the end of three identity-shaping episodes in Exodus 2, and set against a larger backdrop of wartime ideology and ethnocentric policies targeting the Hebrews (and the children of Israel) in Exodus 1, Moses' words represent more than an isolated moment of autobiographical reflection on identity construction in the context of alienation. Although Moses self-identifies as a sojourner in a foreign land, the bearer of that identity and its memory is not Moses, but his son Gershom, who embodies this uttered identity in the meaning of his very name. Moses' words thus function as an interpretive trope for the community to which Moses belongs, the community that must carry on the work of liberation and turn exile into exodus. The significance of Gershom cannot be fully understood in isolation from the preceding narrative events that brought Moses to Midian, the ensuing events in Midian, and the discourse about exodus that returns Moses to Egypt. Moses is a repeat survivor of political violence; he is an endangered, exposed, and adopted child. But he is also a refugee—an embodied casualty and subject of violence. All of those realities constitute the narrative history leading up to his presence in Midian, the interpretive framework for Gershom's narrative genealogy, and Moses' commentary on that genealogy. Just as Moses' experiences of endangered exposure, alienation, and adoption are mapped onto the national story (Israel endangered in Egypt, alienated in the Wilderness, and adopted in the Mountain area), so too Gershom's identity as a literary and literal child is mapped onto the Exodus community.

The narrative that births Gershom is shepherded and attached to Zipporah's material and epistemological body, the body of a non-Hebrew mother. Though partially marginalized within her geopolitical and patriarchal setting, she is an entrepreneurial woman who encounters Moses and identifies him as an Egyptian engaged in rescuing oppressed subjects (Exod. 2:19). Her predisposition toward enhancing rescue continues when she performs saving rituals for Moses and Gershom when they all embark on a communal return to confront and overcome colonizing erasure (Exod. 4:22, 24–26). She is the activist, analyst, and religious practitioner whose material, intellectual, and social body informs and guides the costly but generative work of communal rescue and life enhancement. Her actions as a shepherd and her intervention and commentary on behalf of Moses/Gershom at the intersections of life and death extend the actions and commentary of her narrative ancestresses: the midwives, Moses' biological mother, Miriam, and the Egyptian princess (Exod. 1:16; 2:1–10). Further back, Zipporah is connected to matriarchal narratives, especially the actions of the eponymous Egyptian *ger* ancestress, Hagar, whose story represents the experience of survival around intergenerational and interregional motherhood, expulsion, child exposure, and adoption (Gen 16; 21:8–21).[4] Zipporah represents the latest narrative ancestress to labor for the triumph of life; she is one of the biblical narrative's "mothers of the movement"[5]—mothers that have to fight to receive their children, either posthumously or preemptively, from the jaws of death and alienation.

The communal child—Gershom—that she births also represents an epistemological embodiment of the experiences that have defined Moses' life: close encounter with death, alienation, and isolation. Through Moses' commentary (Exod. 2:22), historiography and memory are present in real bodies as much as in discourse. Textual, geographical, and human bodies are not just correlative but also co-constitutive. To read one without reading the others is to misread. Moses alone—as the mobilizer of ancestral memory under Yahweh's tutelage—can neither fully understand the character and scope of Exodus nor adequately contribute to its significance without positioning his own historical

---

4. Following the divine promise about Abraham's children becoming *ger*, we read about the ethnic, regional, and genealogical relation between Hagar, Sarah, and Abraham (Gen. 15–16). See Phyllis Trible and Letty M. Russell, eds., *Hagar, Sarah, and Their Children: Jewish, Christian, and Muslim Perspectives* (Louisville, KY: Westminster John Knox Press, 2006).

5. The expression is obviously modern and refers to African American mothers whose sons and daughters were killed by gun violence—whether accidental or via police violence—and who decided to raise their voices in protest and demand legislative changes in gun policies.

86   LET MY PEOPLE LIVE

genealogy within a larger unfolding narrative that lives in the human
and geographical body of another—Gershom. Gershom is not just a
biological name; it is a communal body that bears the marks of the
work of liberation (Exod. 22:21; 23:9). It is this community—not just
a single narrative—that holds the memory and the history of Moses
and Zipporah. Disembodied and displaced hermeneutics is resisted.
The Exodus story, recast through *gershomite* identity, is about reengag-
ing Egypt as a fragmented and fragmenting space, as a displaced and
alienated space, but also as a place where liberation is already ongoing
in the narrative presence and activities of the midwives and Miriam and
the Egyptian princess and the Hebrews in Egypt. *Gershomite* identity
and epistemology function to define exodus group identity and hermeneutics in three important ways: to protect the endangered, to remember the discarded, and to liberate the multiple that are confined in the
singularizing body of the nation, colony, or empire.

Rabbinic tradition gives us insight into this mode of hermeneutics.
As Louis Ginzberg shows in *The Legends of the Jews*, biblical characters
were often given multiple names in the midrashic tradition, to signify
that the characters and their names functioned to represent complex
communal relations. In this rabbinic tradition, Moses' parents and
kindred give him multiple names: his father names him Heber to
commemorate the reunion between Amram and Jochebed after their
divorce; Jochebed names him Jekuthiel to express her fulfilled hope
that Moses would be returned to her after the exposure; to Miriam,
the child was Jered because she descended to the stream to ascertain
his fate; to Aaron, he was Abi Zanoah because his father had cast off
his mother and then taken her back; to his grandfather, Moses was Abi
Gedor because the heavenly father built a breach in Israel to rescue
them from Egyptians attempting to throw Hebrew children into the
water; to his nurse, Moses was Abi Soco because he was concealed in
a tent for three months; and to Israel, he was Shemaiah ben Nathanel
because in Moses' day, God heard the sighs of the people, delivered
them from oppression, and gave them the law. Names function as epistemological tropes through which rabbinic authors explore and reflect
on nonlinear, dynamic processes of identity construction.[6]

Moses' name that we are most familiar with (Exod. 2:10) comes at
the culmination of a cluster of genealogical, socioeconomic, cultural,
and political negotiations involving members of his Hebrew subgroup

---

6. Louis Ginzberg, *The Legends of the Jews*, vol. 2, *Bible Times and Characters from Joseph to the Exodus*, trans.
Henrietta Szold (Champaign, IL: Project Gutenberg, 1998), 269–70.

and members of the house of Pharaoh. He is given an Egyptian name with a Hebrew etiology.[7] More than that, Moses is named not right after his birth (Exod. 2:2), but after he survived a threat to his life, was exposed, and then singularly rescued and placed in Pharaoh's court. His name reflects larger social dynamics about endangered existence, marginalization, and singularity in the story. In an intriguing essay on Moses, H. Zlotnick-Sivan posed the following question: "why did the redactor(s) of this phase of Israelite 'ancient history' cast Moses as an Egyptian alumnus and subsequently as a deliverer from Egypt and not, say, Babylonian or even Persian bondage, especially if one subscribes to an exilic or post exilic date of the Pentateuch redaction?"[8] The question is crucial because, as Zlotnick-Sivan notes, Egypt occupies only about a third of the narrative corpus of Exodus (Exod. 1–15). Much of the narrative takes place in the Wilderness and Mountain areas, where Egypt functions as a memory trope.

The birth and naming of Gershom introduces a new beginning in the story, a beginning in which Moses transfers his identity and experience onto Gershom through the identity-forming moment of naming the child. As the naming of Gershom reflects the implications of forced migration on adult Moses, who is at once separated from the center of imperial power but also living in the shadow of the imperial force (the Mountain), unsettling anxieties about identity formation continue to animate the story. Upon encountering Moses in the vicinity of the mountain, Jethro's daughters leave him behind and return home. Jethro asks his daughters a probing question: "Where is he?" (Exod. 2:20). This is a question about the lost, displaced, or isolated sibling, recognizable in the Cain-Abel story (Gen. 4:9). But instead of switching a lost biological baby for a geographical adult, Jethro's accompanying question, "why did you leave the man?" (Exod. 2:20), effectively recognizes the role that his daughters are urged to play in moving the story away from the singularizing force of Mountain space (cf. Psalm 22:2).

As the story of Gershom increasingly comes into narrative and communal embodiment, and eventually into narrative and embodied view (birth), it decenters single hero narration and moves toward

---

7. Herbert Marks, "Biblical Naming and Poetic Etymology," *Journal of Biblical Literature* 114, no. 1 (1995): 29–31, argues that the use of etymology in the story is a literary motif that captures makeshift beginnings, not original beginnings, and therefore attends to the elements of "disguise and doubling" of identity in the succeeding scenes.

8. H. Zlotnick-Sivan, "Moses the Persian? Exodus 2, the 'Other' and Biblical 'Mnemohistory,'" *Zeitschrift für die Alttestamentliche Wissenschaft* 116 (2004): 190–91.

entrenching communal interregional and intergenerational narration. In his etiological and hermeneutical commentary about Gershom, the geopolitical epistemology and identity around "erasure/exile/singularity" is embodied as "survival/exodus/community." In this geopolitical and interpretive conferral of identity and subjectivity, exodus as a partial return from colonial exile becomes concurrent with exodus as a redesign against erasure, alienation, and singularity. In the narrative person of Gershom, the story of Moses surviving erasure and overcoming alienation and singular existence becomes a communal story. The postcolonial nightmare might yet be turned into a dream world of liberation and communal thriving.

THE *OGBANJE*: GERSHOM'S AFRICAN KIN

In one of the great classic modern novels, *Things Fall Apart*, we read—at a time of distress, indeed of despair, for the exiled protagonist Okonkwo—that "Mother is Supreme," a phrase that would ring as shallow, perhaps even insulting, to the hypermasculine Okonkwo. In fact, Okonkwo not only disdains the casual artistic lifestyle of his father and his son, which he reads as feminine, and the occasional storytelling by his wives, but he also seems set on violently wrestling everything into submission. However, the phrase "Mother is Supreme" is not exclusively about challenging Okonkwo's patriarchal gender ideology or personal mannerisms, though the phrase certainly does that. "Mother is Supreme" also functions in the narrative as a critical epistemological and memory trope that infuses the depth of cultural life-forms into the wreckage of intimate violence and diaspora. The phrase comes at the end of an intergenerational and interregional portrait of Okonkwo's return to his maternal homeland. His maternal uncle, Uchendu, paints the portrait: "Why is Okonkwo with us today? This is not his clan. We are only his mother's kinsmen. He does not belong here. He is an exile, condemned for seven years to live in a strange land. And so he is bowed with grief." And then—one can almost feel the power of sarcastic phraseology, of internal cultural critique, and perhaps even of tonal inflection—Uchendu continues, "Can you tell me, Okonkwo, why it is that one of the commonest names we give our children is Nneka, or 'Mother is Supreme'?" Okonkwo does not know the answer to the question.[9]

9. Chinua Achebe, *Things Fall Apart* (New York: Anchor Books, 1994), 133.

The cultural and political significance of this narrative portrait of Okonkwo's exile in relation to identity dislocation and memory is its genealogical and spatial irony: a very successful man with a well-established socio-cultural identity associated with separation and departure from maternal kinship identities (mother-land, mother-folk) is bowed with grief as he temporarily reengages and finds refuge in motherland, which has become his place of exile. The portrait of Okonkwo's exile in his motherland, the description of his interactions with his maternal kinfolk, and the exploration of his ignorance about the raison d'être of "Mother is Supreme" constitute a narrative and cultural episteme about survival through motherhood (genealogical and cultural) and about learning-to-remember as an act of communal transference and conferral of identity; in reconnecting with motherland, but especially with the epistemology associated with the trope of motherhood, Okonkwo is invited to respond creatively to exile. Given that Okonkwo was banished from the land by the earth goddess Ani for committing a violent act, the exploration of "Mother is Supreme" allows Okonkwo and his gathered community to address the ideology, not just the act, of violence, including patriarchal violence.

Although set in precolonial Africa, Achebe's work is a critique of colonial violence and its epistemological underpinnings. "Mother is Supreme" is a memory mnemonic that conflates several tropes—gender, genealogy, culture, and geography—about individual and collective identity, linking those tropes to alienated and marginalized bodies (motherhood, motherland) and portraying those bodies as places and epistemologies of beginnings that predate and overcome violence and marginalization. The construction of the colonial and postcolonial nation-state as patriarchal departure from, and rejection of matriarchal origins and epistemes, is a function of ignorance, and therefore of unaccountable remembering. Ironic, iconic, and proverbial in its significance, the phrase "Mother is Supreme" functions to provide constructive cultural perspective to the exiled hero, and therefore to move away from single hero forms of identity formation embodied and enacted in the character of Okonkwo. The gathered assembly to which Okonkwo's body is attached must reconstitute individual and communal selfhood in the face of exile-at-home. Thus, Uchendu's invocation and exploration of a culturally pervasive concept attuned to layered constructions of communal identity in diaspora-home dialogues and spaces is at once nostalgic and creative. Uchendu's character explores motherland and motherhood as places, as epistemologies, and as embodied subjects of beginnings and of redesign (return) for the future of his diaspora-home community.[10]

As a "prevailing semantic paradigm,"[11] the trope of "Mother is Supreme" functions as a form of African postcolonial memory with three constitutive parts. First, there is conjunctive memory. This is memory as communal mobilization around ideological and structural coherence of identity formation. The galvanizing ethos of conjunctive memory is a drive toward holism of life, a process that recognizes the traumas of loss, marginalization, and isolation but that insists on hope-full productions and reproductions of life where colonial exile is historicized, internalized (though not integrated into the sense of self), and held to accountable restructuring. It is partly his resistance to such work that causes Okonkwo to finally commit suicide, an act that his peer, Obierika, interprets as a direct function of maddening colonial ideology and practice. The anticolonial thrust that Okonkwo represents must learn new forms of postcolonial memory in which the community ultimately claims custody of its otherwise lost, marginalized, and isolated bodies.

However, conjunctive memory does not function in isolation from other forms of memory. Memory structured around "Mother is Supreme" is cognitively and affectively disjunctive from patriarchal and colonial ideology (e.g., homeland and promised land as "fatherland"), and therefore it functions as a necessary corrective to such epistemes.[12] Achebe beautifully provides such a corrective in his portrayal of Okonkwo. For all his male chauvinism and predilection to domineering violence on or against the other—gendered or not—Okonkwo is fond of his daughter, Ezinma, born to Ekwefi, a free-thinking woman and devoted mother whose love for wrestling attracted her to Okonkwo. Ekwefi and Okonwo endured many years of life's hardships together. Ezinma was the tenth and only surviving child in a line of *ogbanje*— a child who died and was believed to have returned in the form of another child. As mother, Ekwefi engaged in a different kind of wrestling with the recurring cycle of birth, loss, and rebirth, which proved distressful to her physical body and the gendered communal body, and required ritual ceremonies and interpretive moves to interrupt.[13]

---

10. Achebe, *Things Fall Apart*, 133–35. I use community here in a generous sense, ranging from face-to-face interactions to social groups—tribal, ethnic, national, etc.—that share some form of collective ideology not necessarily based on personal acquaintance or knowledge.

11. The phrase "prevailing semantic paradigm" is Jan Assmann's *The Mind of Egypt: History and Meaning in the Time of the Pharaohs*, trans. Andrew Jenkins (Cambridge, MA: Harvard University Press, 2002), 6.

12. Adéléke Adéèkó, "Great Books Make Their Own History," *Transition* 100 (2008): 40.

13. Achebe, *Things Fall Apart*, 75–86.

Okonkwo's fondness for Ezinma portrays the narrative hero as already deeply involved in, and bonded with, notions of home and alienation, presence and absence, return and departure—all embodied in his daughter and in a recurring painful process of birthing, singularly experienced by the physical body of the mother. This is the basis of a second form of memory, disjunctive memory. Disjunctive memories are not mobilized by structural ideological coherence but by their contingent attachment to the recurring capacity to return, to recreate space for communal belonging beyond existing parameters of patriarchy or colonialism. Through his fondness for Ezinma, Okonkwo learns to recognize how his own identity as a father is inseparable from the difficult, creative work of Ekwefi. Okonkwo learns to remember his identity in relation to the multigenerational rhythms of life generated and endured by Ekwefi and embodied in Ezinma. The trope of "Mother is Supreme"—narratively embodied in Ezinma—challenges Okonkwo's patriarchal ideology and his single-hero attempts to undo colonialism, and invites him to commit to alternative modes and rhythms of communal belonging that originate outside of existing dominant ideologies and power structures.

Although disjunctive memory inhabits and emerges from the margins of social, political, or ideological space, its elusiveness makes the distinction between the center and the periphery of social identity permeable and changeable. Because disjunctive memory develops and operates in response to being abandoned or discarded—mentally, ideologically, and physically—its galvanizing ethos is survival, a defiant refusal to die: in "Mother is Supreme," *supremacy* functions as a powerful cultural, social, gendered, and political right to survival, a functional and conceptual antidote to erasure, alienation, and singularity. This is the basis of a third form of memory, adjunctive memory. Adjunctive memory—in the sense of concurrent, not auxiliary—is memory that navigates and emerges from the internal coherence of conjunctive work and the uneasy coherence of identity around marginalized existence. Adjunctive memory works around the simultaneity of familiar and unfamiliar identities and experiences. The relationship between Okonkwo, Ekwefi, and the returning changeling (Ezinma) illustrates this reality of communal identity formation around subjects and ideologies that are supposed to be lodged in the past, buried in the earthy soils that give the community its geographical identity and cultural fervor (conjunctive memory), but these identities continuously recur as powerful, if elusive, presences (disjunctive memory). Through

92 LET MY PEOPLE LIVE

adjunctive memory, there is a conferral of the supremacy of motherhood on the *ogbanje* child, who no longer simply represents survival of
erasure and belonging beyond marginalization, but also the capacity to
forge life that is intergenerational and hospitable, not just generation-
ally accommodating.

THREE SCENARIOS OF *GERSHOMITE-OGBANJE*
SUBJECTIVITY IN EXODUS 2

I want to examine the biblical narrative in Exodus 2 as depicting and
responding to colonial, postcolonial, and imperial scenarios. Within
this narrative, three scenarios construct (2:1–10), deconstruct (2:11–
15), and reconstruct (2:16–22) communal identity formation and
meaning. I will use the foregoing literary and epistemological construct
of *gershomite-ogbanje* identity to read these three scenarios as modes of
African reactions to colonial, postcolonial, and imperial manifestations
of erasure/loss, alienation/marginalization, and singularity/isolation.

From Endangered to Adopted: Identity in Exodus 2:1–10

Hugo Gressmann argues that the story of Moses' birth and adoption
originally existed as a legend about a single hero that was secondarily
linked to the threat against the entire Israelite population.[14] Since
Gressmann's publication, several critical refinements of his theory have
developed further insights into the genre, rhetorical, and socio-political
functions of the story.[15] Developed at the height of the historical-
critical method of biblical interpretation, which also coincided with the
period of official colonialism, Gressmann's theory about the primacy of
single-hero legends and the secondary attachment of communal threats
to such legends is at once insightful and highly problematic: it explores
the hero-community relation as sequenced rather than concurrent. A
gershomite-ogbanje postcolonial reading challenges single hero focus or
primacy, prioritizes the narrative history to which leading characters

---

14. Hugo Gressmann, *Mose und seine Zeit: Ein Kommentar zu den Mose-Sagen* (Gottingen: Vandenhoeck &
Ruprecht, 1912), 1–16. For critiques and expansions of Gressmann's theory, see Brevard S. Childs, "The Birth of
Moses," *Journal of Biblical Literature* 84, no. 2 (1965): 109–15; Jonathan Cohen, *The Origins and Evolution of the
Moses Nativity Story* (Leiden: E. J. Brill, 1993), 5–27; Athalya Brenner, "Female Social Behaviour: Two Descriptive
Patterns within the 'Birth of a Hero' Paradigm," *Vetus Testamentum* 36, no. 3 (1986): 267–69.
15. Meir Malul, "Adoption of Foundlings in the Bible and Mesopotamian Documents: A Study of Some Legal
Metaphors in Ezekiel 16:1–7," *Journal for the Study of the Old Testament* 46 (1990): 97–126.

A POSTCOLONIAL AFRICANA READING OF EXODUS 2

belong, and anchors the communal nature of heroic narrative—its capacity to mobilize an endangered community to challenge oppression and create new futures.

The story (Exod. 2:1–10) constitutes the beginning of the larger narrative that ultimately produces Gershom and Moses' associated commentary about his alien experience. One of several Levite women, perhaps a single mother,[16] is strapped for economic resources but also faced with horrifying governing demands that sons be thrown into the Nile—the economic engine that subsidizes the nation and its political autocrat. She apparently reaches her wits' end after hiding her beautiful, healthy son for three months. The oppressive gaze and apparatus has apparently become so intrusive and restricting that she cannot hide her child anymore. What she loses is not the capacity to produce and nurture life; her loss is the capacity to do so unencumbered by the menacing and colonizing gaze of ethnic erasure. She responds to the exacting and threatening political decree the best way she knows how: she builds a basket, reminiscent of Noah's ark and evocative of makeshift rafts bearing modern-day survivors, escapees, and returnees. Then she puts her son in the basket and, with Miriam functioning as a witness and informant-narrator, the woman-mother puts her son in the reeds of the Nile. It is a daring act of solidarity with her experiential narrative predecessor and eponymous ancestress, Hagar, who exposes Ishmael near water, under analogous circumstances of duress, distress, and creativity (Gen. 16:7; 21:15). Her decision to transition her son and daughter from secretive life in the shadows of Pharaoh's emerging ethno-nationalist ideology and its death decrees, into the public space, is risky and highly consequential. Her decision is indicative of the structural, rather than sporadic, modes of communal duress occasioned by Pharaoh's death-decree, to which she responds. In her production of communal futures, she has decided to engage rather than hide from the nation's ethnocentric structures. Through her double placement of Moses (in the ark at home and in the ark in public) and her added placement of Miriam in close proximity, Jochebed is not simply anticipating the communal experience that transitions from Passover to liberation; she is narratively and structurally producing and conjuring this experience. Her actions of hiding Moses and then releasing him into

---

16. It is inconclusive in the narrative whether or not Moses' mother is a single mother. The text is ambiguous about Moses' father and certainly does not accord him any active part in raising Moses. Like Hagar's story where a child being separated from its mother is closely related to economic distress and being a single mother, so too here Moses' mother acts alone to secure a future for her son.

the public space set the stage for structured responses to political violence and identity formation. When we see Moses in the public space, we cannot overlook Miriam and/or Jochebed actively producing the values that shape that public space.

Circumstance leads to seemingly random and uncertain opportunity: a well entouraged Egyptian princess comes to bathe, and soon the boy is rescued and brought into the "national" house—the very house that threatened to kill him and his kind. This is not a story of a singular hero and his isolated providential rescue, secondarily linked to the community. It is rather a story of precise strategic thinking and action, embodied by multiple characters who populate the public site and the discourse of adoption; it is a communal story of counter-erasure and resistance to marginalized and singularized existence. Although the princess' identification of the boy as Hebrew may evoke his possible phenotype or cultural embodiment, what is consequential for Africana is that public identification of Moses as Hebrew signals, and makes official, the princess' understanding (alongside Jochebed's and Miriam's) of identity formation in relation to institutional policy. Pharaoh's policy and decree, not primordial genealogy or phenotype, are the prime factors in understanding Moses' exposure and its implications on discourse about identity formation. It is Pharaoh's violent policies that are rightly under scrutiny; it is these policies, attached to phenotype, that attract deserving critique in anticolonial and antiracist hermeneutics.

Because of standing policy, the exposed boy is in political and cultural distress, evident by the fact that he is found crying. The cry is a political and cultural cry wrapped up in a targeted body, and it requires more than momentary and isolated redress and interpretation. To perform the hermeneutical task of triple survival—cultural, political, and ideological—represented by the triple placement of Moses (in the basket at home, in the reeds of the Nile, and in the house of Pharaoh), arrangements are made to reconnect the hidden, exposed, and distressed child with his ethnic group under the tutelage of Jochebed, Miriam, and the Egyptian princess. In pursuit of this communal response to erasure, marginalization, and singularity, the story's architects put the rescued communal child in the innermost space of political power, to compel reconsideration of the internal makeup and ethos of the governing institution. Adoption transforms Moses from an endangered/marginal/single boy in distress to a prince in the house of Pharaoh.

It is not the first time in the Hebrew Bible that oppressed Hebrews access the corridors of power in violent, marginalizing governments.

But it is the only time in the Hebrew Bible that such access is explored, through adoption, as a quasi-genealogical pursuit, rather than through hierarchical subjugation as a cup bearer or through imperial service as the "court Jew." Indeed, Moses' adoption into the house of Pharaoh comes in the wake of political amnesia about Joseph's rise to power in the Pharaoh's courts (the quintessential marginalized and singularized cupbearer story in Genesis). It also comes in the wake of the violent policy threatening an entire generation of Hebrews. To overcome this double threat, the storyteller forges an even more intimate link between Hebrews and Egyptians. This signals that the ideology of erasure and the policy of genocidal violence that placed Moses in the public place of danger must be permanently and effectively resisted from within the structure itself. Transition from such necessary and effective resistance to redesign is possible through collective action that reimagines the structure, the membership, and the authority of governance, rather than by continuing to interpret and celebrate its existing forms of intramural, episodic rescue actions.

How far into the belly of the state and its governing structure must one go in order to effectively radicalize it for the work of liberation? Perhaps the question is slightly misstated. Given the encompassing power of colonial and imperial mythologies, subjugated persons are already deep within the infrastructure, and the question is whether Moses' presence in that site of power will result in assimilation or will trigger transformative reorganization of the nation or empire. The question is epistemological and ideological: How much more effective, meaningful, and enduring is transformation etched to geopolitical insiders (those who find identity around the concept of the nation as a political entity) than to geocultural insiders (those who build identity around cultural tropes both within and beyond the nation-state)? How do race, ethnicity, and culture feature in the African postcolony? That is where the communal story puts Moses after adoption. The story of simultaneous native and alien identity begins to evoke the most salient aspects of embodied ethic for the postcolonial, feminist, or womanist subject: it is no longer enough to simply explore how to survive while sharing space with the structure that threatens to eliminate you; one must ask how to redesign the structure.

The story engages rather than ignores economic anxieties, ethnic/racial trauma, and communal vulnerability from violent exposure, the effects of which are partially addressed through adoption. This is not a story of complete escape from violence; rather, this is a story of narrow

96   LET MY PEOPLE LIVE

escape, fueled by acts of political compassion and acts of critical discourse and cultural agency that create new paradigms of identity formation around intraethnic nurture and interethnic structure. Moses'
adoption, after he grows up, evokes legal and institutional privileges
and protections against threats of enslavement.[17] Indeed, the language
of adoption inaugurating Moses' adult life is similar to the language of
the divine adoption of kings elsewhere (2 Sam 7:14; Ps. 2:7). Moses
does not become a king, but that possibility was not lost on the rabbis.
In *midrashic* tradition, the princess says: "I have brought up a child,
who is divine in form and of an excellent mind, and as I received him
through the bounty of the river in a wonderful way, I have thought it
proper to adopt him as my son and as the heir of thy kingdom."[18] In its
pursuit of structural redesign, the story opens up a new layer of analyses: Will Moses become a Pharaoh? And how might Exodus as a story
set within Pharaoh's wartime ideology and praxis (Exod. 1:10) be reimagined if Moses, the preeminent leader, is portrayed as a Pharaoh-in-
the-making? Because political transition is only a part of exodus work,
the narrative begins to place Moses outside of the corridors of power.
Miriam advocates that his presence in places of power must be contingent on his ability to be intimately connected to, and nourished by, his
nursing mother, and thus connected to the voices and resources that
sustain and enrich life within the marginalized and endangered community. Once removed from official spaces, Moses and the oppressed
community experience another dimension of the power of violence and
the effective traumatic memory on fragmented communal identity,
beyond the political.

Alienation and Counter-Adoption: Identity in Exodus 2:11–15

Two distinct but interrelated views frame analyses of violence in this
episode in which Moses kills an Egyptian man who was beating a
Hebrew. The first view examines violence *by* Moses and raises questions
about the legitimacy of violence as a tool of deliverance and, related
to that, the moral and political authority of a violent person. In his
Commentary on Exodus, Thomas Dozeman describes Exodus 2:11–15a

---

17. The Ananiah archive from Elephantine describes a similar process of adoption, in which a certain Jedaniah,
a Hebrew slave (called *lad* and *son*) of Takhoi is adopted by Ananiah. The text repeatedly has Ananiah saying of
Jedaniah, "my son he shall become." See Bezalel Porten, *The Elephantine Papyri in English: Three Millennia of
Cross-Cultural Continuity and Change* (Leiden: Brill, 1996), 234–35.
18. Josephus, *Jewish Antiquities* II, 9.6–7; Ginzberg, *Legends,* 271–72.

as "a tale of failed leadership" that "sketches Moses' initial inclination toward violence, how such action influences his identity and undermines his authority. The message is that violence begets violence."[19] A second view recognizes Moses' initial act of violence but also highlights the violence *toward* Moses. For William Propp, the story's violent incidents function to frame the ensuing narrative in two ways: first to set up Moses' appointment by the deity in the next chapter, showing the "futility of attempting to rescue Israel without divine aid" and the "necessity for a society to be guided by divinely inspired law;" and second, "conversely, Israelite hostility toward Moses, first articulated by the wicked Hebrew, becomes a leitmotiv for the rest of the Torah."[20]

With all its impulses for forward movement, anticipating divine liberation (which itself is partially violent), the episode also evokes a strong sense of narrative memory. Specifically, the story anchors its socio-cultural and political genesis not just in a generic folkloric world of memory ("in those days," Exod. 2:11, author's translation), and not just in contemporary acts of violence (by or toward Moses), but more specifically in political memory about Moses' maturity, "when the child grew up"—a phrase that echoes and situates his official public adoption (Exod. 2:10).[21] The episode begins where the adoption story reaches its narrative finale and its institutional anchor. It is a "going out" that is as much about Moses' embrace of his socio-cultural affinity (he goes out to see his kin) as it is about the political manifestation of his institutional persona (he observes their hard labor). Furthermore, the sequence of events over two days and the reference to events from the previous day by Moses' interlocutor—the enslaved Hebrew who witnessed Moses killing an oppressive Egyptian—frame interpretation as an ongoing endeavor, attuned to unfolding events. Narrative sequencing creates a sense of inner narrative memory, the basis for such interpretation: "Do you mean to kill me as you killed the Egyptian?" (Exod. 2:14). Meaning is explored not just in relation to chronological time and context but also in relation to layers of memory associated with the traumas of violence. Events that are sequentially in the

---

19. Thomas Dozeman, *Commentary on Exodus* (Grand Rapids, MI: William B. Eerdmans, 2009), 86.

20. William H. C. Propp, *Exodus 1–18: A New Translation with Introduction and Commentary* (New York: Doubleday, 1999), 168, italics in original.

21. The use of *wygdl* in 2:10 and 2:11 has been part of the primary reason for making source-critical arguments about the adoption story and this story. The double use of *wygdl* results in two meaning: in 2:10 it suggests growing up enough to be weaned and in 2:11 it suggests growing up to adulthood. See John Van Seters, *The Life of Moses: The Yahwist as Historian in Exodus–Numbers* (Louisville, KY: Westminster/John Knox Press, 1994), 30. Examples of such double usage include Gen. 21:8, 20; 1 Sam. 2:21; 3:19. According to the book of Acts (7:23), Moses was forty years old when he fled Egypt. The book of Jubilees (47:1; 48:1) says he fled at the age of forty-two.

past in a linear-temporal sense and presumably no longer part of active public social consciousness (e.g., Moses' killing of the Egyptian on the first day) may turn out, through inner narrative memory, to have been latent (in a Freudian sense) or concealed (as in Moses' hiding of the dead Egyptian's body).

Whether repressed or concealed, violent memories may be reengaged through inner narrative analyses. Thus, in addition to undermining Moses' political and legal authority, and serving as a *Leitmotiv* for much of what follows, this narrative episode requires reexamination of the preceding adoption narrative: what becomes of the adoption story when (1) Moses is saddled with personal anxieties about the political processes that have defined and contributed to his adoption persona; when (2) a member of the subgroup to which Moses' adoption story assigns him becomes influentially and effectively critical and resistant to his use of authority derived from violence; and when (3) the representative of the adopting institution seeks to kill Moses. In other words, how does Exodus 2:11–15 redefine colonial adoption for individual and communal survival in the postcolony?

Again, scholarly perspectives are varied, yet sometimes overlapping. For Brevard Childs, the biblical author clearly demonstrates high stylistic and literary skills in crafting a narrative that echoes elements of the birth-exposure-adoption story. Nevertheless, Exodus 2:11–15 is only "loosely connected" to the preceding birth and adoption story.[22] George Coats, for his part, sees the episode as part of a "Moses Tradition" that presupposes the adoption story; it portrays Moses as someone who, though in a privileged position, is nevertheless "aware of his relationship with the oppressed people."[23] And for Trent Butler, the episode, along with the preceding adoption story, is part of a critical "tradition," even a "movement" in ancient Israel against Moses.[24] This "anti-Moses" tradition, Butler argues, existed alongside a dominant "pro-Mosaic" tradition that now permeates much of the Pentateuch,

---

22. Childs, *Book of Exodus*, 29–30.

23. George Coats, *The Moses Tradition* (Sheffield: JSOT Press, 1987), 24.

24. Trent Butler, "An Anti-Moses Tradition," *Journal for the Study of the Old Testament* 12 (1979): 9–15; "Anti-Moses Tradition," *Lexington Theological Quarterly* 14, no. 3 (1979): 33–39. Butler, "Anti-Moses," 38, writes that each of these narratives "gives a peculiar identity to Moses. He is the child of nameless parents reared in the court of the Egyptians. He is a clever murderer who sought to claim the right to be ruler and judge without proper credentials, but was discovered and disowned. He is an Egyptian married to a hated Midianite, producing a son whose name indicates that the family belongs to the foreign, landless, lower ranks of society. Such language in the right hands, spoken in the proper tones of sarcasm, could be used to discredit Moses." See, however, Cornelis Houtman's argument about Moses "who is so eminently qualified to be the leader of the people" and yet has to deal with people who show that "they do not want his leadership and help," in Houtman, "*Exodus*," vol. 1, Historical Commentary on the Old Testament (Kampen: Kok Publishing House, 1993), 292, 294. The other anti-Moses texts include Exod. 2:16–22; 4:24–26 (fragmented); 18:1–12; and 18:14b–23.

A POSTCOLONIAL AFRICANA READING OF EXODUS 2   99

both movements addressing Moses' dominating presence and influence on ancient Israel."[25] To varying degrees, Childs, Coats, and Butler recognize a connection between Exodus 2:11–15 and the adoption story in 2:1–10. I want to draw from their insights and then make a further claim: the resonances and dissonances between the two episodes function as ciphers for communal assessments of the relation between the political rescue of culturally privileged individuals and institutional policies that erase non-privileged members of the same community. A *gershomite-ogbanje* reading of the story means that, in spite of its institutional and official character, Moses' singular experience of rescue and adoption is not adequate for addressing violence that has fractured and alienated the community.

Postcolonial Counter-Adoption in Exodus 2:11–15

The story about Moses, a Hebrew-exposed and political adoptee of Egypt, embarking on trips to see members of an oppressed subgroup described as "his kin" constitutes an intriguing subplot in the narrative of Exodus 2.[26] The trips place Moses at the center of two distinct but related events, one economic and the other political: burdensome labor and ethnic/political violence. The narrator is silent about Moses' intentions or direct involvement in alleviating the economic hardship, but provides some details about Moses' involvement in the political dimension of the story.[27] First, Moses intervenes in interethnic violence, mortally striking an Egyptian in defense of a Hebrew man who was himself being struck. Then he is surprised to see *intraethnic* violence on his second visit, and inquires why a Hebrew (described as "wicked"[28]) would attack another: "Why do you strike your fellow Hebrew?"

25. Butler, "An Anti-Moses," 14.
26. The people that Moses goes out to see are described as his brothers, echoing his sister in the adoption story. The group is further described as Hebrew men (Exod. 2:11, 13), identified by Pharaoh (Exod. 1:16) and the Egyptian princess (Exod. 2:6) as an ethnic subgroup in the pre-adoption and adoption stories, respectively.
27. Propp, *Exodus 1–18*, 166, writes, "Moses intervenes in parallel incidents, narrated with typical biblical precision that says little and implies much. We are told, not what Moses feels, but what he does. If one day he precipitously goes to see his brothers' labors, we know his disquiet and commiseration have been growing. If he strikes an Egyptian, we know he is outraged. If he hides the body, we know he is afraid. The style of narration invites the reader into characters' minds, precisely by *not* divulging their thoughts." This silence, especially with respect to the economic hardship, constitutes a glaring gap that later interpreters filled. The Midrash, for example, portrays Moses as being "touched unto tears" upon seeing the hardship, as providing encouraging words to his people about a hopeful future, and as using his political status as an adopted son to negotiate with Pharaoh to lighten the labor, and eventually secure a Sabbath. See Ginzberg, *Legends*, 277–78.
28. The Hebrew *rš* carries a sense of legal offense (cf., Exod. 9:27; 23:1; Deut. 25:1; 1 Kgs. 8:23; Prov. 24:24). The NRSV has "the one who was in the wrong"; Childs, *The Book of Exodus*, 28, has "the offending party." In his rebuttal, the Hebrew man challenges Moses' authority as a judge, hence the legal sense of the charge.

The rhetorical and *retrospective* irony in Moses words is that they echo his violent act from the previous day. What the story separates through narrative chronology and temporal sequence over two days, as well as through ethnic identity, the story connects through thematic echo of violent social experience. In a postcolonial setting, interlocution transgresses not just colonial time but also its production of ethnicity. Aligning himself with a dead Egyptian, the Hebrew man questions Moses' role in establishing political and judicial authority derived from violence: "Who made you ruler and judge over us? Do you mean to kill me just as you killed the Egyptian?" (Exod. 2:14). The storyteller uses Moses' visit to see his kin to shift the location of, and the personnel involved in deliberations about, Hebrew fortunes from the courts of Pharaoh to workplaces. In contrast to the adoption episode, this counter-adoption episode explores how ethnicity—in its primordial, circumstantial, and constructivist formulations[29]—can be mobilized in intragroup and intergroup dynamics to critically examine the layers of sporadic and institutionally backed violence in the colony and postcolony.

The rhetorical and *prospective* irony in the Hebrew man's words is that they anticipate Pharaoh's life-threatening reaction, forcing Moses to become "exposed" again, this time beside a well in Midian. The cumulative effect of violence and violence-generated discourse is socio-political alienation for Moses, from his Hebrew "brothers," from the Egyptian he killed, and from Pharaoh, the political representative of Egypt. This triple alienation echoes his triple placement in Exodus 2:1–10, first in a basket, then in public, and in Pharaoh's house. The triple alienation thus performs the cultural, social and political functions of countering single-hero adoption—the narrative of the postcolonial petit bourgeoisie—and laying bare its inadequacy to effectively and sustainably resist colonial ideologies and systems. When the episode ends with Moses away from Egypt, away from the ethnic group to which his adoption story assigned him, and away from the institutional setting for his adoption, his counter-adoption is complete. The story is liberative not because Moses is adopted as a single hero, but because the community retains its capacity to challenge such understandings of liberation. There is more to the story.

---

29. For discussion on primordial, circumstantial, and constructivist modes of ethnicity, see Richard Jenkins, *Rethinking Ethnicity: Arguments and Explorations*, 2nd ed. (London: Sage, 2008), 147–52; Francisco J. Gil-White, "Are Ethnic Groups Biological 'Species' to the Human Brain? Essentialism in our Cognition of Some Social Categories," *Current Anthropology* 42, no. 4 (2001): 515–53; Andreas Wimmer, "The Making and Unmaking of Ethnic Boundaries: A Multilevel Process Theory," *American Journal of Sociology* 113, no. 4 (2008): 970–1022; Chris Lorenz, "Representations of Identity: Ethnicity, Race, Class, Gender and Religion: An Introduction to Conceptual History," in *The Contested Nation: Ethnicity, Class, Religion and Gender in National Histories*, ed. Stefan Berger and Chris Lorenz (New York: Palgrave MacMillan, 2008), 34–43.

A POSTCOLONIAL AFRICANA READING OF EXODUS 2   101

Just as Moses' adoption was the culmination of a cluster of socio-cultural, economic, and political negotiations involving members of his ethnic subgroup and members of the house of Pharaoh (2:7–10), so conversely here his exile ("re-exposure") is the culmination of a cluster of rejections of the hermeneutics of single hero rescue by members of his ethnic subgroup and the singularizing Pharaoh (2:14–15). It is not that ethno-political and institutional identities and structures have ceased to exist; it is that they have performed the specific social function of defining Moses as a cultural, political, and regional alien. Colonial adoption and postcolonial counter-adoption have converged to produce a community that is highly attuned to, and perceptive of, the forms and layers of alienation that animate its discourse on identity formation, belonging, and activism on behalf of liberation.

Perception and Cognitive Blur at the Workplace (Exod. 2:11–12)

The counter-adoption episode repeatedly uses the language of "seeing" to frame Moses' first visit. Moses sees hard labor; he sees interethnic violence; and he sees that there was "no man" to observe him—that is, he sees the markers of alienation, erasure, and singularity. As objects of Moses' vision, these epistemologies and realities echo his adoption story: the first seeing evokes his own economic distress and needs (2:6–7); the second recalls the life-enhancing interventions of his biological and adoptive mothers (2:2, 6); and the third evokes memory of his dual ethnicity, Hebrew and Egyptian (2:6, 10). In their present context, however, these echoes function as narrative contrasts. I will examine them in turn.

First, Moses goes out to his brothers and *sees* their alienating tasks; he sees distressful economic experience. The Hebrew idiom ("to look at") that connects Moses to the economic burdens of the subgroup—which Pharaoh refers to as "people of the land" (Exod. 5:5)—suggests more than disinterested, fact-finding, supervision, or observation. Rather, it implies significant involvement and emotional impact on the one seeing; it is seeing that summons Moses' moral and ethical sense of self, and leads to identity formation.[30] Usage of the idiom elsewhere in exilic literature portrays the sense of envisioning something that is

---

30. John I. Durham, *Exodus* (Waco, TX: Wood Books, 1987), 18, writes that Moses saw their burden "at first hand." Gordon F. Davies, *Israel in Egypt: Reading Exodus 1–2* (Sheffield: JSOT Press, 1992), 119, 125, agrees with Durham's translation and goes on to argue that Moses' "empathy for the Hebrews over against the Egyptians is established early on when he 'sees their burdens at first hand.'" Childs, *Exodus*, 29, has "looked with sympathy." Terence E. Fretheim, *Exodus*, Interpretation: A Bible Commentary for Teaching and Preaching (Louisville, KY: John Knox Press, 1991), 43, notes that the language of seeing here is also applied to God (Exod. 2:25; 3:7, 9; 4:13; 5:19), suggesting that Moses' actions foreshadow or anticipate God's actions.

102 LET MY PEOPLE LIVE

hopeful and liberating (2 Kgs. 10:16; Isa. 52:8; Jer. 29:32; Mic. 7:9) or distressing and unpleasant. In the case of the latter, the subject expresses a desire *not* to see it (Gen. 21:16; 44:34; Num. 11:15; 2 Kgs. 22:20; Esth. 8:6). In creating its first narrative memory marker, the story has come full circle. Having benefited from the structured economic agreement following his encounter with the Egyptian princess, Moses is now in the position of a prince and comes face to face with the harsh economic reality of his kin. It is a distressful situation that he will later on, in the context of the national story, rather not see and, in fact, argue for its alleviation, even at the cost of his life (Num. 11:15). For now, Moses' perception of Hebrew hard labor creates the first layer of discrepancy between his institutional status and the alienating experience of the ethnic group to which his birth and adoption story associate him, in the shadow of Pharaoh's oppressive policies. The economic benefits of colonial adoption (Exod. 2:7–9) are discrepant and unavailable to all Hebrews; what Moses' family had in a patronage adoption story, the subgroup does not.[31] For my Cameroonian postcolonial hermeneutics concerned with the quality of life for the entire community, this discrepancy is problematic and systemic; it echoes the embittered life associated with Pharaoh's theorizing about exodus and wartime economic policy (Exod. 1:10).

Second, Moses *sees* interethnic violence—an Egyptian striking a Hebrew, one of his brothers. The phrase "his brothers" here echoes "his sister" and the role she played in the adoption narrative (Exod. 2:4, 7). The expression implies a form of social categorization that goes beyond family relations. The prepositional phrase, "one of his brothers" (lit. "from among his brothers") suggests a layer of identification that associates Moses with ethnic Hebrews, as opposed to Egyptians.[32] The use of ethnic distinctions in association with violence is initially developed as part of Pharaoh's policy against Hebrew children (Exod. 1:16). The conflict of ethnic identities advocated by that policy is initially undermined and transformed into a confluence of identities in Moses' adoption narrative. The empire/nation that kills is replaced by the empire/

---

31. Dozeman, *Commentary*, 87, notes that although the hard labor here recalls that of Exod. 1:11, there is a sense of intensified slavery in Exod. 2:11, a notion developed in the midrash.

32. In fact, in the adoption story, a similar prepositional phrase characterizes Moses' relationship to the ethnic subgroup. Upon opening the basket and seeing a young man crying, the princess says, "this must be one of the Hebrews' children" (2:6) a phrase that is echoed in the prepositional phrase, "a Hebrew man, from among his brothers." The partitive *mem* of m'hyw simultaneously singles out Moses and associates him with Hebrew men. See similar uses of the preposition in Num. 16:2; 25:6; 1 Sam. 24:28; Josh. 2:2, etc. Ginzberg, *The Legends*, 281, indicates that the adoption story had taken cultural significance and acceptance, so that people referred to Moses as "son of the princess."

A POSTCOLONIAL AFRICANA READING OF EXODUS 2

nation that rescues, led by members of the marginalized community. Here in Exod. 2:11, Moses sees a violent contrast of the very categories of social identification that represent the narrative finale of his birth-adoption story (Exod. 2:2, 10). What compassion constructed in the adoption story, violence deconstructs here.

Third, Moses *sees* a vacuum, the vacuous nature of a political strong-man, which crumbles under sustained examination. Over two days, he sees events around which there was "no one" or "no man" (*'n 'š*). These events range from individual acts of violence (2:11, 12, 13) to questions about political authority associated with violence (2:14). In the fog of recurring violence and ensuing debates, Moses sees a total-izing mirage, a blur. Because the narrator has hitherto associated see-ing with action (Exod. 2:2, 5, 6), one not only expects some form of action on Moses' part, but also that such action will have private and institutional dimensions. That is, Moses' action may, on the one hand, be covert—echoing his biological mother's (*'šh*) discrete actions upon seeing her healthy child (Exod. 2:2). Such action has more to do with honorific survival than with political liberation; her actions are unoffi-cial, discrete, and even sub-cultural, but qualitatively healthy and based on an alternative (nonviolent) sense of communal self. On the other hand, consistent with the institutional character of Moses' adoption story, such action cannot and will not remain discrete and isolated, but be recast for public and institutional significance (Exod. 2:6). The story requires communal assessment beyond the actions of a single individ-ual—the colonial and postcolonial strongman.

Through his triple seeing, Moses reengages the alienating economic, violent ethnic/racial, and political singularizing layers of the adoption story; he becomes the persona around and with whom narrative charac-ters and readers explore these multiple aspects of adoption. Upon seeing ethnic violence, Moses turned "this way and that" (Exod. 2:12). Then, seeing that there was no one, he killed the Egyptian man and concealed the body. The fact that Moses turned "this way and that way" suggests that he skulked to make sure there were no eyewitnesses; the event remained part of his personal memory but not collective memory, and fit into one aspect of the adoption story as a story of survival *through* secrecy (cf. Exod. 2:2). On another level, the ensuing phrase "there was no one" leaves open the possibility that Moses might have been looking for someone else with whom to save the Hebrews. The irony is that, besides Moses, no other narrative character has been constructed to navigate these layers of private and public ethics, to creatively engage

104   LET MY PEOPLE LIVE

the dynamics of subgroup and national relations in the colony and postcolony, and to structure multiplicity toward flourishing.[33] Moses is the product of the community. As Dennis Olson argues, the secrecy associated with the killing of the Egyptian shows that Moses had "no intention of committing a courageous and public act of open defiance and self-sacrifice which will mean the inevitable sacrificing of his status as a son of the daughter of Pharaoh."[34] The inability to confine violence and its interpretive and ethical challenges to the realm of secrecy serves as the narrative vehicle for the cumulative sense of Moses turning "this way and that way"—metaphorically holding together two identities in ways that reengage and challenge the ethical and institutional assumptions of the adoption story.

Ethnicity and the Construction of a Political and Judicial System (Exod. 2:13–14)

Moses' second trip to observe the Hebrews is marked by a poignant moment of potential change in political practice. The interjection (*hnh*, "behold," "look") that characterizes his perception of intraethnic struggle (Exod. 2:13) is more than intellectual fascination or curiosity, as made evident by the drastic policy changes that ensue from Pharaoh and the princess looking at the Hebrews (Exod. 1:9; 2:6).[35] The interjection signals moments when Hebrew activity is seen and understood through the gaze of Egyptian officials—precisely, when a subgroup or an oppressed group's experience is not understood on its merits but recast through the oppressor's institutional gaze, leading to new policy decisions. The conversation between Moses and the Hebrew man rightfully addresses the legitimacy of Moses' political and judicial authority. Is Moses at risk of becoming a political strongman? The prepositional phrase used to challenge Moses' attempted "setting over" of political and legal authority at the workplace in Exodus 2:14 echoes the ethnocentric "setting over" of labor force authority by Pharaoh in Exodus 1:11.[36] Now placed in the mouth of a Hebrew man in the context

33. Ronald Hendel, *Remembering Abraham: Culture, Memory, and History in the Hebrew Bible* (Oxford: Oxford University Press, 2005), 67–71.
34. Dennis Olson, "Violence for the Sake of Social Justice? Narrative, Ethics, and Indeterminacy in Exodus 2:11–15," in *The Meanings We Choose: Hermeneutical Ethics, Indeterminacy and the Conflict of Interpretations*, ed. Charles H. Cosgrove, Andrew Mein and Claudia V. Camp (Harrisburg, PA: Bloomsbury Academic, 2004), 140.
35. Davies, *Israel in Egypt*, 126.
36. In 2:3, Moses is "set among" the reeds on the banks of the Nile after being nursed and hidden for three months. The context suggests an act of survival, not the establishment of a political structure.

of political conflict, the prepositional phrase frames a question ("Who made you ruler and judge over us?") that reflects subgroup anxieties and resistance to political structures of oppression and exploitation. It is unclear whether the group referred to as "us" by Moses' challenger is exclusively Hebrew or includes Egyptians. As Olson argues, "Moses' identity here mirrors the reader's experience of indeterminacy in evaluating Moses' use of violence to defend the vulnerable and less powerful," and this prevents easy categorization in which questions of right and wrong are framed in dualistic categories of us versus them.[37]

What seems clear, though, is that the man's anxiety regarding Moses' authority stems from institutional violence that transcends individual personalities. In fact, as the story moves into a second (šny) day and presents two (šny) Hebrews struggling, Moses' conversation with the Hebrew man illustrates the need to avoid easy homogenizations of subgroups and their internal politics. The language of social identification shifts from Hebrews as brothers (Exod. 2:11) to Hebrews as neighbors: "Why do you strike your fellow Hebrew?" (Exod. 2:13). Without challenging Moses' neighborly language about group association, the Hebrew man questions Moses' political and judicial authority. The social and political meaning of Hebrew is unstable and is to be determined with each occurrence and each context. In the context of interethnic identity constructed to reflect a sharp contrast between ethnic groups, Hebrew carries the sense of a biologically or politically cohesive identity. Yet, second level analyses (signaled by the second day) allow for assessing the implications of shifting identity (ethnic and social) on the establishment of political and judicial systems. Can Exodus produce a political and judicial system that attends to the specific challenges of the Hebrews and to the interethnic relations that challenge Pharaoh's ethnocentric policies?

Alienation and Residence by a Well (Exod. 2:15)

Coming out of his interactions with Egyptians and Hebrews, Moses is a vulnerable man, anxious about subgroup perceptions of him and Pharaoh's threats against him, the result of which is impending exile, a break from the adoption story. Violence and threats of violence have taken Moses through a series of multiple fragmented social identities— interethnic and intraethnic, political and economic, institutional and

37. Olson, "Violence," 144.

106   LET MY PEOPLE LIVE

private. The fragmentation continues after "Pharaoh heard this matter/ word" (Exod. 2:15, author's translation). It is unclear whether "this matter/word" refers to Moses' violent act on the first day (referenced by the Hebrew man) or to the potential policy-altering debate between Moses and the Hebrew man on the second day. That is, it is unclear whether Pharaoh is reacting to discourse about Moses' violence against an Egyptian or to the fact that memory (continuing discourse) about such violence also serves as a galvanizing force for Hebrew resistance to the establishment of structured political authority at the workplace on the second day. Perhaps both aspects are implied. In any case, the narrative is evoking the sense of a traumatic history that doesn't go away.

The subgroup to which Moses belongs no longer supports his authority as a political representative of Egypt—authority afforded him by the adoption story. Furthermore, violence and its cultural and political interpretations cause Pharaoh to intervene and bring the counter-adoption motif to its logical conclusion. Although initially *faced* with multiple fragments of his identity, turning this way and that way (Exod. 2:12), Moses runs into so much institutional and legal resistance that he ends up fleeing from the *face* of Pharaoh (Exod. 2:15). In a narrative plagued by violence, Moses' exile (alienation), not his death (erasure), is crucial to performing the final narrative act of counter-adoption. The narrative about Moses' two day trips and his encounter with two men functions to perform double exposure for Moses. The first exposure mimics and contrasts with the protective shield that his mother afforded him (Exod. 2:2); the second exposure mimics and contrasts with the protection afforded him by the Egyptian princess (Exod. 2:10). The first exposure is ethnic; the second is national. What is left is geographical exposure at the Nile and the resulting adoption, which is now performed in the Midian story. Moses flees into exile and is re-exposed, this time with emphasis on the convergence of *ethnic/ national/geographical* identity.

Re-Adoption as Riposte to Isolation in Exodus 2:16–22

In 2:16–22, narrative texture, setting, and perspective change once again. Narrative nomenclature defines Midian as a different place, a foreign land. The story has crossed regional boundaries and developed geographical distinctiveness. Another piece of data is added to the reconstruction of memory: Moses the Hebrew is now Moses the

A POSTCOLONIAL AFRICANA READING OF EXODUS 2   107

Egyptian (Exod. 2:19); his national identity is partially experienced as alien identity. Almost as if to suggest cognitive, political, and cultural latency (in a Freudian sense[38]), Moses' Hebrew identity is unmentioned; and his Egyptian identity and actions (2:19) are no longer a function of political stature but of *alien*ation. It is as an *Egyptian refugee* that Moses is re-adopted—this time into the family of a local priest. Re-adoption adds to the story's kinships of strangers, transitioning Moses' social identity from refugee to sojourner.

The transforming power of this modality of existence is signaled by the morphological similarity between Moses' navigation of geography ("foreign land") and genealogy: his action of resisting alienating acts (*grš*) by shepherds who harass the priest's daughters (Exod. 2:17), and his son's name, Gershom (*gršm*), which references Moses' alien status (Exod. 2:22). The relation between identity construction and ongoing struggle over geography and its resources becomes genealogical and hermeneutical (*gēr hāyîtî bĕʾereṣ nokrîyâ*—"I have been an alien in a foreign land"). Pejorative anxieties about geography (*ʾereṣ nokrîyâ*, a strange/othered land) are linked to, and explored as, a partially protected and integrated identity and transformed into a form of socio-political existence that appropriates alien (*gēr*) identity as a riposte and challenge to local and global oppression or marginalization.[39] *Gershomite* subjectivity cannot and does not claim self-defining transformation by simply "returning" to or reclaiming ancestral space and memory, but by also grappling with the enduring power of globalized—and/or imperialized—cultural and territorial otherness attached to the identity of the migrant community.[40] Claiming interpretive agency, the community interprets the simultaneity of its alien-native identity in response to violent geographical and genealogical mapping and remapping.[41] These defining vectors of simultaneous ancestral and

---

38. Freud developed his idea of latency to explain the temporal lapse between the Armana period (where he located the traumatic events of Akenaton's monotheism) and the return of that traumatic memory under Moses. Sigmund Freud, *Moses and Monotheism*, trans. Katherine Jones (London: Hogarth Press, 1939), 35–41, 108–10.

39. Some uses of *nokrîyâ* include person of foreign nationality/ethnicity (Gen. 17:12, 27; Exod. 2:22; 12:43; 18:3; Ezra 10:2, 10, 11, 14, 17, 18, 44; Neh. 9:2); persons outside of one's family household (Gen. 31:15; Exod. 21:8; Prov. 23:27; 27:2). See Jopie Siebert-Hommes, *Let the Daughters Live! The Literary Architecture of Exodus 1–2 as a Key for Interpretation* (Leiden: Brill, 1998), 121–27; Rolf Rendtorff, "The *Gēr* in the Priestly Laws of the Pentateuch," in *Ethnicity and the Bible*, ed. Mark G. Brett (Boston: Brill, 2002), 77–87.

40. See Reinhard Achenbach, "Gêr—nåkhrî—tôshav—zâr: Legal and Sacral Distinctions regarding Foreigners in the Pentateuch," in *The Foreigner and the Law: Perspectives from the Hebrew Bible and the Ancient Near East*, ed. Reinhard Achenbach, Rainer Albertz, and Kakob Wöhrle (Wiesbaden: Harrassowitz Verlag, 2011), 29–51. At the family reunion in the wilderness (Exod. 18:3–4), Moses' children (Gershom and Eliezer) embody the convergence of intergenerational and interregional identity in response to violence.

41. Adriane Leveen, "Inside-Out: Jethro, the Midianites and a Biblical Construction of the Outsider," *Journal for the Study of the Old Testament* 34, no. 4 (2010): 399–404.

displaced identity provide ideological and hermeneutical structures for the Africana returnee-remainee, and they inform the Exodus story as *gershomite* or *ogbanje*. These vectors work to reintegrate identities of otherness into communal whole, to create disjuncture from oppressive systems, and to envision viable futures for humans and the environment together.

CONCLUSION

Three narrative scenarios in Exodus 2 constitute three social and interpretive dynamics that attempt to turn the postcolonial nightmare into a dream again. First, the scenarios mark the overlap between private and public identities, played out in spaces where distinct ethnic identities meet and where discussions revolve around violent constructions of "subgroup," "national," and geographical identities. In the adoption scene at the Nile, Miriam's strategic improvisation creates the occasion for a confluence of ethnic identities and economic structures to ensure life-enhancing institutional responses to the conditions of distress afflicting the Hebrews. In the counter-adoption scene among the enslaved Hebrew people, violence and threats of violence fracture interethnic and intraethnic identities, and there is communal resistance to new political and judicial structures based on the authority of violence. And in the re-adoption scene, exogamous marriage and geographical alienation function to structure the relation between outsider and insider and to bring together the triple markers of identity (ethnic, national, and geographical) in the birth of Gershom. The narrative has created a *gershomite* community.

The second interpretive dynamic revolves around the role that an oppressed subgroup—acting in resistance to sporadic and long-term slow violence—plays in shaping communal identity. In the adoption scene, Miriam deploys her cognitive and narrative abilities to diagnose Moses' fate in public and propose solutions; and his biological mother nurses him for survival and adoption into Pharaoh's house. In the counter-adoption scene where Moses re-enters the public space as a political adoptee of Egypt, his kinfolk resist his actions and attempts at establishing a political and legal structure based on violence. When Pharaoh threatens to kill him, Moses flees into Midian where Jethro's daughters—themselves already involved in local struggles against marginalization—encounter him and begin the process of redirecting his identity toward protective community care (as a shepherd). In the re-adoption scene, Zipporah becomes the narrative and embodied bearer and producer of new identity—one that transitions Moses from an alien to a sojourner. In all these three instances, the story moves forward because of the ingenuity and actions of the oppressed or marginalized.

A third interpretive dynamic involves institutional reaction to Moses' association with endangered or marginalized subgroups. In the adoption scene, the Egyptian princess formally adopts Moses, names him, and brings him into the house of Pharaoh—a process that uses the trope of expansive geopolitical genealogy rather than political servitude (e.g., cup bearer) to place Hebrews in positions of power overseeing the very political structure that once threatened to kill them. In the counter-adoption scene, Pharaoh threatens to kill Moses—an act that, in the post-adoption setting, is effectively an attempt at kinship fratricide. Pharaoh's policy of exposure at the Nile is expanded territorially and becomes exposure at a well in Midian. And in the re-adoption scene, the Midianite priest, Jethro, provides the religious and institutional setting for integrating multiple identities—Egyptian, Midianite, and Hebrew—that have suffered forced displacement.

Gershomites are members of a community that bears, through narrative and embodied subjectivity, the memories of Moses as an Egyptian refugee, as an alienated kin, and as a survivor-returnee. This is the community to which Moses hands down exodus hermeneutics, a community that he enlists into the work of liberation that predates his birth and predates the institution and infrastructure of erasure, alienation, and singularity. *Gershomite* identity thus represents and embodies repurposed memory of the generative work and ethos of its narrative ancestresses—the midwives, Zipporah, Miriam, the Egyptian princess, Jochebed, and Hagar—characters that contribute to exodus discourse and survival in the midst of violence. It is in this sense that I understand Barbara Johnson's claim that the Bible posits "foreignness as somehow necessary for nation building."[42] To the extent that "foreignness" and "strange land" play a vital role in constructing national stories, Moses' exile into Midian—that is, the deconstruction of his colonial adoption—serves as the first stage in that process. In other words, foreignness and land are like a double-edged sword that severs and binds at the same time, carving out the cultural space between the home that one chooses and the home that chooses one. It is *as* an alienated Egyptian

---

42. Barbara Johnson, *Moses and Multiculturalism* (Berkeley: University of California Press, 2010), 9.

that Moses returns *as* a Hebrew; he is an *ogbanje* whose return summons and signifies the community's ongoing work of liberation. Diaspora is no longer a matter of unending alienation; it is also a matter of ongoing reconstructed return.

This narrativized body, this *gershomite* or African *ogbanje* body, is a simultaneously local and trans body (divine, spatial, and human). It produces a story that is attuned to, and valorizes, *seeing* ongoing communal affliction, *hearing* the voices of a groaning kin in distant lands, *remembering* covenantal commitments that summon ancestral life, and *coming* to partner with new generations of actors to effect religious, social, cultural, and geopolitical transformations. This portrait of the Africana body illustrates the necessity of interregional and intergenerational framing of exodus work. This body—informed by epistemological and hermeneutical approaches that overcome erasure, alienation, and singularity—gradually commits itself to a theology dedicated to triple conscious liberation work. Such work embodies three dimensions: communal and structural changes (conjunctive memories) against erasure, communal and structural changes (disjunctive memories) against alienation, and communal and structural changes (adjunctive memories) against singularity. Yahweh formally enters the story as an active subject-character committed to the premium value of community thriving. Yahweh sees and recognizes injustice in the community; hears and responds to the voices of those who cry out; reactivates unifying memory bonds; and forges new social and political networks to challenge oppression, marginalization, and isolation (cf. Exod. 2:23–24; 3:7–8). That work resides and lives in *gershomite-ogbanje* identity and hermeneutics and in its relation to different bodies—divine, human, and earth/land.

4

Afroecology and Exodus

INTRODUCTION

Afroecology is a term associated with the AgroEcology Fund, a non-governmental organization located in the southeastern region of the United States whose purpose is to support practices and policies that promote organic farming. Agroecology is farming that "centers on food production that makes the best use of nature's goods and services while not damaging these resources" and strives "to nurture a healthy landscape in which to grow the world's food and fiber. . . . guided by an ethos of bio and cultural diversity featuring small farmer-centered applied research and policies that protect their livelihoods."[1] Afroecology is part of the academic apparatus of agroecology. It is associated with "The Down-South AfroEcology Training School (DATS)" which was "designed to strengthen the agroecology movement within the United States through the engagement and education of Black farmers in the Southeast region who are either currently farming organically, seeking to transition to organic practices, or are not currently farming. *DATS uses the term Afro Ecology instead of agroecology to better reflect their focus on incorporating culturally relevant delivery methods.*"[2]

---

1. "An Ecological Approach to Agriculture," Agroecology Fund, https://www.agroecologyfund.org/what-is-agroecology.

2. Agroecology Fund, https://www.agroecologyfund.org/grantees-1/2017/3/20/down-south-afroecology-training-school-dats, emphasis added.

111

Drawing from the intersection between afro and agro as indicative of the co-constitutive relation between Afri-culture and agri-culture, I want to reflect on the political and ecological dimensions of the Exodus story, informed by Africana interpretive subjectivity and imagination.

WANGARI MAATHAI AND THE GREEN BELT MOVEMENT

Wangari Maathai was affectionately known as the mother of trees. When she started the Green Belt Movement (GBM) in 1977 to fight deforestation in Africa, she was responding to a crisis of life and survival, especially among the poor and marginalized women in Kenya:

> I wasn't motivated by my faith or by religion in general. Instead the motivation came from thinking literally and practically about how to solve problems on the ground. It was a desire to help rural populations, especially women, with the basic needs they described to me during seminars and workshops. They said that they lacked clean drinking water, adequate and nutritious food, income, and enough energy for cooking and heating. . . . Personally, however, I never differentiated between activities that might be called "spiritual" and those that might be termed "secular." After a few years I came to recognize that our efforts weren't only about planting trees, but were also about sowing seeds of a different sort—the ones necessary to heal the wounds inflicted on communities that robbed them of their self-confidence and self-knowledge.[3]

Maathai's reflective commentary on her extraordinary life-work crystalizes what the trained biologist, civil servant, educator, mother, wife, and advocate understood to be rich work at the intersection of environmental regeneration, gender justice, anticolonial critique, and deep postcolonial cultural analyses around urban and rural communities in Kenya and across Africa. "Education, if it means anything," the Nobel Laureate writes, "*should not take people away from the land*, but instill in them even more respect for it, because educated people are in a position to understand what is being lost. . . . As I told foresters, and the women, you don't need a diploma to plant a tree."[4] Maathai's resistance against epistemology detached from land—or that simply exploits the land—is

---

3. Wangari Maathai, *Replenishing the Earth: Spiritual Values for Healing Ourselves and the World* (New York: Doubleday, 2010), 13–14.

4. Wangari Maathai, *Unbowed: A Memoir* (New York: Anchor Books, 2006), 138, italics added.

AFROECOLOGY AND EXODUS 113

instructive for understanding the futility and absurdity of formulating postcolonial (political) liberation and human flourishing without sustained attention to care for the land—its character, subjectivity, needs, voice, and abilities to survive and flourish.

Maathai's journey in, with, and through the Green Belt Movement grew out of multiple strands of personal and communal engagement with her environment: she had lost a familiar fig tree because a new land owner (colonialist) felled it to make room for growing tea: "I mourned the loss of that tree. I profoundly appreciated the wisdom of my people, and how generations of women had passed on to their daughters the cultural tradition of leaving the fig tree in place. I was expected to pass it on to my children, too."[5] Without the material tree, and its symbol as a custodian and producer of cultural belonging, knowledge transmission lacked relevance and potency; the loss of the tree was synonymous to the loss of wisdom and cultural identity. That loss was also associated with colonial erasure: "I remember how colonial administration had cleared indigenous forests and replaced them with plantations of exotic trees for the timber industry," and that also became postcolonial erasure: "After independence, Kenyan farmers had cleared more natural forests to create space to grow coffee and tea."[6] Because deforestation disproportionately affected women—who are often tasked with being custodians of cultural identity and memory but also with providing economic strategy and support for families—Maathai's work with women's organizations in Kenya and abroad became the organizing structure for the GBM.

Maathai framed her environmental work beyond the national story of liberation, arguing that the survival of the nation from colonial pillage could not be achieved without investment in environmental sustainability. She drew from Jomo Kenyatta's slogan—*Harambee*—about community collaboration; from the work of previous generations (e.g., The Men of Trees organization, founded by chief Josiah Njonjo); and from a desire to respect previous generational struggles against colonial rule, by planting trees that formed the first "green belt" in Kenya.[7] Tree planting was an anticolonial act. Maathai thus provides what can be described as a poetics of thinking with trees at the intersection of environmental care, women's empowerment, sustainable liberation, anticolonial resistance, and communal renewal:

5. Maathai, *Unbowed*, 122.
6. Maathai, *Unbowed*, 123.
7. Maathai, *Unbowed*, 130–32.

114   LET MY PEOPLE LIVE

As women and communities increased their efforts, we encouraged them to plant seedlings in rows of at least a thousand trees to form green "belts" that would restore to the earth its cloth of green. This is how the name Green Belt Movement began to be used. Not only did the "belts" hold the soil in place and provide shade and windbreaks but they also re-created habitat and enhanced the beauty of the landscape.[8]

Thinking with the trees of the GBM involves three epistemologies: First, trees are rooted and thus represent resistance to ecological diaspora—soil erosion and exposed earth (earth without its green cloth). To think with trees is to think about a sturdy earth capable of resisting erasure. Second, to think with trees is to think communally; the green "belt" functions as communal memory and activity that resists marginalized identity. The convergence of the GBM with national and international women's empowerment illustrates the symbolism of the green belt as a mode of collective bonding in resistance against alienation. And third, to think with trees is to engage and develop the aesthetic character of the earth; it is to allow for, and enhance, the aesthetic subjectivity and a poetic of the earth. Thinking with trees challenges arbitrary dualisms and recognizes how trees grow simultaneously in multiple directions—downward, outward, and upward—and thus constitute an alternative epistemology to singularity. Importantly, Maathia understood her work of tree planting as a poetics of thinking with water and its flow into multiplicity.[9]

At about the same time that Maathai urged citizens across the African continent to plant trees, a number of political leaders and activists also began talking about planting trees across the entire continent, just south of the Sahel. The project, which was finally adopted by many African countries and supported by activists across the world, has been named "The Great Green Wall."[10] From Senegal in the western end of the continent to Djibouti in the eastern end, the GGW has become a symbol of Africa's revitalization, a kind of ecological panafricanist metaphor for afroecology. This eco-pan-africanism has resonance with the Exodus story. In the next chapter, I will sit with, and engage, the character of Miriam, as she navigates multiple earth-sites in the Exodus story, and produces an exodus approach that is rooted in afroecology. But for now, I want to examine the implications of afroecology on my reading of the Exodus story.

8. Maathai, *Unbowed*, 137.
9. Maathai, *Unbowed*, 119.
10. Great Green Wall, https://www.greatgreenwall.org/about-great-green-wall.

HERMENEUTICAL REFLECTIONS

Formulations about the material impact of climate change on human and non-human life are not new. The science around climate change has gained unanimous consensus among modern scientists, and this consensus has added value to the urgency with which one must engage the material realities of a world rapidly exploited, a world with rapidly diminishing resources. Africa and Africans—both continental and diasporic—are intimately familiar with the intersection of multiple forms of exploitation of human and non-human life-forms. The question as to whether there is a viable, healthy, flourishing future for Africa, African-descended persons, and the world is not new to Africana thought and political history. Many times, these questions have gained prominence in popular imagination and discourse and then subsided. But, as Aliou Niang has argued in *A Poetics of Postcolonial Biblical Criticism*, there are also many ways in which these questions have remained ingrained in the cultural, material, religious, and political ontology, subjectivity, and ecology of Africa and her many children.[11]

In *Israel's Poetry of Resistance*, Hugh R. Page Jr. writes,

> Whether they are physical, emotional, spiritual, imagined, eschatological, or of some other type, diasporas require complex negotiations between locations and social groups. Removal from an actual or illusory homeland, through either coercion or voluntary relocation, is often an occasion for rethinking identity. It can also lead to a reassessment of the relationship between those living remotely and the kin they have left behind. Feelings of grief, loss, and disorientation are not uncommon by-products of such experience.[12]

Page's theorizing around the "complex negotiations between locations and social groups" is useful for exploring Africana experience of ecological diaspora in relation to Exodus. It is not simply a question of nature and culture that is at stake here—of Israel being removed from one geographical/ecological location to another. Rather, what is imagined and explored is the way discourse about ecological crisis affects Africa (and Exodus-Israel); and how that discourse addresses the histories of

---

11. Aliou Cissé Niang, *A Poetics of Postcolonial Biblical Criticism: God, Human-Nature Relationship and Negritude* (Eugene, OR: Cascade Books, 2019), 35–69.

12. Hugh R. Page Jr., *Israel's Poetry of Resistance: Africana Perspectives on Early Hebrew Verse* (Minneapolis: Fortress Press, 2013), 15.

extraction, displacement, urbanization, colonization, and migration that have defined African/a identity formation.

The central issue, made particularly acute for postcolonies and their subjects, is what to do with the traumas that have been unleashed at the violent intersections of politics, religion, race, and ecology. The postcolonial crisis is as ecological as it is political and does not allow for theorizing postcolonial survival and thriving apart from the crisis of the Anthropocene. The response to the ecological, political, ethnic, and racial crisis that consumes the world is not to retreat into ecopolitical enclaves of nativism (a form of singularized thinking), or indulge in sharp binary divides (that assign decay/erasure to one space versus another), or—for exodus narration—treat the Wilderness as merely a place of trial and transition (a form of temporary alienation). The solution, I believe, lies in developing a communitarian hermeneutical theory infused with an ideological and ethical commitment to human and non-human flourishing. This commitment may manifest itself in the form of the sustainability of holistic living; it may also manifest itself in the form of negation and resistance against oppressive and extractive machineries. Such work is inherently communal, not singular. Its power is collective and contextual, not privatized and alien. Its green knowledge is intersectional and elastic, not binary. It finds interpretive kinships in the areas of race, gender, colonialism, food, and economic analyses of texts and peoples.[13]

Melanie Harris's monograph on ecowomanism and her edited volume explore the intersections of womanist thought, environmental ethics, and intergenerational identity formation.[14] A vital step toward creating accurate environmental history, argues Harris, is including the contributions of people of color—"black environmentalists"—whose work and struggles navigate the intimate paradox of the horrors of Black lives lynched and an enduring Africana spiritual connection to the earth. Harris frames ecowomanism as deconstructive of oppressive systems around the tripartite of race-class-gender, and constructive in its insistence on "strategies of resistance, spiritual resilience, and intellectual genius solutions for survival."[15] This formulation is similar to Madipoane Masenya's *eco-bosadi* hermeneutics,

---

13. For example, Rob Nixon, *Slow Violence and the Environmentalism of the Poor* (Cambridge, MA: Harvard University Press, 2011), 1–44; Dwight N. Hopkins, "Holistic Health and Healing: Environmental Racism and Ecological Justice," in *Faith, Health, and Healing in African American Life*, ed. Stephanie Y. Mitchem and Emilie Townes (Westport CT: Praeger, 2008), 16–31.

14. Melanie Harris, *Ecowomanism: African-American Women and Earth-Honoring Faiths* (Maryknoll, NY: Orbis Books, 2017); Melanie Harris, ed., *Ecowomanism, Religion and Ecology* (Leiden: Brill, 2017).

15. Harris, *Ecowomanism: African American*, 3, 4, emphasis in original.

developed from her South African context and location but richly applicable across the livelihood of African descended persons.[16] Drawn from the Northern Sotho word for womanhood, Masenya's *bosadi* hermeneutics engages four intersecting injustices: racism, sexism, classism, and African culture (patriarchy). When threaded through with ecological sensibilities, intentionality, and creativity, *eco-bosadi* seeks to unmask and challenge male-oriented anthropocentric readings of biblical and non-biblical texts in favor of a "universe-orientated framework of God's care and sustenance for the whole of creation including humankind."[17]

In a short and provocative collection of essays on African bioethics, the Cameroonian philosopher and bioethicist Godfrey Tangwa writes,

> The pre-colonial traditional African metaphysical outlook can be described as eco-bio-communitarian. . . . Within the African outlook, human beings tend to be more humble and more cautious, more mistrustful and unsure of human knowledge and capabilities, more conciliatory and respectful of other people, plants, animals, inanimate things, as well as sundry invisible/intangible forces, more timorous of wantonly tampering with nature, in short, more disposed toward an attitude of *live and let live*. . . . Within this worldview, the distinction between plants, animals, and inanimate things, between the sacred and the profane, matter and spirit, the communal and the individual, is a slim and plastically flexible one.[18]

The relation between this eco-bio-communitarian theory and its geopolitical and historical praxis is a richly vexed one in Africa, generally, and in Cameroon in particular. The bio and cultural diversity that has sustained African history through multiple geopolitical permutations over centuries and millennia is the same biodiversity that has endured massive abuse and exploitation, and survived. The impetus for ecological hermeneutics implies understanding the communitarian "live and let live" as more than simply about accommodation; praxis is infused with an ethical demand: let live.

Three hermeneutical approaches unfold here. First, there is a proactive stance toward enhancing human and non-human life. It is more

---

16. Madipoane Masenya (Ngwan'a Mphahlele), "All from the Same Source? Deconstructing a (Male) Anthropocentric Reading of Job (3) through an Eco-*bosadi* Lens," *Journal of Theology for Southern Africa* 137 (July 2010): 46–60.

17. Masenya, "All," 57–60.

18. Godfrey B. Tangwa, *Elements of Africa Bioethics in a Western Frame* (Mankon, Bamenda: Langaa Research & Publishing CIG, 2010), 57, italics in original.

than rhetorical deployment of metaphors from dendrology or anthropology (e.g., humans are like trees, or human behavior has roots) to describe the relation of humans to the environment.[19] This proactive stance is understood and structured as intimate kinship and affinity between human life and non-human life, what Harris calls ecoautobiography and its deployment in producing ecomemory.[20] Like all kinship relations, proactive investment in *nurturing ecological life as inherently human and non-human* is critical to the sustainability, survival, and flourishing of eco-kinship. This proactive stance motivates the development of new knowledge and a communal praxis of solidarity in defense of vulnerable and endangered human and non-human life-forms. The political story cannot stand, survive, or be meaningful without the ecological story. Exodus is epistemologically and materially grounded in the earth, for survival and flourishing. But the exodus earth is more than a site or stage of political liberation; the earth is participant and subject in the story.

Second, there is a homeopathic hermeneutic that insists on renewal emerging in protest against fissuring, cracking, and burning/flaming landscapes; structured around splitting, flooding, and polluted waters; and structured around assembling and dispersing clouds. Dwight Callahan's use of hermeneutical homeopathy as an interpretive methodology deployed by enslaved African Americans to read/draw life out of the death-dealing uses of Scripture by slave owners is applicable here.[21] The homeopathic hermeneutic means that Yahweh's command to Pharaoh—"let my people go"—is liberative for the people who depart but also for those who remain; for the humans and animals that leave Egypt, but also for the land of Egypt itself; for the land of Canaan, but also for the people of Canaan. As we see with the plagues, Pharaoh's oppressive system is bitter for humans and for Egypt's environment. Pharaoh's original sin is that he institutes an ideology and praxis of governance that inserts rupture and alienation into the human-earth/land relation: The intense oppression of the Hebrews coincides with diminished straw (Exod. 1:14; 5:6–18). This ruptured relation eventually forces Moses out of the land and sets the stage for Yahweh's command that Moses return to Egypt from the land of Midian (Exod.

---

19. See, for example, Arthur Walker-Jones, *The Green Psalter: Resources for an Ecological Spirituality* (Minneapolis: Fortress Press, 2009).

20. Harris, *Ecowomanism: African-American*, 27–38.

21. Allen Dwight Callahan, *The Talking Book: African Americans and the Bible* (New Haven, CT: Yale University Press, 2006), 40.

AFROECOLOGY AND EXODUS 119

4:20). Moses returns to liberate the people but also to institutionalize a liberation narrative that begins in Egypt. As evident in the stories of Miriam and the Egyptian princess (around the Nile) and Zipporah (around the well), responses to human and ecological ruptures and alienations in Exodus are not portrayed as exclusively extraterritorial; they are also developed as responses to local environmental and human traumas. Lack of appreciation for the local character of Exodus' ecology contributes to marginalizing ideologies and praxis.

Third, there is a hermeneutic of translatability. This means that ecological survival depends on recognizing and enhancing the multiple forms that life takes, including the ways in which air, land, and water, for example, are not simply elements of the environment, but active subjects. The *land* of Egypt itself becomes the place where liberation begins, which makes the endpoint of liberation an earthy place that is equally accessible and assessable for its capacity to produce and sustain a liberated community. Egypt is a land remembered as flowing with milk and honey (Num. 16:13), the antecedent environmental place that makes the promissory place of the promised land imaginable in concrete ways (Num. 16:14). In the Exodus story, the devastated land of Egypt is connected to the Wilderness and then connected to the promised land, flowing with milk and honey. The multiplicity of "exodus" lands—Egypt, the Wilderness, the Mountain—signals the need for examining the interconnected tissues that hold these lands together in Exodus narrative flows.

EXODUS PLAGUES: A NARRATIVE ECOLOGICAL "PRELUDE" TO WILDERNESS

Exodus is a story that is granularly attached to its environments. The story moves from Egypt—a land experiencing political and environmental crises—toward a land metaphorically portrayed as flowing with milk and honey. The movement of peoples from one geographical location to another coincides and intersects with major changes in non-human life and its forms.

The intersection is epistemological. Geographical locations are named and renamed on the basis of their capacity to sustain human and environmental life in flux. Thus, the material land of Egypt becomes a house of slavery, because Pharaoh's politics of oppression intersect with a land overrun with environmental disasters that the narrator calls

120   LET MY PEOPLE LIVE

plagues. As the exodus community continues on its journey, they learn not just from divine laws and statutes but also from meteorological phenomena: quaking mountains (Exod. 19:18; 32:20), moving clouds and fires (Exod. 13:17–22; 40:34–38), and a cracking earth (Num. 16:32; 26:10).

The intersection is also hermeneutical. In their current narrative location in Exodus, the plagues are not simply signs of the Exodus deity and his cohorts locked in mortal combat with another strong man, Pharaoh, and his cohorts. It is certainly that. But there is more. The plagues also represent the subjectivity of a convulsing earth, subjected to rampant exploitation; the plagues also represent the material evidence of the failure of certain political ideologies—the politics of ethnocentrism that adopts the infrastructure of nation-statism to implement demagogic policies that create privileged futures. Similar intersection of nationalism and visitation of a plague unfolds in the golden calf story (Exod. 32:21, 35), which relaunches the exodus community on its journey. Again, political and ecological storylines move together.

The motif of exodus environments that takes the community from the land of Egypt (now plagued), through the Red Sea (now convulsing), into the wilderness (Exod. 25:22) soon experiences anew the intersection of political trauma and environmental trauma. First, the people encounter no water and then bitter water, which they cannot drink (Exod. 15:23). The bitter water conjures memories of bitter lives under oppression (Exod. 1:14) and bitter Passover herbs (Exod. 12:8). Furthermore, inability to drink the water in the wilderness (Exod. 25:23) is reminiscent of the Egyptians' inability to drink the polluted water during the plagues (Exod. 7:18, 21). The bitter intersection of the plagued land and political oppression emerges in the narrative place of the wilderness and the ideological subjectivity of Wilderness.

The presence of polluted water functions as a site, subject, and act of memory about that which is lost; and the presence (production) of sweet water functions as a site, subject, and act of regenerative futures. (This regenerative feature will be discussed in the next chapter.) The people's response upon finding no water, then bitter water, is not a classic political cry for liberation, with anticipated manifestation and embodiment in an extraterritorial land. Instead, the response to the lack of water and the presence of bitter water is communal complaint/ murmur (Hebrew: *lûn*). The recurrence of this trope (Exod. 15, 16, 17; Num. 14, 16, 17) in Wilderness space suggests that the narrative meaning of *lûn* includes communal responses, the sounds that dried-up or polluted environments make. The community's demands for good food and clean (sweet) water (Exod. 15, 16, 17; Num. 14) and for proper structuring of political and religious power (Num. 16, 17) are repetitive because they constitute legitimate demands for systemic responses to social and environmental crises, to which departure from the inhabitability and abuse of environment is a foundational prelude. Through shared narrative embodiment of bitterness—political oppression and environmental plagues—the subjectivity of the dried-up land in the Wilderness merges with the voice of the community it hosts, and it erupts as repeated murmurs. The urgency behind these murmurs is not limited to fear of death from Pharaoh's "horse and rider" or Moses' staff, but extends to include fear of death-dealing conditions of environmental spaces and material ecosystems subjected to violence and war. If the political and ethical urgency for liberation from Egypt is that oppression can alter the character and identity of a people, and even attempt to permanently foreclose their capacity to flourish in accordance with divine creative promises, the urgency about liberation in the Wilderness is that the livelihood and subjectivity of water and food have been so drastically changed: the water is dried up (erased) or bitter (polluted); and food no longer grows from the ground but rather rains down from above, prompting questions (manna—"What is this"?) about its potential manifestation as a form of unsustainable economic patronage.

Exodus is, in many ways, informed and influenced by Pharaoh's political behavior and epistemology. With the transition from Egypt to the Wilderness, however, the political voice of Exodus is no longer the primary point of reference; instead, the earth becomes the subject of engagement and inquiry. The political, economic, and social traumas of oppression and the tremors of a convulsing world converge in Exodus 7–11 and ultimately transition to the wilderness (cf. Exod. 14–15). As Egypt becomes uninhabitable from disasters attributed to political and ideological self-aggrandizement, the Wilderness emerges as Exodus' logical unnatural spatial location. In the Wilderness, the exodus community does the intersectional work of connecting political and ecological experiences of oppression, alienation, and isolation. Wilderness is a place and a subject in exodus narration (cf. Isa. 35:1).

The pillars of cloud and fire in the Wilderness move into the Mountain areas, which constitute part of Exodus' ecological character, range, and discourse. Political and religious power is reconstituted in the

Mountain, where legislative and ritual activities unfold around quaking mountains and unpredictable movements of clouds and fires. The environmental grandeur of the Mountain—its narrative and material capacity to instill a form of structure and sovereignty to Exodus—compels reflections on the absurdity of imagining and creating exodus legislation "at the top" without regard for the livelihood of the community at the bottom of the Mountain and its fiery rituals and tent-making activities.

Framed in and around these environments, Exodus' narrative is connected to ecological pathways that oscillate between earthy memory (of the land of Egypt) and earthy imagination (of a land lodged in promise). Exodus discourse is coordinated and processed as much by the covenantal and statutory words of its deity, Yahweh, as by the ability of migrant bodies to endure, navigate, and transform harsh environments into flourishing ones. But Exodus is also defined by the capacity of its own environments to survive human-engendered destruction and to flourish. In addition to exploring communal survival through the elasticity of the divine word—its capacity to gather intergenerational and interregional bodies and spaces—the story also reflects on divine presence through the fragile elements of nature itself: the presence of the deity is associated and synchronized with pillars of clouds and fire around tents of communal gatherings; legislative activity and covenantal obligations intensify around quaking and fiery mountains even as "heaven and earth" are summoned as subject witnesses advocating life rather than death (Deut. 30:19); ritual statutes and prophetic utterances emerge in response to polluted waters and a fracturing earth (Exod. 14–15; 32–33); food production and storage models are developed and tested for their reliability as intergenerational sources of nourishment and healing (Exod. 16); etc. Exodus is not just a political and cultural story of human migration and exile and liberation. It is also, quite fundamentally, a story about the earth/land—its experiences of trauma and the possibilities of regeneration.

AFROECOLOGY AND EXODUS

Recent African migration trends—both within and beyond nation-states and the continent—are intimately related to worsening climate change. According to the *Journal of Climate,*

AFROECOLOGY AND EXODUS

Africa is less responsible for the occurrence of anthropogenic climate change than any other continent but more vulnerable to its effects on account of its high population, low adaptive capacity, and multiple converging stressors. Africa is furthermore an interesting case study for climate change due to its unique climatological features. It is the only continent that has almost equal parts in the Southern and Northern Hemispheres and thus is home to a wide variety of climate zones. It consists of the Sahara Desert and Sahel in northern Africa, the Namib–Kalahari Desert in southern Africa, tropical rain forest in equatorial Africa, and grasslands and savanna in between. The prevalence of land surface effects, internal climate variability, and sensitivity to global sea surface temperatures make the continent climatically complex.[22]

I want to examine what the journal describes here as the continent's complex climate variability and then relate that to theorizing and interpreting Exodus in relation to environmental changes and activity. I will organize my reflections around water, land (specifically the desert), and air.

Engaging Water, Thinking with Water

Go to Pharaoh in the morning, as he is going out to the water; stand by at the river bank to meet him, and take in your hand the staff that was turned into a snake. Say to him, "The LORD, the God of the Hebrews, sent me to you to say, 'Let my people go, so that they may worship me in the wilderness.' But until now you have not listened. Thus says the LORD, 'By this you shall know that I am the LORD.' See, with the staff that is in my hand I will strike the water that is in the Nile, and it shall be turned to blood. The fish in the river shall die, the river itself shall stink, and the Egyptians shall be unable to drink water from the Nile."

(Exod. 7:15–18)

This confrontation between Yahweh and Pharaoh at the waterside is narratively portrayed as a precursor to life in the wilderness. Ecological devastation is what ultimately compels this transition. This means recognizing the geopolitical impact of the Nile and the Red Sea—twin water bodies that represent the intersections of politics and environment in Exodus. This intersection has interpretive significance for

---

22. Natalie Thomas and Sumant Nigam, "Twentieth-Century Climate Change over Africa: Seasonal Hydroclimate Trends and Sahara Desert Expansion," *Journal of Climate* 33 (2018): 3349.

124 LET MY PEOPLE LIVE

Africana. Africa is home to the longest river in the world, the Nile, around which ancient and modern urban cities developed. With a drainage area estimated at 1,293,000 square miles, the Nile rises south of the Equator and flows northward through northeastern Africa, impacting over ten countries, including parts of Tanzania, Burundi, Rwanda, the Democratic Republic of Congo, Kenya, Uganda, South Sudan, Ethiopia, Sudan, and Egypt.[23] That is, the Nile directly impacts about 20 percent of countries in Africa, weaving and meandering across geopolitical landscapes and postcolonial boundaries, as if in defiance of anthropogenic boundary-making and policing of the colonial and postcolonial nation-state. As Ewald Blocher has argued,

> The natural environment that the Nile traverses is made up of different topographic and climatic zones; not only does the river flow from sub-tropical to arid regions but it simultaneously crosses artificially constructed borders. Like a lifeline, the Nile flows through numerous politically divided regions and, in the process, is cut up into smaller geographical pieces.[24]

In the macro movement of Exodus, the Nile is connected to the Red Sea at the point where the narrative addresses the temporal-spatial depths of rupture that permanently delink the migrant community from Egypt. These bodies of water sustain an oppressed community but also function as ecological coroners—they release trapped or dead bodies on their shores, the bodies of the rescued Moses and liberated Israel, and the bodies of Pharaoh's dead army—as if to summon and compel communal assessment: The liberated Israel turns around and acknowledges the dead bodies on the seashore (Exod. 14:30).[25] To think with such waters requires theorizing around the "co-constitution of water as a substance and water as poetics."[26] The language of such material poetics includes such words and expressions as "flow," "deep/depth," "undercurrent," "flood," "circulation," "dry," "bubble," "freezing up," "evaporate," "leakage," and "seepage."[27] Some of this language is lyrical and rhythmic, as deployed in Exodus' song at and about the sea (Exod. 15:1–12).

---

23. Magdi M. El-Kammash, Harold Edwin Hurst, and Charles Gordon Smith, "Nile River," https://www.britannica.com/place/Nile-River.html.

24. Ewald Blocher, "Dammed Water: Water as a National Commodity," *Rachel Carson Center Perspectives* 2 (2012): 36.

25. In the tragic unfolding of this role as ecological coroner, the Mediterranean Sea has been the subject-space where dead migrant bodies are washed up in recent years.

26. Cecilia Chen, Janine MacLeod, and Astrida Neimanis, "Introduction: Toward a Hydrological Turn?" in *Thinking with Water*, ed. Chen, et al. (London: McGill-Queen's University Press, 2013), 9.

27. Chen et al., "Introduction," 10.

AFROECOLOGY AND EXODUS 125

Thinking with the forms, rhythms, and subjectivity of water "requires relational thinking" because water "literally flows between and within bodies, across space and through time, in a planetary circulation system that challenges pretensions to discrete individuality."[28] Thus one interprets in ways that recognize the capacity and character of "watery places and bodies" to be "connected to other places and bodies in relations of gift, transfer, theft, and debt. Such relationality inaugurates new life, and also the infinite possibility of new communities."[29] There is a deep intersection at work here in Exodus: the transition from a watery body or community to a desert or wilderness community has implications for the subjectivity of the people and the environment. Political liberation without ecological liberation is unfinished and almost entirely flawed.

On the "Other" Side of Water: Thinking with Deserts

We must go a three days' journey into the wilderness and sacrifice to the LORD our God as he commands us.

(Exod. 8:27)

Connected to the story of water—in fact, on the other side of water—is a specific kind of land: the wilderness. The song of the sea transitions from water (15:1–12) to land (15:17–19). Here, I want to briefly focus on a particular form of land that has defined African epistemologies and politics—the desert.[30] Africa boasts the largest non-polar desert in the world, the Sahara Desert. It shares borders with the Atlantic Ocean on the west, the Red Sea on the east, the Mediterranean Sea on the north, and the Sahel Savannah on the south. The enormous desert spans eleven countries: Algeria, Chad, Egypt, Libya, Mali, Mauritania, Morocco, Niger, Western Sahara, Sudan, and Tunisia. Constituting about a third of the total landmass of Africa, the Sahara has functioned as a pathway in inter- and intra-continental migrations galvanized around religion, nationality, culture, and economics.[31] It has sustained movement and history. "The history of the desert," writes Ghislaine Lydon, "just like that of the ocean, is marked by continuous exchanges."[32]

---

28. Chen et al., "Introduction," 12.
29. Chen et al., "Introduction," 12.
30. In Isaiah 35:1, the words *wilderness* and *desert* are analogous and interchangeable.
31. Irene Díaz de Aguilar Hidalgo, "The Niger-Libya Migration Route: An Odyssey Shaped by Saharan Connections and European Fears, 2000–2017," *Framework Document* 1 (2018): 1–31.
32. Ghislaine Lydon, "Writing Trans-Saharan History: Methods, Sources, and Interpretations across the African Divide," *The Journal of North African Studies* 10, nos. 3–4 (2005): 295.

126   LET MY PEOPLE LIVE

Like water bodies (the Nile, the Atlantic) that inform and shape
Africa/na, the Sahara is not a natural habitat for humankind. Navigating the Sahara puts different kinds of pressures on the human and
cultural body; it is not flooding/drowning that the community fears
but rather dehydration. The desert, as a dehydrated body, is partly the
natural kin of the abused water systems. The body that succumbs to the
Sahara is not bloated and floating on the shores; the wilderness body
is brittle and exhausted. It is not a fattened body but a starved and suffocated body, drained by a politics of extraction and environmental
slow death. The crisis of the wilderness is not always spectacular and
sporadic, but it is rather gradual and incremental. An afroecological
reading of the desert (Wilderness) examines the importance of the relationship between exhaustion and resiliency in Africana exodus work,
between desert spaces and watery spaces. In biblical metaphor, the desert is not just a place where new pathways open but also where streams
and springs flow (Exod. 15:22, 27; cf. Isa. 41:18; 43:19).

Thinking with Air: Can We Breathe?

Then the LORD said to Moses and Aaron, "Take handfuls of soot from
the kiln, and let Moses throw it in the air in the sight of Pharaoh."
(Exod. 9:8)

So Moses stretched out his staff over the land of Egypt, and the LORD
brought an east wind upon the land all that day and all that night;
when morning came, the east wind had brought the locusts. The
locusts came upon all the land of Egypt and settled on the whole
country of Egypt, such a dense swarm of locusts as had never been
before, nor ever shall be again. They covered the surface of the whole
land, so that the land was black; and they ate all the plants in the land
and all the fruit of the trees that the hail had left; nothing green was
left, no tree, no plant in the field, in all the land of Egypt.
(Exod. 10:13–15)

One material space for African/a ecological theorizing is the Congo
Basin, which spans six countries (Equatorial Guinea, Cameroon,
Central African Republic, Democratic Republic of Congo, Republic
of Congo, and Gabon). Although invoked in colonial racist ideology (e.g., in Joseph Conrad's 1899 novel *The Heart of Darkness*) as
a pathway into an unknown and supposedly morally depraved space,
the Congo Basin is metaphorically known in scientific and ecological

circles as the "world's second lung" because of the amount of its water discharge, the amount of carbon dioxide it takes in, and the amount of oxygen it releases, without which much of Africa would be a desert.[33] Of the top ten largest wetlands in the world, three are in Africa: the Congo Basin (fourth), Lake Chad Basin (eighth) and River Nile Basin (ninth).[34] Since the adoption of the Ramsar convention on Wetlands (1971), several countries have adopted the goals of preserving wetlands, including the implementation of environmental flow assessments (EFA)—how much of a river's original flow regime should continue down into its flood basin in order to provide valued ecosystem service.[35] Wetlands are viewed as crucial to the ecosystem and its services. Sunday Kometa and Jude Kimengsi have drawn on the historic work and legacy of the Ramsar Convention (ratified in Cameroon in 2006) to advocate collaborative work between urban development planners and environmental conservation experts in Cameroon, particularly in the Ndop wetlands.[36]

A key contribution of wetlands to planetary flourishing is their production of oxygen. Breathing is a divine act, a gift of the highest order. The act of breathing, the organs that perform it, and the conditions that enhance or inhibit this act have compelled human and divine attention since ancient times. As civilizations emerged and social systems developed, the life-force, the breath, that animates and inspires human and non-human beings and flourishing has remained a subject of unrelenting focus and attention. Theologically, this is what connects created life to the Holy One. As humans, we have developed institutions, traditions, and rituals to structure this relationship of shared life and to permanently connect it to other humans, to non-human creatures, and to the Divine. In the Exodus story, there is a trope of communal reflection on its aerodynamic character. Yahweh reminds the people how they were carried "on eagle's wings" and brought to the deity at the time of major environmental devastation and political oppression in Egypt (Exod. 19:4). This experience of birdlike mobility constitutes an interpretive mode of exodus gathering as aerial movement, a rising up. The movement of the wind represents at once the devastation of

---

33. Maathai, *Replenishing*, 37.

34. Paul Keddy, et al., "Wet and Wonderful: The World's Largest Wetlands Are Conservation Priorities," *BioScience* 59, no. 1 (2009): 42.

35. Keddy, et al., "Wet and Wonderful," 39.

36. Sunday Shende Kometa and Jude Ndzifon Kimengsi, "Urban Development and Its Implications on Wetland Ecosystem Services in Ndop, Cameroon," *Environmental Management and Sustainable Development* 7, no. 1 (2018): 21–36; Emmanuel M. Nyambod, "Environmental Consequences of Rapid Urbanisation: Bamenda City, Cameroon," *Journal of Environmental Protection* 1, no. 1 (2010): 15–23.

128 LET MY PEOPLE LIVE

the land and the social force of resistance against Pharaoh's ideology. As one reads in Virginia Hamilton's *The People Could Fly*, aerodynamic mobility constitutes resistance to oppression at the intersection of race and environment.[37] This eco-political tradition has continued in the form of the "I Can't Breathe" protests and their connection to the enduring work of the Black Lives Matter (BLM) movement. As a movement and mode of communal breathing, in resistance to communal choking, the BLM, founded by three Black Women—Alicia Garza, Patrisse Cullors, and Opal Tometi—has become a powerful communal and global lung that reaches deep down into systems of national and international citizenship and pumps breath into the contorted or suffocating human, social, and ecological bodies. I have identified this work as an unending commitment to Never Stop Breathing.[38] The intersection of ethnic/racial and ecological devastation in Exodus produces a form of Wilderness, not just for the people but also for the environment. Exodus' aerodynamic form includes the importance of oxygen for survival and endurance (Isa. 40:31).

Elsewhere, the symbol of political and ecological survival—Noah's ark—is closely associated with flying creatures: a raven and a dove. The raven "went to and fro" until the waters dried up, while the dove went to "see if the waters had subsided" (Gen 8:7–8). This bird-sending account is similar to other accounts in ancient Mesopotamian flood stories and has informed analyses of the relation between the birds and their function in assessing the in/habitability of previously flooded spaces.[39] The aerodynamic capacities of the birds become a metaphor for navigating flooded space (the raven is "going out and returning" until the land is dry), and the gradual, phased-out process of ultimately inhabiting previously flooded space. Thus, unlike the apparently one-directional travel performed in the metaphor of the eagle in Exodus (19:4), the community imagined in this environmental text is engaged in various kinds of returns. The raven's multiple returns are intimately linked to departures from an earth that is gradually becoming dry. The raven's capacity to survive outside of the temporary safety zone of the ark is signified by its non-singular returns. The raven's audience is not Noah—the secluded community inside the ark—but a community of

---

37. Virginia Hamilton, *The People Could Fly: American Black Folktales*, illus. by Leo Dillon and Diane Dillon (New York: Alfred Knopf, 1985).

38. www.neverstopbreathing.org.

39. See David Marcus, "The Mission of the Raven (Gen. 8:7)," *Journal of Ancient Near Eastern Studies* 29 (2002): 71–80.

living beings, ecosystems, and epistemologies outside the ark, a community that, like Elijah's, is also experiencing a gradual drying up of the earth and its waters (1 Kgs. 17:1–6). For its part, the dove's returns to the ark are also multiple, but they are given linearity: the bird's returns are temporary, sequential, and ultimately cease. The transition from the dove's temporary return to its ultimate failure to return is embodied in the presence of the olive tree. The airborne life and character of the story unfolds around engagement with the distress of disappearing water and the ultimate hope of emerging trees. The two birds transition from survival to liberation in ways that are multiple but consistent in their repeated engagement with the elements of nature. This "ecological moment" associated with "life in the air" has material relevance and presence on the ground—it is connected to a community that is working to survive political and ecological devastation. For the exodus community, ongoing movement work of liberation is continuously linked to, and analogized with, the movement of the wind/spirit/breath. It is that movement that fuels survival and thriving inside of Egypt and beyond Egypt, in the Wilderness and beyond, and in the Mountain area and beyond.

CONCLUSION

The oppressive systems that Exodus identifies, describes, and addresses are political and environmental, and the battle for human and environmental flourishing is waged in the courts of political power (Exod. 1; 5–6), but also in fields and waterfronts and reservoirs (Exod. 2; 7–11). The story's depictions of oppression and embittering distress, of fragmentation and interregional survival, and of environmental disaster and transition into the wilderness and mountain area is associated with the development of economies of extraction in local and global spaces. Pharaoh's refusal to let the people go—his refusal to allow human and environmental flourishing—is motivated by his infatuation with war, his infatuation with national boundary-making (1:10), and the economic incentives associated with such warring machinery (Exod. 5:3–5). The oppressed, marginalized, and isolated community's increasingly distressful cry is matched by unrelenting political demands for the land to produce straw for bricks to supply an insatiable building project of political and military aggrandizement. Both realities of political and ecological distress also meet around the equally insatiable search for, and control of, waters. It is this clash that initially puts Moses among the reeds (2:3), and that ultimately puts the migrant community and Pharaoh's army between the parted waters of the Red Sea (Exod. 14–15). Thomas Dozeman has shown that the manifestation of the exodus deity's power over the forces and elements of nature—water, land, and air—infuses much of the story, particularly the plagues narratives. In the final battle around the Red Sea, the story "explores Yahweh's power over the chaotic sea itself to destroy Pharaoh and his army."[40] The "Sea of Reeds," or Red Sea, functions as an important mythological trope and geospatial site for the emergence of Exodus' ecological identity and subjectivity (Exod. 2:3, 5; 10:19; Num. 14:25; Isa. 19:6).

The stories about Moses in the Nile (reeds) and Pharaoh's army in the Red Sea depict watery spaces as at once shielding endangered bodies from a threatening political system (Exod. 2:1–10) and holding the bodily remains of a crumbled political system of oppression (Exod. 14–15). In performing those tasks, the waters and marshlands function as the story's ecological midwife-coroners, releasing—in isolated and systemic fashion—caged or trapped or dead bodies along its shores. Exodus' ecological diaspora is plain to see. The uninhabitability of Pharaoh's geopolitical "house of bondage" is intricately related to the uninhabitability of the polluted and plagued Egypt. These realities become part of the topography of all of Exodus' geopolitical spaces, including its routes, fortresses, and waters, and the extractive economies associated with those places.[41] The narrative transition and liaison between the Nile (Exod. 2) and the Red Sea (Exod. 14–15) represents a fluid and expansive transition that connects political oppression to ecological extraction (the making of straws and bricks) to ecological abuse (the plagues) and to ecological convulsion (the Red Sea).

As Herbert Robinson Marbury writes in *Pillars of Cloud and Fire*, "God uses two distinct beacons—a pillar of cloud and a pillar of fire—to lead the Children of Israel to Canaan. Each sign appears when its form is most visible—a cloud during the day and fire at night." Marbury connects these meteorological phenomena to the social work of liberation by African American activists striving to reform or drastically

---

40. Thomas B. Dozeman, *Commentary on Exodus*, Eerdmans Critical Commentary (Grand Rapids: William B. Eerdmans Publishing Company, 2009), 298.

41. For more details, see Lester L. Grabbe, "Exodus and History," in *The Book of Exodus: Composition, Reception, and Interpretation*, ed. Thomas B. Dozeman, Craig A. Evans, and Joel N. Lohr (Leiden: Brill, 2014), 70–77. On Israel's economies of extraction, see Roland Boer, *The Sacred Economy of Ancient Israel* (Louisville, KY: Westminster John Knox Press, 2015).

AFROECOLOGY AND EXODUS 131

alter the fabric of the nation.[42] The political work of these meteorological phenomena is also ecological. Whereas the Nile episode (Exod.
2:1–10) transitioned Moses from the basket in the reeds to the political
house, the Red Sea episode (Exod. 14–15) transitioned Israel out of the
house of Pharaoh (his military infrastructure) and into the wilderness.
Fearful, alienated, and endangered, the exodus group begins to synchro-
nize its movements with environmental and meteorological phenomena—the pillar of cloud and fire and the standing walls of water—that
serve as exodus coordinates and that enable them to develop crossover
mechanisms to escape political clash and environmental disaster. They
walk on dry land because the sea splits for a moment and then returns
in a flooding rage that sweeps the Egyptian army. The surviving community, now located on the other side of the geopolitical and environmental war, looks back and sees the bodies of Pharaoh's colonizing
soldiers sprawled on the seashore (Exod. 14:30), the same spatial location where Moses encountered Pharaoh at the beginning of the plagues
(Exod. 7:15). The story has effectively removed political Pharaoh from
the scene; he is no longer the primary reference point for understanding
liberation. Attention turns more decisively to exodus' environments,
which no longer function as subsidiary sites of political struggle but as
co-subjects of reference in the unfolding narrative. Political liberation
without environmental liberation is half-baked liberation.

In responding to challenges raised by the Red Sea community,
Moses (and Aaron) are often summoned to intercede on behalf of the
people, to perform social acts that ensure communal survival, chan-
neling and distributing the power of generative liberation. Moses and
the exodus deity engage in ritual and non-ritual activity that include
assessment of human interaction with the non-human world: striking
rocks to produce water (Exod. 17); interpreting and being influenced
by clouds and fires around the tent of meeting (Num. 14; cf. Acts
2); summoning food to fall from the sky, raising questions about the
nature and durability of manna for intergenerational sustenance (Exod.
16); and planting trees besides waters and covenantal objects (Exod.
15:25; Num. 17).

The murmuring tradition might be read as an ecological turn in
Exodus narration, where engagement with the material subjects/objects
of the natural world is juxtaposed with discourse about the divine statutes, ordinances, and voice that frame the ecological turn as a turn

---

42. Herbert Robinson Marbury, *Pillars of Cloud and Fire: The Politics of Exodus in African American Biblical
Interpretation* (New York: New York University Press, 2015), 6.

toward communal healing. The magnitude and the fragility of this turn makes it a test: that is, a continuing demand or requirement of the community to navigate the ecological space for the purpose of thriving (Exod. 15:25b–27). The relation between the un/inhabitability of social and political space in Egypt and the un/inhabitability of ecological and environmental space in the wilderness is no longer simply transitional and temporary, but it has become an ongoing challenge to the community to develop inhabitable spaces. The interpretive turn around the Red Sea puts the material substance of water and trees next to the textual substance of legislation, communal storytelling, and healing.[43] To further explore this narrative space and voice called Wilderness, and its interpretive significance for a reading that moves beyond a diaspora frame ("let my people go") to a bio-framing ("let my people live"), I will focus in the next chapter on the character of Miriam and her material and rhetorical proximity to water and trees.

---

43. Carol Meyers, *Exodus* (Cambridge: Cambridge University Press, 2005), 129: "the message is that both water and regulations are essential for survival."

5

Miriam

The Water-Woman and Exodus Ecology

INTRODUCTION

In 2015, a colleague and I took students on a cross-cultural immersion course to Ghana. We visited several historical sites, including the Kwame Nkrumah Mausoleum and the botanical garden in Accra. But it was the visit to the Elmina Castle that provoked some of the most unexpected feelings and thoughts in me. I had read about the history of the place—its colonial structure, its transformation of the local landscape, and its infamous door of no return—the material space that represented the colonial and racist ideological channel of Africana experiences of erasure, alienation, and singularity. When we entered and moved through the dungeons and up to the second level where there used to be a chapel, I suddenly felt really sick. My body must have changed somehow, because a student came up to me and asked whether I was OK. I said no. I wanted to escape because that sort of place is not conducive for human survival. I mention this episode because it points to the ways in which ecology—natural and constructed—can produce unwell bodies. To be a healthy or a sick body is not always about autoimmune deficiency; it is also about the pressures that bodies face when placed in certain ecological spaces. The extent to which human and ecological bodies interact and intersect is a part of my Africana Exodus/exodus analysis.

My aim in this chapter is to focus that analysis on Miriam as a sisterly ally, a prophetic catalyst, and a believed/disbelieved subject of

134   LET MY PEOPLE LIVE

eco-hermeneutics. Miriam is a significant figure in Exodus lore. Earliest memories identify her, alongside Moses and Aaron, as one of the programmatic forerunners of Yahweh's twofold activity of bringing Israel up from the land of Egypt and redeeming the people from the house of slavery (Mic. 6:4). Pseudo-Philo's *Biblical Antiquities* (20.8) associates Miriam with the water at Marah, Aaron with the pillar of cloud, and Moses with manna. The gushing rock (the "moveable well") that provided water for the Israelites became known as the Well of Miriam.[1] Given this memory, why the narrative paucity about Miriam in Exodus? Is she the embodiment of suppressed or liminal, but nevertheless powerful, memories of survival in Second Temple Jewish and early Christian communities? Deidre Good, following the work of the thirteenth-century Parisian, Peter Abelard, has in fact provocatively written about the possibility of a "miriamic secret."[2] Good argues that, by name and by traits, Miriam shares narrative subjectivity and epistemology with other female characters in ancient communities. By name—etymology, morphology, and cultural significance—Miriam is connected to a cultural and linguistic repertoire that puts her in conversation with other biblical characters, including Mary, the mother of Jesus, and the Magdalen.

> Mar-yam is the form of Mary's name that was always (as far as we know) used in the old Creeds in the Syriac churches. . . . it is likely that no Syriac variants of the name Mary/Miriam were ever used in the Bible.
>
> Readers of the Syriac Bible would thus view Mary the mother of Jesus as having the same name as Miriam in Exodus and Mary Magdalene. Where there are three names in English there is one in Syriac. In this respect, the Syriac mirrors exactly the original Palestinian reality: In Palestinian Hebrew or Western Jewish Aramaic, the name of Jesus' mother and the others would have been exactly the same as Miriam in Exodus. The shift from Miriam to "Mary" is a by-product of the move from Hebrew/Aramaic to Greek (and then Latin).[3]

Miriam is both an individual subject and a representation of epistemological and narrative kinship woven across the fractures, displacements, and misalignments of exodus history and geography. Like water that cleanses and refreshes in its flow but also collects debris along the way,

---

1. James L. Kugel, *The Bible as It Was* (Cambridge, MA: Harvard University Press, 1997), 364.
2. Deidre Good, ed., *Miriam, the Magdalen, and the Mother* (Bloomington: Indiana University Press, 2005), 3–24.
3. Good, *Miriam*, 12.

Miriam embodies the flows of exodus herstory/herstories and herstoriographies that do more than sit at the nexus life and death, that, in fact, insist on the story's capacity to find new life-forms and new nomenclatures of affinity and generativity in some of the most austere places.

In addition to the epistemology of nomenclature, Miriam shares narrative traits with her canonical sisters. These traits include narrative and social roles as sisters, prophets, and believed/disbelieved subjects. As sister, she is more than a travel companion; she is a trailblazer of the flow of exodus work (Mic. 6:4). As prophet, she is visionary, orator, and powerful leader on behalf of the dispossessed and marginalized (Exod. 15:20). And as believed/disbelieved, she sits at the intersection of canonical and repressed (disbelieved) traditions.[4] How Miriam fares in this analysis is critical to eco-exodus hermeneutics.

In *Exploring Ecological Hermeneutics*, Norman Habel argues that "a radical ecological approach to the text involves a basic hermeneutic of suspicion, identification, and retrieval," which bears similarities to feminist hermeneutics and situates readers "as creatures of Earth, as members of Earth community in solidarity with Earth."[5] A hermeneutic of suspicion in an ecological reading recognizes the anthropocentric character of the biblical text and seeks to overcome two basic assumptions: that humankind is superior to non-human creation, and that nature is simply an object of human exploration and investigation. Identification or empathy moves the reader to recognize "the prior ecological reality of our kinship with Earth: that we are born of Earth, and that we are living expressions of the ecosystem that has emerged on this planet." Retrieval allows the reader to refrain from ascribing the term *anthropomorphism* to the subjectivity of non-human characters in the text. The reader seeks to discern the voice of Earth and embark on reconstructive endeavors that may allow one to "hear Earth as the narrator of the story."[6]

In the Wake, Christina Sharpe's expansive engagement with Africana modes of being, includes analyses of the role of water (the Atlantic Ocean) as the time and space of residence for Black bodies traversing in slave ships. Even as the ship moved, the bodies that entered the body of water remained there in residence, materially and epistemologically

---

4. Good, *Miriam*, 14–21.
5. Norman C. Habel, "Introducing Ecological Hermeneutics," in *Exploring Ecological Hermeneutics*, ed. Norman C. Habel and Peter Trudinger (Atlanta: Society of Biblical Literature, 2008), 3.
6. Habel, "Introducing Ecological Hermeneutics," 4–5.

connected to water and separated from water.[7] As human bodies merge with the body of the ocean, residence time—the time that it takes for human blood that has entered the ocean to finally leave—becomes ecological time. I will argue that Miriam functions as the subject and epistemological catalyst for examining Exodus' engagement with water as part of exodus "residence time" linked to ecological time. In Egypt, Miriam is strategically located along the Nile, where she watches Moses among the reeds and engages the Egyptian princess about a process to recognize and compensate the nursing work of Hebrew women. By her narrative location and rhetorical formulations, Miriam is central to how Exodus intersects around economic, cultural, and ethnic/racial security. The future of the oppressed community is a result of Miriam's ability to survey and theorize about the flow of liquid nursing associated with Moses' mother (Exod. 2:6–10) and the larger epistemological framing of the land of promise as a land flowing with milk and honey (Exod. 3:8). This is true when the exodus community is at another defining transitional moment at the Red Sea. Miriam summons the seaside community to sing something of a new song, to repurpose its deadly and near-death experiences around oppressive politics and devastated ecologies. Through Miriam's prompting and leadership, the community articulates Exodus as an eco-political story of transition from liberation to healing (Exod. 15:26). Her prophetic reengagement with the waters of the Red Sea, and her production of a textual body (song) about water, offers a communal experience of divine healing, embodied as a change in the very character of the water, from bitter water to sweet water (cf. Exod. 15:25). Miriam's reformulations around water in Exodus are consistent with her memorialized role in Micah 6:4 where she summoned the elements of creation as witnesses (Mic. 6:1–2) to a communal formation linking creation to new birth and steadfast love (ḥesed) (Mic. 6:6–8).

Etymologically, Miriam's name is associated with water (*yam*). Whether this association is experienced as bitter (perhaps allusive to the Hebrew root, *mrr*) or beloved (allusive to the Egyptian *mry(t)*, "the beloved") is undecipherable in a conclusive manner. Rita Burns has argued, persuasively, that the name should be understood in relation to ancient Egyptian uses of *mry* ("beloved") in association with deities.[8] Like the name Moses, the name Miriam is wrapped in

---

7. Christina Sharpe, *In the Wake: On Blackness and Being* (Durham, NC: Duke University Press, 2016), 41.

8. Rita J. Burns, *Has the Lord Indeed Spoken Only through Moses? A Study of the Biblical Portrait of Miriam* (Atlanta: Scholars Press, 1987), 9–10.

mythology and geography. In the genealogical and ecological flow of exodus, Miriam comes out of the communal womb—the activism and resistance—of many other women in Exodus, including the midwives and her own biological mother. Her physical and embodied proximity to water and watery spaces is matched by her persistent rhetorical capacity to give voice to the waters—how they flow, how they are taken up and used for nurture, how they open up to swallow (or host) the victims of a failed political system based on ethnocentric ideology. Miriam is the resilient beloved one who also carries within her the embittered experience of an oppressed and exploited community and its ecologies.

Levitical genealogies (Num. 26:59; 1 Chr. 5:29) give Miriam kinship and ancestry, and therefore memory. She is part of the fruit of the communal womb that produced Israel's leadership team. When that leadership team is tested in Numbers 12, Miriam is subjected to harsh treatment that puts her in a watery space that Yahweh analogizes to being spat on by her father. This hypothetical scenario portrays Miriam's character and voice as a liquid woman—a woman who generates and sustains flow—as exodus companion and as progenitor who is displaced yet critically necessary for the community. When she finally exits the community—when she dies and is buried at Kadesh (Num. 20:1)—her absence (her burial) signifies a major drying up of community life, described as a lack of water. Does the Wilderness overcome the water? Can anyone nurture Miriam's dried body, even as she nurtured Moses and the exodus community around water? Anthony Rees has shown how engagement with the Wilderness in Numbers provokes and conjures complex feelings of "dis-satisfaction, dis-comfort, and even disdain."[9] The wilderness experience comes after the plagues and the Red Sea battle, which transition Israel out of Egypt and remove political Pharaoh from the scene. Henceforth, Israel will need to engage the land itself in order to forge its futures. Here Madipoane Masenya's *eco-bosadi* hermeneutics proves fruitful. *Eco-bosadi* challenges patriarchy's oppression of women and the earth, and it subjects both forms of oppression to critical examination in search of liberating futures.[10] The first space where such future-making work begins anew in Exodus is the Wilderness.

---

9. Anthony Rees, *Voices of the Wilderness: An Ecological Reading of the Book of Numbers* (Sheffield: Sheffield Phoenix Press, 2015), 3–4, 118.

10. Madipoane Masenya (Ngwan'a Mphahlele), "All from the Same Source? Deconstructing a (Male) Anthropocentric Reading of Job (3) through an Eco-*bosadi* Lens," *Journal of Theology for Southern Africa* 137 (July 2010): 56–57.

Having been produced by her mother's biological and cultural womb and then strategically placed by the waters of the Nile, Miriam becomes a leader in womanist affect and creativity (cf. Exod. 15:20). This reading is a recast of Exodus in which Miriam is not only the first woman prophetic voice but also the first to shift the mode and manner of exodus narration from political resistance to eco-political living and flourishing. That is, her song is antiphonal not just to the voices of other women singing but also to the song of Moses. While Moses leads the people from water to land (Exod. 15:1, 19), Miriam's song initiates movement from bitter water to sweet water (Exod. 15:21, 27), a narrative and creative echo and synergy with her emergence—and the emergence of exodus work—around the eco-political space of the Nile and the wilderness. It is perhaps this ecowomanist thrust to exodus, memory narration, and creativity that the song of the sea gestures to.

Isabel Mukonyora has given voice to such work in her reflections on the theology and rituals of a Christian community called the Masowe Apostles that embarks on annual migrations through several central and east African countries to enact and embody Wilderness as "reach[ing] out to God." Mukonyora writes,

> [In] walking to the outskirts of the city of Harare, removing their shoes and spending four to six hours praying on the dirt with the sun shining and the wind blowing, they perform their knowledge of God. The term *sowe* is used to describe the sacred places used for prayer, which can be on the edge of a golf course, small forests, or dry meadows—wherever there is unoccupied land with which to give expression to the idea of children of God on the margins of society. Masowe Apostles are theologians of liberation whose understanding of God is thus lived, dramatized, and embodied.[11]

Miriam sits at the intersection of water and dry land, between the reeds of the Nile and Pharaoh's house, on the one hand, and between the Red Sea and Wilderness, on the other. She is connected to the material subjectivity and force of the water and the land. She rhetorically and materially sits at the place of marginalized existence, with marginalized subjects, but she also rhetorically and materially embodies resilience and transformation.

---

11. Isabel Mukonyora, "Dramatization and Embodiment of God in the Wilderness," in *Faith in African Lived Christianity: Bridging Anthropological and Theological Perspectives*, ed. Karen Lauterbach and Mika Vähäkangas (Leiden: Brill, 2020), 271, 272.

CONTRA NECROECOLOGY: MIRIAM AND EXODUS 2:1–10

Pharaoh's consecutive decrees requiring that Hebrew boys be killed at birth, or be thrown into the Nile (should they survive the first decree), constitute two attempts to control ethnic identity at the intersection of politics and ecology. To saturate the birth stool with death is to control biological and cultural stories of beginnings and to handicap their promise; to saturate the Nile with death is to control ecological stories of achievement and pollute the character of life. At that narrative moment, when the crumbling political story intersects with the ecological story, Miriam bursts into the scene. Because Jochebed—and likely numerous other mothers—could no longer fight exclusively political battles, she put Moses in the reeds along the Nile. Miriam emerges, spatially and narratively, as a second-first act of badass womanist resistance to Pharaoh's two decrees. While Jochebed represents the resistance to necropolitics formulated and enacted through the infrastructure of the political house, Miriam represents resistance to necroecology—ecological death. Miriam's mother could no longer hide her son in the house; political resistance alone was insufficient. Through Miriam's positioning at the Nile, the story begins to make its ecological case.

When the Egyptian princess comes down to the river—when she departs from the political house/infrastructure of erasure and situates herself next to the ecological space—she brings not just the political institution with her but also its decree. And once the Egyptian princess empathetically rescues and identifies Moses the Hebrew—a logical deduction from Pharaoh's standing policy that Hebrew boys be thrown into the Nile—Miriam interjects and proposes to bring a Hebrew woman to nurse the child. Miriam uses her oratorical and strategic knowledge to engage the Egyptian princess and advocate something more than episodic rescue from the water. To remove Moses from the water is to remove Pharaoh's death decree from the water. But Miriam wants more—she wants to institutionalize the role of nourishing water in exodus work. Policy, not phenotype or a happenstance of history, is what attached death to the Hebrew body and its habitat—from the womb to hidden places in the home and finally to the open places of the Nile. Situated at the intersection between national houses structured around necropolitics, Miriam connects the water-rescue scene back to Pharaoh's house and thus back to the political institution and policy that saturates the waters with death and distress. The nursing mother that Miriam secures (Exod. 2:7) is able to produce milk (cf. Job

140   LET MY PEOPLE LIVE

3:12) in the face of marginalized and endangered existence, and this structures the movement of Moses' rescue from water to water.

Miriam's analytical, insightful, and embodied utterances in Exodus 2 suggest that her labors in exodus narration revolve around the possibility of communal and environmental regeneration beyond the politics of death that saturate the waters, and beyond the politics of singular momentary rescues understood as departures from polluted water. In that sense, she represents a form of communal strategic improvisation that extends and transforms Exodus' "residence time" in water; she continues the movement work of the midwives, who guarded other watery spaces—the wombs of the Hebrew women. She realizes the connection between political death and ecological death. Miriam's narrative and physical proximity to water represents the voice of regeneration and its capacity to resist and alter Pharaoh's environmental pollution policy. The water can nurse healthy bodies rather than simply function as a coroner for dead bodies. Miriam is the catalyst for epistemological and practical framing around water and with water. It is a risky move that puts her in a position where she might be erased from the story that moves from water to land; she also risks her work being displaced by the patriarchal and imperial systems and ideologies that move the story from multiplicity to singularity.

Through its initial unfolding as a narrative about male rescue and political maturity (Exod. 2:10), Miriam's voice is silenced and her presence marginalized in the clashes and discussions around new authority (Exod. 2:11–15), exploitative and oppressive economic structures (Exod. 5:1–6:12), and ecological devastation in the plagues. The enduring political and economic clashes are relocated spatially around water (Exod. 7:15) and manifest in the form of water pollution/infusion with death (Exod. 7:17–24). In bitter narrative irony, the political and ecological story unfolds without the analytical voice, the strategic insights, and the prophetic articulations of the water-woman, Miriam. This remains true until the community that endures and partially survives the plagues is trapped between a pursuing army and a massive body of water, the Red Sea (Exod. 13–15). Motivated by the urgent need for full liberation, the exodus community—and its story—will grapple with the narrative erasure of the water-woman.[12]

In the seaside battle, Moses' staff reenacts the power to break open new spaces by splitting the waters. This ultimate battle at the

---

12. See Christine Trevett, "Wilderness Woman: The Taming of Miriam," in *Wilderness: Essays in Honour of Frances Young*, ed. R. S. Sugirtharajah (New York: T&T Clark, 2005), 26–44.

sea—perhaps a battle over/for water—illustrates a tragic intersection between the violent politics of nation-state and environmental disaster. In this struggle, Passover and its agricultural practices effectively cluster and then usher Israel out of the political yoke of pharaonic economic oppression (Exod. 12–13). Additionally, Yahweh proposes safety measures that political leadership in Egypt could deploy to mitigate adverse effects of the environmental disaster, including shelters for open field animals (Exod. 9:16–21) or the apparently secluded land of Goshen (Exod. 8:22 [8:18, Masoretic Text]; 9:29). But the long-term livelihood of the exodus community and its environments requires more than temporary pockets of safety zones. Exodus' concern about ecological survival requires more robust engagements with the story's environments: its material resources, its waters *and* clouds *and* animals *and* marshlands *and* wildernesses *and* sands *and* reeds, all connected to the community's long-term livelihood. Pharaoh's inability to participate in Passover rituals connecting the survival of the community to herbs and animals, and his inability to properly respond to changing environmental phenomena—the gathering pillars of clouds and fire and the standing or rising waters at the Red Sea—prompt him to pursue a policy of colonial domination (Exod. 14:2–3). Here, the story thoroughly rejects Pharaoh's political ideology in its narrative and poetic depictions of the destruction of Pharaoh's army at the sea; the political story turns to the ecological story for help.

In Moses' song of the sea—the song that celebrates Yahweh casting "horse and rider" into the water (Exod. 15:1)—the poetic submersion of pharaonic governance into the depths is powerful and potentially the ultimate manifestation of victory.[13] As Ian Wilson has argued, the song of the sea, which has "an interest in geographical, temporal, and redemptive liminality" also had a socio-mnemonic function in postexilic Judah: "the Song stands as a conspicuous landmark of Judah's salvific relationship with Yahweh. It memorializes the exodus as the primary redemptive event in Israel's past, but it is also an integral part of that past moment, an event in and of itself, which occurs just after the Sea-crossing."[14] The song presents the poetic expectation that the submerged structure of political and environmental devastation

---

13. On Exodus 15 as a victory song, see Martin L. Brenner, *The Song of the Sea: Ex. 15:1–21* (Berlin: De Gruyter, 2012), 36–46; Brian D. Russell, *The Song of the Sea: The Date of Composition and Influence of Exodus 15:1–21* (New York: Peter Lang, 2007).

14. Ian Douglas Wilson, "The Song of the Sea and Isaiah: Exodus 15 in Post-Monarchic Prophetic Discourse," in *Thinking of Water in the Early Second Temple Period*, ed. Ehud Ben Zvi and Christopher Levin (Berlin: De Gruyter, 2014), 126, 130.

142   LET MY PEOPLE LIVE

and pollution will not rise back up again. The water is saturated with unnatural and politically motivated death, and the watery substratum becomes the metaphoric depths of deadly ethno-nationalism. Moses' song narratively removes Israel from that depth. He moves the community from water (Exod. 15:1) to dry land (Exod. 15:19). The structure of the song transitions from past victory (in the watery space, 15:1–12, 18) to future-oriented space (culminating in land, Exod. 15:13–17). Thomas Dozeman sees, in this shift, the influence of the Deuteronomist, for whom the primary focus of the latter part of the song is Yahweh's leadership in the wilderness and the conquest of the land.[15] Pursuant to this logic of water-to-land movement, Miriam's song communally celebrating Yahweh's victory over Pharaoh in the water (Exod. 15:20–21), followed by a narrative journey culminating in communal camping around watery spaces (Exod. 15:22–27) would seem out of place. Yet, her song inserts a different vibrant interpretive framing to the subjectivity of the sea in exodus storytelling. Instead of the sea-song functioning as a singular linear movement to the wilderness and conquest narratives, Miriam's song focuses on events around the sea as integrally vital, not simply transitional. In badass womanist mode and epistemology, Miriam's song stands in contrast to a conquest motif; it also introduces a parallel layer of interpretation that impacts the remainder of Exodus 15 and its relation to Wilderness life. Miriam's song and communal narrative commentary, consistent with her physical and rhetorical proximity to water, produces movement from water (Exod. 15:21) to another water (Exod. 15:27) and opens another vector of exodus interpretation and storytelling that is not about political rescue and conquest but about the transformation of an ecosystem that has endured abuse in the process of political struggle and ecological devastation. As her song unfolds, political transformation is connected to revitalized ecosystems in the form of springs and palm trees (Exod. 15:27).

Miriam compels the reader to look at the depths. Her song creates an environmental exodus vision in which rescue through and from rising waters ushers in legislative and statutory work to create healthy communities around clean waters and palm trees (Exod. 15:27). It is not just the human community that is rescued; it is the regenerative power of the earth itself that is cleansed and restored. This regenerative power begins with the divine instruction to Moses to plant a tree next

15. Thomas B. Dozeman, *God at War: Power in the Exodus Tradition* (Oxford: Oxford University Press, 1996), 154–55.

to the water. Moses used his staff to split the waters (Exod. 14:16); now he is inspired to cast a tree into the water to make it fit for drinking (Exod. 15:27). A revitalized ecology is critically important to Exodus interpretation.

THE GREENING OF MIRIAM IN THE WILDERNESS: NUMBERS 12

The narrative in Numbers 12 about Miriam's changed body is astonishing—it casts a different perception of Miriam as a prophetic leader than we have in the book of Exodus. Moses is said to have taken a Cushite woman as wife. For reasons that are unclear, Miriam and Aaron rebuke Moses (Num. 12:1).[16] Although God summons Miriam and Aaron, Miriam alone is bodily impacted: her skin becomes leprous. This bodily transformation is associated with an ecological event, as it occurs when the divine cloud rises from the tent. A striking feature of this story is that Yahweh vouches for Moses' authority because— unlike other prophets to whom Yahweh speaks through dreams and riddles—Yahweh speaks to Moses "mouth to mouth" (Num. 12:8). Yet, the dissimilar method of prophetic authority that distinguishes Moses is countered by the similarity in embodied experience around the prophetic call narratives of Moses and Miriam. Miriam's leprous body (Num. 12:10) recalls Moses' leprous body (Exod. 4:6) when Moses was unable to speak "face-to-face" with God in the bush (Exod. 4:10–12). What, then, is the basis of the distinction between Miriam and Moses? And why does the distinction necessitate separation from the community? As interpreters note, Miriam's separation is based on fear of pollution rather than medical contagion.[17] Moses and Miriam experience bodily eruption when they are placed in unnatural ecological spaces and coverings. For Moses, the transformation is a function of local covering, as he puts his hand in a cloak he is already wearing; for

---

16. Moshe Reis argues that Miriam and Aaron rebuked Moses because he abandoned his conjugal responsibilities to the Cushite woman. See Reis, "Miriam Rediscovered," *Jewish Bible Quarterly* 38, no. 3 (2010): 187. Wilda C. Gafney, *Womanist Midrash: A Reintroduction to the Women of the Torah and the Throne* (Louisville, KY: Westminster John Knox Press, 2017), 133, argues that Miriam's rebuke of Moses is over his abandonment of Zipporah (Exod. 18:2). Reading this story in the context of mixed marriages (interracial marriages in South Africa), Funlola Olojede argues that the otherwise reputable Miriam is portrayed as someone with a "dark side" who succumbs to racist stereotypes about a Cushite woman. See Olojede, "Miriam and Moses's Cushite Wife: Sisterhood in Jeopardy?" in *Feminist Frameworks and the Bible: Power, Ambiguity, and Intersectionality*, ed. L. Juliana Claassens and Carolyn J. Sharp (New York: Bloomsbury T&T Clark, 2017), 133–45.

17. Rees, *Voices*, 18.

144   LET MY PEOPLE LIVE

Miriam, the bodily transformation is a function of global covering, as she is enveloped by a (divine) cloud.

In the narrative transition from the ecological space (the burning bush) to the political space (Pharaoh's court), Moses experiences healing when he repeats the initial act of placing his hand in his garment (Exod. 4:6–7). In this Moses-Miriam intertextual analysis, Miriam's healing becomes noteworthy: it comes only after she is separated from a community defined exclusively around the Yahweh-Moses political discourse ("mouth to mouth"), even though there is recognition of other modes of knowledge (wisdom, riddles) within the community. That is, Miriam's separation is a function of the story's attempt to focus on its male, political dimensions to the exclusion of its ecological character.[18] Separating Miriam from the camp, for fear of polluting the sacred space, may address ritual concerns articulated in Leviticus (13–14). But the separation prevents the community from engaging the nature of divine presence in the clouds (and their waters). For, as it turns out, Miriam's separation—her alienation—also prevents the community from moving forward. As Gafney puts it, "The daughters and sons of Israel vote with their feet on the banishment of Miriam: they refuse to move them. Or they vote with their behinds: they sit on them."[19] Either way, the exodus community—as a body—is stuck because of the unhealthy gendered, eco-marginalizing political dimensions of the story.

Three experiences speak to triple consciousness that animates the story. First, Miriam is compared to a stillborn baby, eaten at birth. This speaks to the possibility (threat) of erasure (Num. 12:12). There is nothing wrong with the motherly womb that has produced Miriam; but there is something about her disfiguration that is primed on eating her substance and erasing her. Second, she is alienated from the community, placed outside for seven days, as if separated from the work of creation itself (Num. 12:14). The normal birthing process that puts the child outside the mother's body/womb is negatively analogized in a communal body that alienates her, marked by the father's saliva. Creation is undermined by alienation. And third, although she and Aaron critique Moses, she alone is punished, which speaks to the experience of oppressive singularity.

---

18. When Moses engaged the burning bush, he was overcome by fear and covered his face (Exod. 3:6); and when he was asked to engage the ground with his staff, the experience was traumatizing and caused him to flee (Exod. 4:3).

19. Gafney, *Womanist Midrash*, 134.

Aaron and Moses request healing for Miriam. This request prompts the deity to invoke a hypothetical scenario of a parent spitting (*yaraq*) on Miriam's face: "But the LORD said to Moses, 'If her father had but spit in her face, would she not bear her shame for seven days? Let her be shut out of the camp for seven days, and after that she may be brought in again.'" (Num. 12:14). The story analogizes a cultural experience with an ecological experience, both of which converge around Miriam. The cultural analogy is clearly one of shaming. The expression—spit in the face of someone—is used only one other time in the Hebrew Bible (Deut. 25:9) in a hypothetical scenario where a widow spits in the face of her brother in-law who refuses to follow through with his levirate obligations to marry and bear children with her. As in Numbers 12, the expression does not stand alone in Deuteronomy; it is accompanied by a social act of dishonor representing the permanent loss of lineage. To spit on someone's face signifies the loss of honor, symbolically representing a foreclosed future.

The etymological meaning of *yaraq*, however, also includes becoming pale or green. The nominal *yereq* is used in Exod. 10:15 to describe the de-greening (the lack of *yaraq*) of trees in one of the plagues. The plague was so devastating that nothing green was left on any tree (cf. Lev. 13:49; 14:37). Elsewhere, the eco-political disaster that Isaiah sees in Moab (Isa. 15:6) includes desolate waters, withered grass, and no "green" (*yereq*). Like the plague in Egypt that deprived the trees of greenery, after locusts settled on them, the settling and rising of the cloud upon Miriam and Aaron leaves Miriam's body leprous. Miriam's body also represents the embodiment of the environment. According to Aaron, she not only faces death but is akin to newly formed life that is eaten up (Num. 12:12). The parental spitting on Miriam represents a form of socially distorted existence, of alienation. Yet, Aaron's words invoke creation, connected to the watery spaces of the womb and of endangered new life. Given the use of *yereq* to describe the ecological trauma associated with Exodus, might the spitting on Miriam constitute a form of Miriamic greening—Miriam's ability to regenerate ecological life where ecological death is prevalent? There is no plausible reason to continue the political journey toward the land of promise if the land's ability to regenerate is excluded from the community, or if the possibility of regeneration and future-blossoming is not available to the marginalized Miriam.

Yahweh's hypothetical scenario of a father spitting on someone's face also has cultural resonance with some African cultural practices

146   LET MY PEOPLE LIVE

of conferring blessing and protection on genealogical or socio-cultural kin. From the Maasai in east Africa to the Diola in west Africa, there are ceremonial events in which people use spittle as a sign of social interaction (greeting and departures) as well as rituals that create blessings and protections for children, or healing ceremonies.[20] Miriam's greening experience—which effectively separates her from the mouth-to-mouth communication deployed by Yahweh and Moses—places her outside of a community that is already oversaturated with anxieties about power that is constructed and deployed largely, if not exclusively, in anthropological and logocentric terms. But an Africana reading suggests that Miriam's greening is linked to ritual spittle as potentially healing. Miriam's engagement with the clouds and with watery substance (spittle) inserts epistemological, ecological, and hermeneutical vitality into the Wilderness narrative: she is placed outside of the community for seven days (Num. 12:15) as if to reenact divine creation space-time (cf. Gen. 1). During this week-long greening process, the community does not move; unlike with the political trajectory associated with Egypt where the depleted land has to be left behind and exited, here the community waits for the plagued land to heal (embodied by Miriam), to become green again and to regain its power and presence within the community. It is possible that this epistemological framework also undergirds Jesus's use of spittle to heal a blind man in a process that deploys the motif of humans as trees (Mark 8:22–24). Jesus takes the man out of the village, and upon healing and connecting him to trees, he sends the man back to his home.[21]

Miriam's greening experience also lends itself to eco-cultural analyses, migration, and renewal, including interlocution with the story of the Samaritan woman at the well. Both stories involve two women in liminal spaces where access to water provided by their parents/ancestors has also become rupturing and unfulfilling. Both stories make allusions to marriage or reproduction, or memories of such, but their narrative function lends interpretive space for communal identity beyond human regeneration; they speak to sustainable cultural and spiritual renewal.[22] In her reading of the story of the Samaritan woman, Mitzi Smith argues that the New Testament narrative—one that is similar to the narrative

---

20. A. H. Godbey, "Ceremonial Spitting," *The Monist* 24, no. 1 (1914): 67–91.

21. Elsewhere in the Gospel of John, Jesus uses spittle and mud to heal a blind man. See Daniel Frayer-Griggs, "Spittle, Clay and Creation in John 9:6 and Some Dead Sea Scrolls," *Journal of Biblical Literature* 132, no. 3 (2013): 659–70.

22. In both stories, there is mention of marriage scenarios: the Samaritan woman had been married before and talked about her marriages; and Moses had married a Cushite woman.

encounter between Yahweh and Miriam—conjures concepts of hospitality and mutuality under duress.

> Jesus' offer of living water to the Samaritan woman with whom he shares the experience of colonization under the Roman Empire signifies a point of convergence and correspondence for colonized peoples who can have access to water, living water, independent of their colonizers. . . . Within this global framework living water is more than a spiritual reality, but becomes a material and human right as well based on its significance for life.[23]

Embodying a dry and presumably thirsty body needing renewal, Jesus asks the woman for water and then promises to provide her with living water, even though he could not access the deep well without a bucket. The Gospel writer John puts Jesus next to the woman (who could access the cultural and material depths of the well) and thus creates a narrative space where retrieved water would come to do more than relieve temporary needs. The Samaritan woman demands life-giving water—water that, although sourced in her deep cultural and environmental tradition, is now difficult to access or highly contested, in part because it has been dried up or polluted in the ethnocentric geopolitics of imperial power and fragmented communities—Jews and Samaritans. The Samaritan woman identifies the well as a material gift from Jacob, "our ancestor" (John 4:12). And yet, in the context of imperial domination, the rich common ancestry came under duress and became scarce. Her demand functions to re-cast the narrative about water in routine social and environmental terms: "so that I may never be thirsty or have to keep coming here to draw water." (4:15). The deep and drying well produces routinized ecological migrants and migration, a reality that the Samaritan woman wants to permanently reverse.

Water as flow, as movement, across cultural and ritual spaces is conjoined with water as depth of intercultural and earthly belonging. It is to this deep transformation of the politics and ecology of exodus that Miriam's greening attests. The community's future depends on its ability to integrate greening Miriam back into its presence as leader, as poet, as prophet, as strategist, as afroecologist. This includes resisting the privileged modes of knowledge production that the story seems to reserve for Moses alone in "mouth-to-mouth"

---

23. Mitsi J. Smith, *Womanist Sass and Talk Back: Social (In)Justice, Intersectionality, and Biblical Interpretation* (Eugene, OR: Cascade Books, 2018), 16.

148   LET MY PEOPLE LIVE

interactions with Yahweh. That singularized mode of communal formation and existence excludes (marginalizes) Miriam, but the story portrays such a community as functionally and essentially stuck—unable to move forward. Beyond more inclusive epistemologies, the story also suggests that political liberation without ecological regeneration is bound to be futureless. The threat to exodus existence and flourishing is intersectional—political, cultural, gendered, human, and ecological.

THE DEATH OF MIRIAM: THE DANGERS OF AN ERASED EXODUS FUTURE

Kadesh is an important location in the Exodus story. It is the site from where the Israelites begin to transition from imagining the promised land to encountering the land as subject. Moses sends spies to explore the strength of the people in the land, their numbers, the quality of the land (whether it is "good or bad"), whether it is fortified or not, whether it is rich or poor, and whether there are trees in it or not. All of the political, economic, and moral information gathered in this spy-encounter with the land returns in the form of fruit from trees in the land (Num. 13:17–20). Even though there is no dispute about the quality of the fruit from the land, there is major debate about how to interpret such secretly gotten indigenous knowledge/evidence and its utility in formulating a politic of land: Does the land devour its inhabitants, or are its inhabitants powerful beyond subjugation (Num. 13:25–33)? Appraisal of the land's indigenous knowledge and character (whether it can be dominated and its people exterminated) intersects with environmental constructions: the land that flows with milk and honey, and has good fruit, is also now a land that devours its inhabitants. The political narrative of domination and extraction is at odds with the land's environmental evidence and its capacity to produce abundantly. That oddity triggers communal rebellion, followed by a threat from Yahweh to destroy the people, and then intercession by Moses on their behalf. The ultimate response to the political and narrative crisis is to turn to the pathway (*derek*) of the Red Sea (Num. 14:25). The crisis of political discourse ultimately finds its resolution in a path toward the sea/water.

Kadesh is also the site where Miriam dies and is buried (Num. 20:1). This is no ordinary death narrative. The water-woman has died, and with that death comes communal distress about water. The community's distress from lack of water intersects with lack of greenery and fruit: no grains or figs or vines or pomegranates (Num. 20:5). The death of Miriam, the oral historian and conjurer of exodus water, has narrative and environmental implications. Although Moses carries out his duties as a prophet and intercessor, deploying both his staff and the assistance of Aaron in a double effort to produce water from rocks, it is here, for the first time and upon Miriam's death, that Moses' future presence in the land of promise is jeopardized. This is where Moses begins to be written out of Exodus' narrative and environmental future. Miriam's death means more than the death of a prophet and narrative strategist; it also means the death of a future. It signals and represents the inability of the political story to secure a future without the ecological story. The memory of post-Miriam Kadesh is that of a community without water, without trees, and, therefore, without a future.

Kadesh produces three crises, each of which point back to the Red Sea community. First, Kadesh represents the crisis of a political future at odds with the ecological evidence. Although the political narrative can secretly glean indigenous information from the land of promise, that information sits at odds with the story's political motif of conquest. That crisis compels the community to seek a path toward the Red Sea (Num. 14:25)—the site where conquest ideologies die/sink. A second crisis revolves around the death of Miriam, the water-woman (Exod. 20:1). The lack of water (the dryness) in the community—the lack of ecological future—that results from her death immediately puts the Kadesh community in an experiential mode of "quarrel," the same mode of communal subjectivity that defined the Red Sea wilderness community (Exod. 15:24). Third, right after Miriam dies in Kadesh (Num. 20:1–13), the community arrives in Meribah, where they argue or quarrel about water. Moses' attempt to draw water from rocks is only partially successful: it provides temporary nourishment but handicaps Moses' ability to lead the people into the land that was promised. Through a communal ritual about discerning generative leadership, Yahweh quells political rebellion against the concentration of powers in Moses (Num. 16:14–17:12; [Masoretic Text: 17:6–21]). This imagery casts back to the Red Sea community in Exodus 15 watching Moses plant a tree beside the water (woman) in an act of communal revitalization.

The Kadesh community's shared pathos with the Red Sea community is a communal response to the death of Miriam, but it is also an attempt to conjure her presence through their vocal complaints about

150   LET MY PEOPLE LIVE

the ecological crisis. In their tears and burial ceremonies, they return to the metaphorical deep pathway of the Red Sea, where we find Miriam and her song.

A POETICS OF EXODUS ENVIRONMENTS: EXODUS 15:20–27

Miriam's song about Israel's survival at the Red Sea (Exod. 15:20–21), the ecological initiatives that follow (Exod. 15:22–25a, 27), and the divine statute and ordinance (Exod. 15:25b–26) constitute intersecting themes of community formation and communal revitalization around water in Exodus 15. Given Israel's traumatic encounters with water and/or the lack thereof, Miriam's song materially and vocally places her again at a critical juncture of community survival and regeneration. Whereas Miriam summoned only one of the Hebrew women and the Egyptian princess to transform Moses' traumatic encounter with water into a story of rescue and nourishment in Exodus 2, here she summons "all the women" (Exod. 15:20) to articulate the nature of this post-water scene. The story of exodus around water expands here into that of an entire community of women who follow in Miriam's footsteps—women who provide epistemological and lyrical form and texture not just to communal life beyond water, but to life with water. Miriam, it seems, has decided to face the persistent threats and traumas associated with water and to turn that trauma around. Like Moses, she also conceives the destruction of political infrastructure as a drowning in the waters (Exod. 15:21). Even as the text separates the Exodus survival story from the sphere of political governance (by removing Pharaoh from the scene), it gradually anchors the migrant's future in environmental activity and then conditions that work of eco-political life-making in the form of statutes. Miriam's song (Exod. 15:20–21) and its statutory and ecological commentary (Exod. 15:22–27) moves through experiences and expressions of erasure survived; it encounters the withering dryness of the wilderness; and it engages in developing statutes and judgments about the pathways of destruction and of healing, intimately related to the environmental act of casting (perhaps planting) a tree in/by the water, to make it sweet and drinkable. The text ends with a community camped by oases and palm trees. To borrow a phrase from Walker-Jones, Exodus 15:20–27 is Miriam's green song: an ecological reading/narration of Exodus that actually produces a people and a land that is healthy.[24]

---

24. Arthur Walker-Jones, *The Green Psalter: Resources for an Ecological Spirituality* (Minneapolis: Fortress Press, 2009), 24.

MIRIAM

A Community by the Waterside:
Resisting Exile as Permanent Erasure

This movement, communally performed under Miriam's leadership, includes an opening celebration and dance that is sequentially linked to the demise of a ruthless horse and rider cast into the sea. The nation-forming staff that Moses wielded was used to divide Pharaoh's colonial waters and direct the community from water to land (Exod. 14:16). Yet the journey toward the Wilderness (the journey "by the roundabout way of the wilderness," Exod. 13:18) puts the Wilderness in interpretive and material proximity to the Red Sea, as well as in proximity to the ideologies and political infrastructure of erasure associated with the Red Sea. While Moses uses his staff to structure communal movement from water to land (Exod. 15:19)—a move that politically frees the oppressed but leaves them economically and ecologically dry, a movement that seeks to depart permanently from the traumas of colonizing waters—under Miriam's prophetic and sisterly redirect, the narrative and communal movement is from water (Exod. 15:21), to lack of water (Exod. 15:22), to bitter water (Exod. 15:23), to sweet water (Exod. 15:24), and finally to residence beside the water (Exod.15:27). With Miriam's song, it is not just the people who are being transformed; the devastated environment is being transformed and regenerated. The staff-controlling deity gives Moses a vision of a tree ('ēṣ) that he must place next to/in the water (Exod. 15:25). Moses must stand next to the water-woman, next to Miriam's ecowomanist and afroecological ethos and construction of communal identity that moves the story from death-saturated colonial water to life-producing water. The trauma around the Red Sea is no longer the sole defining factor; instead, the subjectivity of the water, under Miriam's redirect, becomes part of the narrative flow of the community itself, which travels alongside traumatizing water, then no water, then bitter water, then sweet water, and finally camps around oases of water. Exile is not unmade; rather, it is transformed into exodus.

Humans Are Like Trees: Resisting the Fragility of Alienation

In her embodied prophetic, sisterly, ecowomanist, and afroecological work, Miriam provides an opportunity for Moses to see in new ways. The first time Moses cried in the water (Exod. 2:6), Miriam occasioned his rescue from the water. In this communally engendered song, trail blazed by Miriam and all the women after her, the entire exodus community and Moses are again in the depths of water troubles. The people grumble and Moses cries (Exod. 15:24–25a). Here, Miriam does not attempt to move Moses and the people into a political space; rather, her communal song creates the occasion for Moses to have a new vision from God, which moves him to plant/place a tree beside the water and transform it into sweet water (Exod. 15:25b). At a narrative juncture where the community is increasingly alienated from its ecosystem, Miriam's song engenders human and ecological transformation. Moses and the people are more intimately connected to the land, which no longer functions exclusively as a place of exilic distress and bitter oppressive memory. The dancing water-woman of Exodus 15:20 rewrites the departure from the edge of the Red Sea, reframing it not as departure from water to dryness or even to utopian land flowing with milk and honey. Instead of such movement, Miriam expands water-to-land movement into a water-to-water movement that gradually introduces human and ecological healing into the expanding narrative. This eco-sensitivity and praxis in Miriam's song and narration is evidenced by the palm trees and oases at the end. The water is no longer the symbol of alienation (lament, bitterness, drowning, exposure) but the source of renewal where the community encamps (Exod. 15:27).

The Multiplying One: Resisting Singularity

In the adoption narrative that moves Moses from water to the house of Pharaoh, Miriam's initiative works to transform the political institution. Here the song that she initiates includes a following of all the women and draws in divine action to fashion statutes and ordinances that represent divine power not primarily in its ability to create diseases or rescue a select few from a plagued ecosystems but in its ability to heal the entire community (Exod. 15:25b–26). This is a communal song; it decenters Moses as a single hero and—like the adoption story—portrays him as the product of the community. In Exodus 2, Miriam was the sister who secured the survival of her Levite brother. In Exodus 15, she is still the sister (of Aaron), but she also deploys her role as a prophet and a poet to mobilize the entire community. Here it is not "one of the Hebrew women" that is mobilized but all the women. This is womanism in action—a push to ensure that exodus is a communal achievement, not the privilege of a few.

CONCLUSION

Miriam's name and narrative character represent three distinct but intersecting transformations in the narrative in Exodus. First, she represents and embodies the eco-political transformation of alienation. When she criticizes Moses and is politically alienated from the community, that alienation intersects with the community's ecological alienation from a divine cloud. But she turns that shame and alienation into a greening moment and a future, without which the community cannot move forward. Second, she represents and embodies the transformation of erasure. When she dies at Kadesh, prompting a communal lack of water, the community is forced to return to the Red Sea, where she leads them to face the trauma of loss around the water but also to the gradual transition (flow) from no water to bitter water to sweet water and to residence around water. Life has once again infused the place of death as the people follow where the water woman once led them. And third, she represents and embodies the manifestation of communal identity over and against single-hero narration. She represents more than prophetic authority; she is also a poet and community activist/leader. Her ability to mobilize the entire community around the Red Sea inspires Moses in new ways and sets the stage for understanding the divine statutes and ordinances as mechanisms of communal health and wellness.

6

Facing and Backsiding the Mountain

INTRODUCTION: NARRATIVIZING THE MOUNTAIN

In the biblical narrative, Israel's liberation occurs over the course of little more than a generation or two. The generation that initiates liberation does not live long enough to see its hopes of a free people fully take shape. With the exception of a few leaders, the story leaves its subjects in the Wilderness and/or the Mountain, not the land of promise. It is an odd ending to a story with so much promise, and it signals that ancient Israel never fully experienced sustained freedom from the prying eyes and manipulative policies of imperial regimes. Yet the story is more than a blip on the historiographical narrative it charts. The narrated time exceeds multiple generations (Exod. 12:40–41), the narrated demographic embodies a mixed multitude (Exod. 12:28), and the narrated spirituality aligns ancestral theologies with new ones (Exod. 3:13–16; 20:3–4).

There is something worth analyzing about the Mountain—the place where the narrative ends in the book of Exodus. The exodus community gathers around tents (Exod. 33:7; cf. Lev. 23:42–43; Num. 9:21)—like satellite states—around the Mountain, as if to evoke the image of postcolonial nation states orbiting and negotiating enduring colonial and imperial structures. In exodus imagination, the Mountain is apparently reputable for exacting long-term demands on those it encounters (cf. Deut. 1:6). As evident in Jethro's question to his daughters, early

155

156   LET MY PEOPLE LIVE

return from the mountainside is unexpected: "How is it that you have
come back so soon today"? (Exod. 2:18). The Mountain, read through
an African (Cameroonian) postcolonial lens, is not the site of exodus
imagination or origin; it is preeminently the colonial and imperial
structure that needs exodus redesign work. God summons the community to the Mountain, not to entrench an ethos of Mountainous
invincibility, but as evidence/sign (Heb. 'ôt) of divine involvement in
that ongoing redesign work (Exod. 3:12). This ongoing work is critical to ensuring that the story does not transition into one of imperial
domination. Thus, although mountainside gathering is the place and
time where a liberated people is taken, that journey to the mountain is
also—for Africana—a long interpretive trail to transform the Mountain. That work begins with the Hebrew women, the midwives, and
the princess in Egypt; then it is vigorously pursued by Miriam in the
Wilderness; and finally meets Zipporah's narration in the wilderness-
mountain areas (cf. Exod. 2:16–22). Through Zipporah, Moses the
Egyptian—the man associated with Egyptian royalty—is transformed
into an agent of liberation, not because he is adopted into the royal
family but because his encounter with God in the Mountain compels
him to ally with marginalized communities.

In *God on the Mountain*, Thomas Dozeman sets out the premise
that the interweaving of biblical narrative in Exodus 19–34 as well as
the priestly material in Exodus 35–Numbers 10 constitutes part of
"the Sinai Complex," which is rooted primarily in law yet derived from
a central event at Sinai, namely, the divine revelation of God on the
mountain in Exodus 19–24. The narrative is "structured in a vertical
hierarchy" with the deity located at the top of the mountain while the
people camp at the bottom.[1] It is a narrative complex that gives reason
and meaning to the role of the mountain in shaping the political, religious, and geographical life of ancient Israel. For a community whose
quintessential story of liberation is about rising up against oppression
and structural inequity, the location of the exodus community at the
bottom of a mountainous structure of legislative, ritual, and political
process is anxiety-ridden. Will the story of liberation be suppressed and
permanently pushed underground?

It is significant that Israel's association with the Mountain is marked
by arrival (*bāʾāh*) and departure (*ʿālāh*) for the land of promise (Exod.

---

1. Thomas B. Dozeman, *God on the Mountain: A Study of Redaction, Theology, and Canon in Exodus 19–24*, SBL
Monograph Series 37 (Atlanta: Scholars Press, 1989), 2, 19–35. Dozeman attributes this understanding of the
mountain to pre-deuteronomic tradition

19:1; 33:1), both movements echoing arrival (*bā'āh*) and departure (*'ālāh*) from Egypt (Exod. 1:1; 12:38). Conceptually, the community's association with the Mountain echoes their presence and departure from Egypt. Arrival at Sinai initiates Yahweh's adoption narrative (Exod. 19), followed by laws and statutes (Exod. 20–24) that anchor the covenantal adoption and an embodied ritual creation of that relationship (Exod. 32). It is in the Mountain that the liberated community ultimately confronts the reality that liberation through migration does not fundamentally address the structural forms of oppression; the migratory model is only good for one or two generations.

For the African postcolony—in a parallel to ancient Israel's history around cycles of imperial domination—the work of liberation must have value beyond the delight of the primary generation. When faced with a Mountainous threat to its liberation work, the exodus community does not abandon its work of exodus redesign. Instead, the same community recreates its identity and social relations through constructions of new legal structures (stone tablets), new residential practices (a tabernacle), and the coordination of an exodus itinerary with a mobile divine tent (Exod. 34–40). These mountainside events frame the beginning and end of Moses' persona in exodus narration (Exod. 2–3 and Deut. 33–34). More importantly, these events represent Israel's ongoing theorizing about the Mountain it faces, and the resulting attempts to bring liberation to such Mountains. The worlds of religion, politics, culture, art, legislation, and ecology are mobilized in this expansive work to imagine, create, and sustain new worlds that carry the memories and identities of the past but also represent innovation, blessing, and hope for the future. Henceforth, the Mountain—much like Egypt and the Wilderness—is not just the place where new exodus imagination begins/originates; instead, the Mountain is the structure to which exodus is brought. At stake, for the African postcolony, is how liberation is achievable in a sustained manner in the face, and on the back, of oppression that exceeds the boundaries of colonial and postcolonial nation-states.

AFRICANA FRAMING OF THE MOUNTAIN

In *Out of the Dark Night* Achille Mbembe theorizes Afropolitanism as a conceptual framework for understanding the historical, political, and intellectual trajectories that have informed Africana critiques of

158 LET MY PEOPLE LIVE

colonialism over a century, including anticolonial nationalisms, capitalist and cultural analyses of African communitarianism, and Pan-African alliances across race and nation. Afropolitanism, however, is also a nomenclature—not of what Africa has been but of what it is going to become, given its embodiment of multiplicities and pluralities:

> A name has been found for this *African-world-to-come*, whose complex and mobile fabric slips constantly out of one form and into another and turns away all languages and sonorities because it is no longer attached to any language or pure sound, this body in motion, never in its place, whose center moves everywhere, this body moving in the enormous machine of the world: that name is Afropolitanism.[2]

What constitutes some of the recognizable features of this "complex and mobile fabric" that continues to create world altering shifts in identity, belonging, and community? For one thing, the unfinished fabric of the work of liberation, justice, multiplicity, and hospitality is forged as much through decolonial work inside the gruesome shops and rituals of colonialism and racism and patriarchy as in constructive planetary work on the reverse side of racism, patriarchy, colonialism, and imperialism.

The "complex mobile fabric" of Afropolitanism continues to unfold in ways that signify the unending work of liberation—its methodological parameters, its political character, its forms of community building, its commitments and impetus to transgress colonial and postcolonial boundaries, etc. In his analyses of the political crisis about Anglophone identity and freedoms in Cameroon, David Ngong provides nomenclature and taxonomy for the challenge facing several African countries where marginalized communities within postcolonial nation-states break off to create or advocate independent states. Ngong names this phenomenon, "post-nationalist nationalism":

> [P]ost-nationalist nationalism describes the moment of the fraying of post-independence nationalism in many African countries. It is characterized by movements aimed at creating new states from the ashes of old ones. Disappointed with the trajectory of the state in postcolonial Africa, marginalized groups in many African countries have attempted to create, and in some cases succeeded in creating,

---

2. Achille Mbembe, *Out of the Dark Night: Essays on Decolonization* (New York: Columbia University Press, 2021), 6, emphasis in original.

new states. This includes the emergence of states such as Somaliland from Somalia, Eritrea from Ethiopia (even though Ethiopia was not formally colonized), and South Sudan from Sudan. Post-nationalist nationalism describes a new moment of nationalism that arises from factions that seek to establish their independence from already independent states, such as the case of the Oromo of Ethiopia and the Anglophones of Cameroon. Post-nationalist nationalism seeks independent nation-states not from European colonialists but from what is seen as dominant or oppressive groups within sovereign, post-colonial African states. Contemporary African political theologies have hardly addressed this new nationalism that is often born out of dynamics of marginalization. This new nationalism bears a tenuous connection to the nationalism of the anti-colonial struggle that dominated African politics and political theologies during and immediately after independence.[3]

This kind of contiguous liberation work stretching from anticolonial to postcolonial sensibilities signifies that "nation-states are not themselves seen as liberatory in liberation theology,"[4] although they represent a particular form of political achievement for anticolonial movements. As political, cultural, geographical, and economic embodiments of anticolonial movements, independent African nation-states were and are, in a pan-Africanist view, supposed to forge "new interdependent states" rather than separation and autonomy.[5] Why then the movements toward breakaway states? The reality of post-nationalist nationalism—evident in movements that have fueled breakaway states in postcolonial Africa and fueled violent insurrections and eruptions of white nationalism in the United States—warrants critical analyses of the methods of liberation and forms of institutional embodiment of liberation. Is liberation best embodied in radical transformation of the infrastructure of the nation-state or empire, or in the embodiment of the breakaway faction (nation)? Post-nationalist nationalisms are not simply reactions to the oppressive policies in nation-states; they may also represent a manifestation of totalizing and singularizing ideologies at the intersection of ethnocentric and imperial privilege. Accordingly, their emergence presses the issue of the "finality" of liberation work and its embodiments—political, theological, methodological, spatial, and gendered.

---

3. David Ngong, "African Political Theology and Post-Nationalist Nationalism: The Case of the Cameroon Anglophone Conflict," *Political Theology* 10 (2021): 2.
4. Ngong, "African," 8.
5. Ngong, "African," 11.

160   LET MY PEOPLE LIVE

The work of liberation continues beyond existing structures of colonialism, patriarchy, and imperialism. An emergent question unfolds: What happens when the mobile and mobilized Africana-Exodus body overcomes the infrastructure of colonial, racist, and patriarchal submersion, emerges from the bottom, only to face an ongoing highly incentivized, legalized, and ritualized imperial ideology of singularized supremacy, indulgence of erasure of the other, and permanent marginalization of its "satellite" states? This sort of interrogation, I suggest, can be seen taking place around the Sinai mountain narratives of Exodus. That is, I want to read exodus gathering in the Mountain as intended to redesign empire in the same way that exodus gathering in Egypt compels a redesign of the nation-state for incorporation of the *gershomite-ogbanje* other, and exodus gathering in the Wilderness compels a redesign of the earth for regenerative flourishing. Moses forges more than visions and laws on the mountaintop; he literally takes parts of the mountain back/down to the bottom, where the work of exodus redesign is unfolding. This motif continues into the New Testament, where Matthew's Jesus, just like Moses, scales the mountains for imagination but also motivates his followers to model Mountain redesign (Matt. 17:20; 21:21; cf. Exod. 15). That is, the mountainous narrative—and the journey to the mountain—represents persistent methodological and interpretive work to bring exodus to the Mountain of empire.

FACING THE MOUNTAIN

Yahweh guides Israel to an unnamed mountain linked with Sinai. In front of (Heb. *neged*) the mountain (Exod. 19:2), three modes of seeing unfold that are pertinent to the work of exodus. The first connects Yahweh's actions in Egypt to Israel's experience of aerodynamic movement: "You have seen what I did to the Egyptians and how I bore you on eagles' wings and brought you to myself" (Exod. 19:4). In the decisive moment of transition out of Egypt, Israel saw Egyptian dead bodies on the seashore (Exod. 14:30). Here, that survivor's view of history is attached to the flight of the eagle. This top-down view of exodus movement signals divine adoption as a form of detachment from the grounded realities of political struggle that give historical texture to Israel's identity. In the face of the Mountain, the political story of struggle is partially recast as a story in which humans can fly—escaping the burdens of violence that ravage entire populations. Unlike Moses, whose mountain-facing experience in Midian disabused him of perceiving exodus as escapism and prompted his return to the political story (Exod. 4:19, 21), this mountain facing community is invited to see how liberation—uncritically attached to the mountain—can create a new kind of identity, status, and privileges for a select few. The mountainside community will not only resist this form of exclusive privilege; they will attempt to bring exodus to the Mountain. In scaling its heights and navigating its imperious statue, Moses and the exodus community subject the Mountain to exodus narrative redesign, away from erasure and toward life. As the postexilic prophet Isaiah puts it, communal steadfast belonging can be forged as mountains crumble or as they are removed or displaced (Isa. 54:10); and mountains can be redesigned into places of communal songs of liberation (Isa. 55:12). Imperial erasure must be undone and its structure transformed.

A second seeing/facing of the Mountain unfolds around the legislative text of the first Book of the Covenant (Exod. 20:22–23:19) and its ongoing interpretive tradition (cf. Exod. 24:7). The mountain-facing formulation ("you have seen") used in Exod. 20:22 transforms Moses' privileged one-on-one encounter with the divine atop the mountain from a private to a public event. What does it mean for a community to witness mountaintop privilege, to examine its purpose and determine whether to internalize its logics? Yahweh forbids making gods of silver or gold (Exod. 20:23) but endorses making "an altar of earth ('ădāmāh)" on which to offer burnt offerings and wellness offerings (Exod. 20:24). The prohibition against golden gods anticipates the story of Exodus 32, to which we shall turn later. The prohibition also recalls the mixed multitude that left Egypt with gifts of silver and gold (Exod. 12:36), and it anticipates the building of the tabernacle where the use of precious objects, including gold, is a mark of inspiration (Exod. 35:20–29). In the face of the privilege-forging Mountain, the invitation to see survival around a singular altar for burnt offerings recalls the Akedah, when God summons Abraham to a Mountain where he builds an altar to offer Isaac as a burnt offering, after Ishmael has been sent off into the Wilderness (Gen. 22:1–19). Much like Abraham, the mountainside community faces the possibility of the multiplicity of exodus shriveling into one of exile and survival in singularized form. Moses and the mountainside community will need to resist singularized existence and the privilege of the Mountain.

The exodus community has—through its covenantal texts—learned to draw upon its lived experience of alienation in Egypt to forge social

162   LET MY PEOPLE LIVE

commitments that embrace the alien (Exod. 22:21; Lev. 19:34). But now, in the Mountain, a third form of seeing/facing emerges in the second Book of the Covenant and its interpretive focus on Moses' veiled and unveiled facial embodiments (34:11–36). In Exodus 34:11, which introduces this focus, Yahweh invites the people to see (*hinenî*) the expulsion/alienation (*garaš*) of local populations as Israel advances. This seeing/facing (*hinenî*, Exod. 34:11, 30) of Mountainous power at work causes fear among the Israelites and prevents proximity between Moses and the people (Exod. 34:30). The alienation producing divine empire has replaced the alienation producing pharaonic empire (Exod. 6:1; 11:1). Social alienation merges with geographical alienation, and, in the process, compels Moses to alternate between veiled and unveiled existence. The mountainside community must draw on its *gershomite* identity and epistemology to resist the alienation of populations and instead develop embodied social and interpretive fabrics to carry marginalized subjects into new futures of multiethnic and intergenerational constituents.

These three narrative modes of seeing/facing the Mountain provoke hermeneutical questions: What do liberation-seeking or recently (formerly) liberated communities do when they face imperial structures and logics that repurpose the communal story of liberation from one that produces value for many to one that secures privilege for a few? What must liberation workers do when their subjectivity—their life energy—is so attached to structures of oppression as to warrant permanent remembrance of the oppression and erasure that compelled exodus? Can the liberated subject and her liberation story share the same living spaces (political, ethnic, racial, national, gendered) with exile-inducing structures of empire, colonialism, and patriarchy without sharing imperial logics that create and incentivize the marginalization of populations?

RUPTURE AND REDESIGN IN THE MOUNTAIN AREA

In biblical narrative, the Mountain summons Moses several times before ultimately taking him permanently—it is up the Mountain that he sees the land he was seeking, reflects on how the land itself connected him to ancestors and the divine, and then dies and is buried in the plains of Moab. His grave is unmarked (Deut. 34:1, 4–6). This narrative about rupture around singular experience, alienation from community, and potential permanent loss/erasure remains a sore spot in biblical narration and theological reflection, prompting New Testament Gospel writers to attempt a recovery of missing bodies (Moses, Elijah, and potentially of Jesus) up the Mountain (Matt. 17:4; Luke 9:33; cf. Jude 1:9). Communal gathering in the mountain area requires and performs instant interlocution. Nothing seems fixed. Everything is in flux. That fluidity, set against the Mountain, is ironic, since the Mountain represents fixity and stability. If exodus work requires more than escape from Egypt, if it also suggests that Pharaoh is moveable— that his infrastructure can be cast into the sea—and that the Wilderness can be transformed, then is the Mountain also moveable? Can the Mountain be transformed?

Interlocution in the Golden Calf Story

Exodus 32 is one of the most enigmatic and intriguing passages in Exodus. Its capacity to create instant and highly consequential interlocution about its narrative purposes is unmatched in exodus saga. The making of the golden calf provokes bodily and interpretive gyrations that stretch from the bottom of the Mountain to the top. The event provokes a response—not just in compelling Moses' descent from the mountaintop, but also in re-signifying Exodus and its interpretive depth. Why does a people's exodus-type activity of transformation of communal marginalization (Exod. 32:1) into communal laughter/play (Heb. *ṣāḥaq*, Exod. 32:6; cf. Gen. 21:9) lead to their being portrayed as inflexible ("stiff-necked," Exod. 33:2) and mournful (Exod. 33:4–6)? How can a story about Moses' greatest achievement as a legislator—the bearer of divinely inscribed words (Exod. 32:15)—also threaten to be a story in which Moses asks to be written out of the story (Exod. 32:32)? Why is it that, having both heard the deity's explanation for the communal gathering, Moses and Joshua arrived at contradictory interpretations of the sounds coming from the camp (Exod. 32:18)? How can a story about a people's intentional creation of the calf and celebration of that accomplishment (Exod. 32:1, 6) also become a story about failed leadership that brings sin on the people (Exod. 32:21), and a story of the magical appearance of a calf out of the fires (Exod. 32:24)? Why does Moses successfully negotiate and secure the community's survival against the urges of imperial erasure (Exod. 32:11–14) and then supervise and bless ethnic genocide (Exod. 32:25–29)?

164   LET MY PEOPLE LIVE

There is near scholarly consensus that the story of the golden calf is
one of major crisis. In *Moses the Egyptian*, Jan Assmann writes, "The
primal scene of idolatry is the story of the Golden Calf."[6] Its original
writers may not have intended for the story to attain such a central role,
but that no longer matters in the history of reception of the story: "The
story of the Golden Calf has certainly achieved such status because it
forms the liturgical reading on the Day of Atonement. Can the wrath
of God once again be averted, the covenant continued, life go on for
another year? It is a question of life and death, to be or not to be,
and it is connected with Egyptian idolatry."[7] To build a golden calf,
then, would have been to participate in one of the most gruesome acts
of idolatry. Following this view, Avigdor Shinan and Yair Zakovitch
describe the story of the golden calf as "the worst of all the sins that the
Israelites commit in the wilderness."[8]

Yet, the story also speaks of the sin of leadership failure on the part of
Aaron; the sin is brought on the people, as opposed to being committed
by the people (Exod. 32:21). This sin of failed leadership resonates with
the building of the golden calves by Jeroboam as an act of the northern
kingdom of Israel's separation from the oppressive policies of Solomon
and Rehoboam (1 Kgs. 12:26–30) and the resulting condemnation of
that separation as a cardinal sin (2 Kgs. 17:16). Shinan and Zakovitch
rightly point out that this condemnation originates from, and seeks to
enhance, the southern kingdom and Jerusalem's temple: "Jeroboam was
reinstating an ancient tradition when he erected the calves. Wanting to
defame the northern kingdom, however, the Pentateuch fashioned the
tale of the calf in Exodus 32 as a story about the sin of idolatry."[9]

Carola Hilfrich has analyzed the golden calf story in ways that do not
understand idolatry as a religious-philosophical concept but as a matter
of "cultural sign praxis"—that is, the way we produce and use signs. For
Hilfrich, traditional Jewish discourse on idolatry is in fact a mode of cultural criticism manifested in reading as resistance to the structural function of writing, the reification of the sign.[10] Accordingly, the golden calf
story may function in two modes: from an official stance, it is idolatry,

---

6. Jan Assmann, *Moses the Egyptian: The Memory of Egypt in Western Monotheism* (Cambridge, MA: Harvard
University Press, 1997), 211. See also Jan Assmann, *The Price of Monotheism*, trans. Robert Savage (Stanford, CA:
Stanford University Press, 2010).

7. Assmann, *Moses*, 212.

8. Avidgor Shinan and Yair Zakovitch, *From Gods to God: How the Bible Debunked, Suppressed, or Changed
Ancient Myths and Legends*, trans. Valerie Zakovitch (Philadelphia: Jewish Publication Society, 2012), 101.

9. Shinan and Zakovitch, *From Gods to God*, 106.

10. Carola Hilfrich, "Making Writing Readable Again: Sign Praxis between the Discourse on Idolatry and Cultural Criticism," *The Journal of Religion* 85, no. 2 (2005): 268.

FACING AND BACKSIDING THE MOUNTAIN

departure from the norms of officialdom; but from the bottom, it represents "experimentality and the accommodation of cultural difference" in which the Hebrew people "express a need to accommodate culturally different aspects of their own experience rather than a collectively regressive desire to bow to idols and serve them. Concomitantly, their sign usage could then be seen to involve a popular critique vis-à-vis their leadership's understanding of their praxis as idolatry, which, to them, entirely misses the experimental point of their activity."[11] What might the Mountain have done—or come to represent—to provoke this political, cultural, and religious critique from the bottom?

Leon Kass has gone so far as to argue that, in the context of a newly freed people learning to self-govern, the idolatry of the story was not only inevitable, it was in fact necessary and even desirable—an opportunity for the people to "sin massively" because "a properly executed covenant between God and Israel requires an informed and free choice on behalf of the people. They must choose God as much as God has chosen them."[12] The narrative, ideological, and epistemological context and reality—the Mountain—of that interpretive choice is critical to assessing the story. The people's decision, much like Abraham's regarding Isaac (Gen. 22:1–19), like Zipporah's regarding Moses/Gershom (Exod. 4:24–26), and like Jesus's regarding God in the midst of satanic temptation to self-glorification (Matt. 4:8–10) takes place around the high demands of the Mountain. Like Abraham, the people must ultimately overcome the inclination to erasure associated with the Mountain as the place where Isaac's life is threatened to be taken; like Zipporah, they must overcome the Mountain's capacity to summon and retain people, effectively marginalizing them from community or erasing them. In the mysterious ritual of the foreskin, Zipporah fends off this power of death in the community (Exod. 4:24–26).

Exodus 32 is perhaps the origins story-motif of Mountainous rupture and redesign. First, the motif of an absent physical body—summoned to the mountaintop—creates anxiety and a responsive production of a communal body (Exod. 32:1–6). The removal of Moses from the scene is not the removal of the trope of exodus from community. Instead, removal signals anxiety about the Mountain's capacity—perhaps propensity—to permanently take bodies from the community. Removal puts the community at Africana's proverbial "door of no return"—the

---

11. Hilfrich, "Making," 274.
12. Leon R. Kass, *Founding God's Nation: Reading Exodus* (New Haven & London: Yale University Press, 2021), 533.

decisive moment and site of clash with colonialism, patriarchy, and empire, and the transformation of the captured/oppressed subject under colonial, patriarchal, and imperial domination. From a postcolonial perspective, this is not just a story about a missing individual; it is an episode about what it means to be placed at the bottom of imperial structures and ideologies. Moses' delayed return from that mountaintop *is read* as communal engagement with the unknown: "As for this Moses, the man who brought us up from Egypt, we do not know what has become of him" (Exod. 32:1, author's translation). This unknowability is epistemological and experiential dissonance from the political structure and authority that has summoned Moses (cf. Exod. 5:2). Will Exodus devolve permanently into a story of marginalization and exile as it faces the intransigence of imperialism? Will the postcolony forever exist as a satellite of the empire's structure? The threat of permanent material and epistemological alienation, occasioned from the mountaintop, compels a communal response to redesign the communal future of the postcolony: "Rise! Make gods for us who shall go before us." (Exod. 32:1, author's translation). To overcome the face of the empire, the community at the bottom, the community at the door of no return, begins to redesign its future through an act of material and interpretive rising—to forge conversations across the imperial door, or chasm, of no return. The alienating face of empire, which stands at the top of the Mountain, will be compelled to come down—in the return of Moses with the tablets—and be refaced into a communal mural of a mixed multitude of Exodus-exodus subjects.

A second form of rupture and redesign unfolds around the dangerous allure of toxic singularity at the mountain top—its threatening descent on the people in the form of a colonial and postcolonial strongman—and communal resistance through interpretive memory (Exod. 32:7–18). This passage puts toxic singularity on display. In Exodus 32:7, God tells Moses to go down because "your" (masc. sing.) people, whom "you" (masc. sing.) brought up from Egypt have been ruined (Heb. *šāḥat)*. That Mountainous gaze provokes another articulation of toxic singularity: "Now, let me alone so that my wrath may burn hot against them, and I may consume them; and of you (masc. sing.), I will make a great nation" (Exod. 32:10). Moses is drawn into singularizing discourse and responds to Yahweh about "your" wrath against "your" people, whom "you" brought from Egypt. As the story of exodus falters under the burden of imperial toxic singularity, Moses invokes the Mountain scene as the site where such toxicity is produced (Exod. 32:12) before imploring Yahweh

FACING AND BACKSIDING THE MOUNTAIN

to turn/repent (Heb. *šûb*) from such toxic singularity that threatens to erase multiplicity and undo the work of exodus. In contrast to Mountaintop singularizing ideology, the community at the bottom is portrayed as plural, enacting plurality and connecting multiplicity to oneness (not to singularity). The community turns quickly from singularizing commands and makes a calf "for themselves" and proclaims, "these are your (masc. sing.) gods, Israel, who (masc. plu.) brought you (masc. sing.) from Egypt" (Exod. 32:8). This linguistic and epistemological struggle between singularity and community, signaled by the combination of singular and plural pronouns, provokes the anger of singularizing imperial power, who threatens to erase an entire generation and begin anew with Moses. Moses rejects the singularizing allure and impulse of imperial privilege and summons non-singular narration to redesign the mountainous space (Exod. 32:11–13).

Third, rupture unfolds around the erasure of ritual bodies and the emergence of a textual body that codifies the erasure of names from the otherwise expanding book of life (Exod. 32:19–35). The extermination of members of the community stands as a major narrative and embodied form of erasure. The fact that Moses blesses those who carry out the violence is a real moment of failure on his part, especially since he had resisted the divine incentive to erase the exodus generation and begin anew. In addition to the loss of human life, there is a loss of narrative. When Moses' laws are broken and Aaron's calf is burnt/melted, the fractured pieces are placed in the water, which the people drink (Exod. 32:20). In this political, ritual, and environmental experience of erasure, the liberated and liberation-seeking exodus/exile community internalizes and carries its deity, its laws, its rituals, and its story inside its communal body, much like the exilic prophet, Ezekiel, consumed the divine scroll (Ezek. 3:3) and Jeremiah felt the burning of the divine word in his heart, inside his bones (Jer. 20:9). Survival around the mountain area is as urgent and as hermeneutically significant as survival was in Egypt. The community must again redesign its future against erasure—physical erasure and erasure from narrative. That work begins with Moses' second act of producing the tablets and laws (Exod. 34).

Further Interlocution

The story of the golden calf is retold in Deuteronomy 9 and Psalm 106. In Deuteronomy, the people are blamed for building the golden calf. Moses intercedes for them, a process that takes as much time as Moses needed to receive the stone tablets: forty days and forty nights without food or drink (Deut. 9:18). Moses' physical body—unnourished, gripped with fear, and prostrated (fallen) before the Lord—is also the body that secures communal survival. Furthermore, unlike in the book of Exodus, after Moses burns and crushes the calf into dust, he does not compel the people to drink it; instead, he throws the dust "into the stream that runs down the mountain" (Deut. 9:21). The trauma and the residue of legislative and cultural death is related to the ecosystem where the people reside. The community no longer reads only the stone tablets in order to survive; it also reads Moses' famished, anxious, and prostrating body, along with the flow of its fractured ecosystem. It is the voice of this prostrating body/fragmented land—along with ancestral memories—that Moses channels to secure the people's future (Deut. 9:27–28). The Mountain is an exacting place. To face it is to contemplate and work for legislative goals (including the Ten Commandments and the Books of the Covenant); but it is also to consider how mountaintop legislative "achievement" that is not subjected to the values of exodus life can in fact produce fragile, economically hard-hit communities and prostrating bodies. That exodus value is encapsulated in a compelling need to ensure that the liberated people are not erased from the earth (Deut. 9:28).

In Psalm 106:19–23, the calf story is one of a catalogue of unapproved actions by the Wilderness community, and the celebration of divine forgiveness.[13] Specifically, the calf episode is portrayed as an unacceptable transaction in which the people exchanged "their glory" (Heb. *kebôdām)* for the image of a grass-eating ox. Economic concerns seem to drive the needs of the community and its willingness to prioritize economic well-being over cultural identity ("their glory"). The undernourished community is forgetful of miraculous deliverance stories that do not account for their economic well-being. The psalmist is extremely critical of the production of the calf and, like Exodus 32, depicts a deity that is willing to destroy the people. Moses secures communal survival not by prostrating himself but by standing and turning away the destructive force (Ps. 106:23).

---

13. Gordon J. Wenham, "The Golden Calf in the Psalms," in *A God of Faithfulness: Essays in Honour of J. Gordon McConville on his 60th Birthday*, ed. Jamie A. Grant, Alison Lo, and Gordon J. Wenham (New York: T&T Clark, 2011), 170–75.

HERMENEUTICS ON THE BACKSIDE:
BONDED BEYOND LACUNAE

The narrative about the production of the calf occurs in Exodus 32:1–6. But Aaron's second level description of the process gestures back to mountainside polyphonic interlocution: "So I said to them, 'whoever has gold, take it off'; so they gave it to me and I threw it into the fire, and out came this calf!" (Exod. 32:24). The calf embodies and holds together torn off pieces of the communal body; it is a symbol of the cultural, economic, religious, and political investment of a people at the bottom of a mountain. That investment culminates with the emergence ("coming out") of the calf as the latest iteration of exodus (the verb *yāṣā'* used to describe the calf's emergence in Exodus 32:24 is the same word used for exodus from Egypt in 32:11).

Scholars note that the golden calf story stands in contrast with the story of the priestly material in Exodus 35–40. Both stories, involving Aaron and the priestly class, touch on the politics of exodus narratives, including the potential conflict between Aaron (who builds the calf) and the Levites (who kill idolaters and are blessed for it). James Watts rightly points out that, beside Deuteronomy 9, references to the golden calf story—including those references that chastise the Israelites for idolatry—do not criticize Aaron or impugn his character.[14] Watts argues that, from a rhetorical perspective, the calf story gives the tabernacle construction story a plotline of "creation (Exodus 25–31)/fall (Exodus 32–33)/restoration (Exodus 34–40)," and "the sense of satisfaction that these stories engender would be considerably lessened if they did not include the golden calf story."[15] The same analysis applies to the question of divine presence with the community in Exodus 33. Within the larger narrative arc of Exodus, Watts argues, the initial divine location outside of the camp (in contrast to the tabernacle at the center) functions as a temporary crisis. After Moses protests the divine withdrawal, he is allowed to see God's glory, in anticipation of Israel seeing the divine glory descend upon the tent (Exod. 40), which is elsewhere located in the middle of the camp (Num. 2–3).[16] Thus, although the golden calf episode contains references to sin and violence, within the larger narrative context, Aaron emerges as a heroic

---

14. James W. Watts, "Aaron and the Golden Calf in the Rhetoric of the Pentateuch," *Journal of Biblical Literature* 130, no. 3 (2011): 417–30.

15. Watts, "Aaron," 424.

16. Watts, "Aaron," 426.

character embraced by the Aaronide dynasty of the Second Temple period, in the same way that cultural heroes survive their moral flaws.[17] As the story of a community gathered at the bottom of the mountain, the golden calf story is central to ongoing liberation. The story depicts a community that is prepared to carry its story of liberation into the future, even as it struggles against marginalization, erasure, and oppressive singularization.

THE FUTURE OF THE PAST: BODY-CARRYING BODIES

Women with babies and baskets. Artist unknown. Photo courtesy of Aliou Niang.

It is an iconic picture—an African woman (perhaps a mother, surrogate mother, nanny, aunt, or elder sister) carrying a child on her back, supported by a sling or shawl. This social and cultural deployment of the mother's body is accompanied by—and indeed intended to convey—forms of routine and non-routine intellectual, mental, spiritual, and physical tasks. Portrayed as walking with a basket on her head, likely engaged in educational and entertaining conversations about generational and intergenerational community building, the image represents—in my opinion—an artistic form of motherly supremacy which,

17. Watts, "Aaron," 429–30.

in Chinua Achebe's *Things Fall Apart*, is developed and described as the time-space-body where communal bonding happens in the wake of erasure, diaspora, and isolation. The image also depicts the social and affective connective tissue—the shawl—that binds the mother-baby body in the productions of communal nurture, protection, discipline, and bonding. That is the lesson that Okonkwo, the protagonist of Achebe's novel, learns when he is exiled from his patriarchal village (when he is compelled to abandon patriarchy) and must return to motherland. This reality raises concerns about the impact that such baby-carrying has on the shape of the mother's body, but it also raises methodological interests: how she has to "carry" her own body in order to carry another.

The baby is tightly wrapped on the mother's back and securely fastened to mimic the movement of her body. It is a position of safety and security—regulated for body temperature, age of child, alignment between the two bodies, firmness of the grip, and purpose (veiling the body to keep it warm or from harm). It is one of the ways the adult body manipulates a fatigued or restless infant body and gets it to relax, to experience the rhythmic movement of the adult body, and perhaps to sleep. Whether asleep, partially awake, or fully awake, the child navigates the world through the rhythm of the mother's body. It is a position of affective subjectivity and epistemology. Detached from the land (or unable to navigate its terrain) yet attached to the mother's body (which navigates the land), the child can imagine and dream and see in different ways. Attached by a shawl to the moving body, the child is able to engage the rough terrains of geography, patriarchy, economics, and culture through the body and embodied movement of its mother. Participation in the future does not require individual abilities to see that future but rather the communal ability to carry bodies into that future.

In her study of the relation between baby carrying practices, music, and rhythm, Barbara Ayres speaks of "socially shared personality processes."[18] In navigating the mountain area with Israel, Yahweh participates in redesigning the Mountain: "And the Lord continued, 'see, there is a place by me where you shall stand on the rock; and while my glory passes by I will put you in a cleft on the rock, and I will cover you with my hand until I have passed by; then I will take away my hand and you shall see my back; but my face shall not be seen'"

---

18. Barbara Ayres, "Effects of Infant Carrying Practices on Rhythm in Music," *Ethos* 1, no. 4 (1973): 388.

(Exod. 33:21–23). The poetic character of the synchronized divine-human body is captured in these words: "You shall see my back, but my face shall not be seen." It is the space-time that engages the trailblazing divine and liberating body as also simultaneously a co-resident, or fellow migrant, navigating the fractured textual, geographical, and political terrains that must now be turned into residential places for the liberated body.

In the context and the wake of violence that has wrecked the postcolonial community, the future depends on the narrative capacity of the endangered body or postcolonial community to demand that its trailblazing mountaintop leaders be transformed into co-residents, not strongmen. As postcolonial and cultural hermeneutics have shown, the exodus narrative cannot—and does not—unfold without facing the *ambiveilence*[19] of its colonial and postcolonial weightiness: the weightiness of living and forging life in the shadow of powerful nations and empires, the weightiness of living and forging life in shadowy and fragmented places and texts, where endangered bodies emerging from the colony seek to become a community that is unlike the one they reject. The beckoning weightiness of futures to which Moses invites the divine ("show me your glory") is matched, regulated, and nurtured by the beckoning weightiness of memory (history) to which the divine invites Moses ("you will see my back"). The future cannot be developed as if the traumatic experiences of alienation, erasure, and singularity simply fade away. The people remember that they were aliens, and that memory helps them develop community bonds that transcend and redesign imperial uses and marginalization of indigenous places, times, and bodies. The people remember the violent forms of political and ecological oppression and erasure, and that memory compels them to resist imperial extraction and the erasure of their community's alternative life forms of knowledge and being. The people remember communal endeavors to secure their liberation, and that memory alerts them to the dangers of single-hero narratives.

Linking Objects in the Mountainside

The story of the golden calf ends with a series of troubling phenomena: the Lord strikes the people with a plague (Exod. 32:35)

---

19. The term is Shanell Smith's in *The Woman Babylon and the Marks of Empire: Reading Revelation with a Postcolonial Womanist Hermeneutic of Ambiveilence* (Minneapolis: Fortress Press, 2014).

FACING AND BACKSIDING THE MOUNTAIN

and then threatens to withdraw from the ongoing work of liberation (Exod. 33:3). The community's reaction is a process of mourning and cultural and aesthetic self-stripping (Exod. 33:4–6). In *Killing in the Name of Identity*, Vamik Volkan explores the process of mourning and associated complications, including depression or perennial mourning. Volkan develops the concept of "linking objects," which are "inanimate objects or living beings" that "symbolize the meeting ground between the mental image of what had been lost and the mourner's corresponding self-image."[20] A linking object allows the perennial mourner to externalize the process of mourning associated with loss; it detaches the mourner from the lost object/person and allows the mourner to "postpone the mourning process by giving the image of what was lost a new life in the linking object" and thereby "keeps hope alive for restarting and completing the mourning process at a future time."[21] Volkan then uses metaphors of the human and collective body, clothing, and tents to examine how physical, cultural, and social spaces are constructed, protected, and defended:

> We all wear, from childhood on, two layers of clothing. The first garment, which belongs just to the individual who is wearing it, fits snugly and represents personal identity. The second set of looser outer clothes is made from the fabric of the larger group's ethnic (or religious or ideological) tent. Each member of the group is cloaked by a piece of this same cloth, and it protects the person like a parent or other caregiver. The canvas of the tent thereby shelters thousands or millions of individuals under it as though it were a gigantic single piece, and represents the large-group identity.[22]

Volkan develops this notion of linking objects in his discussion on refugees, where issues of loss and displacement are central to identity formation and meaning-making. Large group identity formation in such camps assumes a shared "subjective sense of sameness" irrespective of whether the members of the camps personally know each other. The refugee camp becomes not just a spatial symbol of displacement but also the locus of new identity formation. A critical part of Volkan's work is his concept of "chosen trauma," which he defines as "a large group's mental representation of a historic

20. Vamik Volkan, *Killing in the Name of Identity: A Study of Bloody Conflicts* (Charlottesville, VA: Pitchstone Publishing, 2006), 53.
21. Volkan, *Killing*, 53.
22. Volkan, *Killing*, 69–70.

174   LET MY PEOPLE LIVE

event that resulted in collective feelings of helplessness, victimization, shame and humiliation at the hands of 'others,' and typically involves drastic losses of people, land, prestige, and dignity."[23] This mental representation, however, does not remain abstracted or disembodied; rather, it becomes a shared experience that is "deposited" in the next generation, in a process of transgenerational transmission: "members of the traumatized group deposit their injured selves, and internalized images of others who were hurt during the traumatic events, into the developing selves of children in the next generation."[24]

What is the political and religious work that linking objects do? The question is acute for a community gathered at the bottom of a mountain. Achille Mbembe's work on necropolitics highlights the fraught reality that colonial and postcolonial violence are linked not just by correlation but also by causation; and that the general instrumentalization of bodies and spaces in the service of political and religious rule connects the colonial potentate, the postcolonial autocrat, and the imperial sovereign. That is the quintessential reality of Africana exodus hermeneutics and the framework of its methodological priorities around redesign—the transformation of systems and structures of oppression into systems and structures of liberation. Because traumatizing realities manifest as a form of oppressive repetitive history that doesn't go away, the creative work of Africana redesign unfolds as undying repetition of the creative work of transformation. The mountainside is not just the site where liberated Israel arrives, it is also the site to which liberation comes. That is, for Africana, the mountain must be redesigned. That work unfolds through (1) repeated attention to the threat posed by mountainous symbols/figures that represent autocratic ideologies and praxis of erasing the 'other'; (2) repeated attention to legal precepts and structures that lack equitable distribution of value, especially for marginalized and oppressed subjects; and (3) repeated, meticulous attention to the construction of political and religious objects/spaces that enhance communal belonging. That narrative and epistemological work develops around the golden calf, stone tablets, and tabernacle-tent narratives, which function as linking objects.

23. Volkan, *Killing*, 173.
24. Volkan, *Killing*, 173.

CAN LIBERATION HAPPEN IN EGYPT
AND AT THE MOUNTAINSIDE?

Moses is introduced in Exodus as a child who survives in hiding underground, is placed in a basket in the Nile, and is recovered and placed in Pharaoh's house, from where he engages the Hebrews on such topics as political power, kinship identity, and justice (Exod. 2:1–15). Although he is forced into exile, he returns to confront the structure of oppression in Egypt. His return is prompted by divine attention to the voices of a marginalized people. The story presents exodus as a departure story. The impression is that liberation cannot happen in Egypt. In Exodus 32, something similar occurs. Moses is removed from the community stationed at the bottom of the mountain and taken to the top. Alerted by the divine to what is happening at the bottom, Moses returns to the community, not with spoken words but with written words about their fate and future. This time, though, the people already have a story and an experience of exodus, which they are determined not to lose. The Mountain threatens that story in specific ways: by its ability to create and incentivize singularity. The mountainous deity can erase the community and start all over with Moses—give Moses a nation (Exod. 32:10). Moses immediately resists the lure of imperial singularity. Moses and Yahweh—both connected to and distinct from the Mountain—know that such singularity is bound to be destructive. The allure of the mountain is powerful. The physical and hermeneutical descent from that singularizing space unfolds around Moses and Joshua, who represent distinct understandings of the communal uprising (Exod. 32:17–18). Is it uprising that produces violence and erasure (as Joshua assumes) or uprising that creates space for multiplicity and dance and song (as Moses assumes, perhaps in resonance with Miriam's communal song in Exod. 25:21)? The descent, however, is also textual. The scripted text in the form of tablets descends from the mountaintop, as if an imperial decree, with its precepts, instructions, and expectations to which all the people respond. That scripted text is attached to material from the Mountain (cf. Exod. 24:12), not from the people. It is as though the Mountain is claiming sole authorship of the story.

In contrast, exodus narrative redesign begins from below, at the bottom of the Mountain. The building of the calf represents that first act of narrative redesign. The object itself is an extension of the material space and possessions (e.g., garments and jewelry) and bodies of the exodus-generating community. This scene recalls the transition out of

176   LET MY PEOPLE LIVE

Egypt, when Yahweh made the Egyptians gracious toward the Israelites and give them materials for the unfolding new life of a mixed multitude of people (Exod. 12:36). What the people create and celebrate is the ability and need for exodus to produce multiplicity that counteracts the erasing singularity of the Mountain. The life and safety of the people precedes the imperial law. Before bringing the laws down, Moses summons a method of multiple narration to frame and redesign a future out of the singularizing mountain. Moses reminds Yahweh of a commitment to Israel's ancestors about creating a future through multiple descendants: "I will multiply your descendants like the stars of heaven" (Exod. 32:13). Moses appeals to Yahweh to turn from divine anger and from the inclination to destroy the people (Exod. 32:11). Killing marginalized people may be a pharaonic tactic of nation-building, or a political ideology embodied by the postcolonial strongman, or a moral attempt to justify imperial erasure of local epistemologies. But that tactic is neither inevitable nor necessary. So Moses poses the question that exposes the consequences of such thinking around the mountain area: "Why should the Egyptians say, 'it was with evil intent that he delivered them to kill them in the mountains and to wipe them from the face of the ground?'" (Exod. 32:12).

Leon Kass argues that Moses and Yahweh are both implicated in the fate of the people: both have long invested in delivering the people, both want to avoid the disgrace of a failed mission, and both are interested in keeping promises made to the people about their futures.[25] There is more to the story, though, than the reputation of its leading characters. The invocation of Egypt and the identification of the Mountain as the location of potential erasure is important. The story is attempting to answer a difficult and perennial question about redesign: Can liberation take place in/with Egypt—the kind of Egypt that the princess represented and that Zipporah narrativized (Exod. 2:5–10, 19)? If exodus is ultimately about redesigning oppressive systems, rather than fleeing them, then the insertion of an exodus motif into the Mountain space and ideology represents a transformation of systems and ideologies of oppression.

Moses has not only rejected the lure of exodus futures singularly tied to his name, he has also invoked multiple storytelling as hermeneutical and material guardrails against such toxic singularity. The last time that any Egyptians spoke about the Exodus story was around the Red Sea:

---

25. Kass, *Founding*, 539–40.

"The Egyptians said, 'let us flee from the Israelites, for the Lord is fighting for them against Egypt'" (Exod. 14:25). Although they could not completely avoid the loss of life resulting from a clash of singularizing powers, the Egyptians' discourse sought to withdraw from Pharaoh's pursuit of singularizing policies, which put him and his forces in conflict with Yahweh. Moses' words represent a similar movement toward communal discourse that decentralizes colonial and imperial power, whether that power is wielded by Pharaoh or by Yahweh.

In redesigning around the Mountain, singularizing liberation language ("*I* am the LORD who brought you out of Egypt") is transformed into pluralizing language ("*These* are your gods who brought you out of Egypt"). Because the story of Exodus—and such godly stories of human, geographical, and divine revelation and becoming "I AM/WILL BE WHO I AM/WILL BE" (Exod. 3:13)—can be coopted by and for imperial purposes, the task of the mountainside community is to ensure that its worship and festival around the oneness of God is not misidentified as loyalty to a singularizing deity, with a single story driven and shaped by a single hero, and locked in an endless battle over incentivized values of singularity. Exodus 32 raises the stakes for such exodus narrative work. What happens if Moses is taken by the mountain? What if Moses' ascent to the mountaintop turns him into an autocrat? Such probing provides an epistemological entry point into postcolonial subjectivity. Must the liberation story produce a postcolonial autocrat? And if it does, how ought the liberated and liberating community respond in godly fashion? Such re-examination and re-articulations become "golden calf" stories—stories of liberation that continuously emerge in response to the challenges of hierarchical mountaintop governance.

That value of resisting erasure, alienation, and singularity can be read as the gift of the divine-human-ecological community at the foundation of the story of Exodus, underlying all its narrative movements. That value is as necessary in the Mountain area as it was in Egypt. The story of liberation and the motif of liberation have trained Israel well. The only question is whether Israel's leadership—human and divine—will live up to the ideals set forth in the motif of exodus. The narrative of Exodus continues to garner relevance across multiple generations and across multiple landscapes because the story addresses, again and again, a perennial question about the need to respond creatively to the un/inhabitability of places of origins and their associated stories, the un/inhabitability of structures of governance and their alternatives, and the un/inhabitability of future places of residence and their

178   LET MY PEOPLE LIVE

expansiveness. If places and structures of origins are permanently lost and future places are already cognitively and materially inhabited or restricted or unavailable or coopted into imperial stories, exodus runs the risk of being perpetually trapped in a peculiar form of trauma—the haunting feeling and triple consciousness of an erased, marginalized, and singularized subject-community whose life is inescapably attached to austerity: past, present, and future.

For this reason, Israel's encampment at the Mountain of God occupies such an important epistemological and hermeneutical space in exodus storytelling, what Carol Meyers calls the "center of the Pentateuch."[26] It is here that a good portion of the structural work of exodus unfolds. As Terence Fretheim puts it, the mountainside encampment initiates new perspectives on legislation, ritual, and relationship for Israel and Yahweh, premised on "no more mountain hideaways; no more palace precincts."[27] The re/construction that defines much of the mountainside narratives (Exod. 19:1–Num.10:10) could be interpreted as a work of theorizing and structuring the narrative power of exodus—its ability to distribute and regularize notions of citizenship and belonging in the face of nation-state oppression, ecological devastation, and ongoing imperial ideologies. Narrative polyphony manifests itself as a form of intergenerational and interregional restructuring accompanied by a decentering of power and governing authority. Jethro's (called Reuel in Exod. 2:18) advice to Moses on mountainside restructuring was prescient: "the task is too heavy for you; you cannot do it alone" (Exod. 18:18). Such restructuring leads to communal survival and ultimate well-being/peace (Exod. 18:23).

CAN LIBERATION HAPPEN THROUGH/WITH THE LAW?

The crises in Exodus—the crises of erasure, marginalization, and singularity—begin around legislative deliberations, instructions and commands driven by Pharaoh and his counselors (Exod. 1:10, 15, 22). In reproducing exodus around the Mountain, the community is described as rising early, providing offerings, creating communal health/well-being, and then sitting to eat, drink, and laugh (Exod. 32:6). Meanwhile, at the top of the Mountain, Moses receives two tablets bearing

26. Carol Meyers, *Exodus* (Cambridge: Cambridge University Press, 2005), 142.
27. Terence E. Fretheim, "Because the Whole Earth Is Mine: Theme and Narrative in Exodus," *Interpretation* 50 (1996): 230–31.

FACING AND BACKSIDING THE MOUNTAIN 179

the written words of God. It is these writings that Moses breaks upon arriving at the camp at the bottom of the Mountain. Why are the mountaintop writings unable to survive communal life at the bottom? Can exodus be accomplished with mountaintop law?

Cheryl Anderson has demonstrated that the Book of the Covenant (Exod. 20–23) and the Deuteronomic Code (Deut. 12–26) show how the law assumed and constructed multiple identities: "One individual could be an Israelite (national identity), free (class identity), and the male head of a household (generational identity). Another individual suggested by the laws could be an Israelite (national identity), debt slave (class identity), and female (gender)."[28] Anderson's *Ancient Laws and Contemporary Controversies* illumines the importance of inclusive approaches to reading biblical laws. The goal of such approaches is to foreground what Anderson calls the "paradoxically marginalized majority"[29] world and realities that animate the biblical text and contemporary readers. In the mountain area, Israel—spatially and politically removed from the institution of slavery and its legal infrastructure—must theorize a new form of power relation that distinguishes the old law maker/master (Pharaoh) from the new one (Yahweh). If Exodus-exodus is to mean more than a change in governing personnel, the liberated community camped in front of the mountain must articulate the qualitative difference in pre- and post-liberation life.

To frame these analyses around the genre of covenantal apodictic and casuistic laws in ancient Israel and the larger ancient Mediterranean legal structures is to situate the mountainside community within the geopolitical and religious context of ancient imperialism. What might it mean to read these Covenantal and Deuteronomic laws in the face and back of the Mountain? Do the laws reflect and mimic imperial documents that (1) provide legal and moral coding to enshrined oppressive systems and (2) celebrate momentary and episodic rescues, even as structural inequities remain (Exod. 21:21)? Do the case laws reflect the creative work of an (oppressed) community and its attentiveness to the plight of the marginalized (cf. Exod. 22:9)? For Dennis Olson, the literary and thematic fractures within the law code suggest that

---

28. Cheryl B. Anderson, *Women, Ideology, and Violence: Critical Theory and the Construction of Gender in the Book of the Covenant and the Deuteronomic Law* (New York: T & T Clark International, 2004), 51.

29. Cheryl B. Anderson, *Ancient Laws and Contemporary Controversies: The Need for Inclusive Biblical Interpretation* (New York: Oxford University Press, 2009), 29.

the process of concrete ethical reflection tends always to be partial, provisional, and in need of being negotiated among conflicting and values. The Ten Commandments represent a polished and abstract set of norms. But the Book of the Covenant reminds us that the actualization of those norms within the community's life is a fluid and ongoing process of specific applications that are not to be frozen into moralistic absolutes.[30]

True. The afterlives of liberation—be they in the forms of national identities or culture or religion or gender or geography—require keen attention to the sorts of mirror-imaging that unfold in light of, but also in the shadow of, monumental historical ideologies and systems of power and privilege. In response to the imperial statutes that Moses is compelled to bring from above, but ultimately break in the camp, Moses will engage in the production of new tablets, only this time they are hewed by Moses to mirror-image the ones he broke (Exod. 34:1). After Moses literally carves out the two structures (tablets) on which the new (revised) laws are written, the content of the "commands" (Exod. 34:11) is preceded by a proclamation of the ethical and intergenerational structure through which the community sees and understands its existence: the merciful and gracious Lord is slow to anger and abounding in steadfast love, which reaches thousands of generations but also brings judgment to third and fourth generations (Exod. 34:6–7). Within the Pentateuch, there are other references to legislative endeavors that address the intergenerational impact of legislation (Exod. 20:5–6; Num. 14:18; Deut. 5:9–10). These formulations represent an attempt to address a structural discrepancy in legislative incentives. It is not just that the process of legislation is unfinalized; it is also that the two tablets (rewards and punishments) that structure legislation are designed to mimic, and respond to, the imperial structure—the imperial Mountain that Moses must climb again. Can good legislation respond effectively to the imperial structure and redesign the Mountain?

Moses meets Yahweh at the top ($r\bar{o}$'š) of the mountain. The Hebrew word can also be translated as "head" or "beginning." So the redesigned structure is brought to the very beginning of the empire's ideology. Legislation that enacts liberation is the kind of legislation that creates long-term, multigenerational value for marginalized communities to

---

30. Dennis T. Olson, "The Jagged Cliffs of Mount Sinai: A Theological Reading of the Book of the Covenant (Exod 20:22–23:19)," *Interpretation* 50, no. 3 (1996): 259.

match and/or exceed the empire's model. The imperial rush to anger in pursuit of erasing one generation and substituting it with another (Exod. 32:10) is replaced by a long-term approach that connects thousands of generations together on the ethical principle of being slow to anger and abounding in *ḥesed* (steadfast love, Exod. 34:6). To thus redesign the tablets of time is to understand legislation as a major tool of liberation work and its capacity to draw on the lived experience of marginalized communities for the purposes of replacing the incentive structures of empire and imperial ideology. Colonial and imperial damage is long term. Therefore, any credible response ought to be longer term in order to produce the political and cultural equity necessary to secure the well-being of entire generations. In response to these changing structures, Moses quickly bows to the ground and worships (Exod. 34:8), an embodied expression that recalls Yahweh's description of the people's activities during the making of the calf (Exod. 32:8). The marginalized body—both Moses' and that of the community at the bottom—redesigns the first/beginning of exodus work by inscribing value that precedes and exceeds the manifestations of imperial erasure.

The new stone tablets, reminiscent of the shattered ones, expand the covenantal relation between Yahweh and the mobile community and regulate their interactions with the settled community in the promised land. The ideology of the erasure of the inhabitants of the promised land is still strongly articulated in the story (Exod. 34:11–28). But that anti-indigenous law terrorizes the people at the bottom and disperses them as well, prompting Moses to reassemble the people (Exod. 34:30–31). The communal re-gathering around the commandments creates a cultural pattern/rhythm of veiling and unveiling Moses' face: that is, of simulating and embodying his constant interaction with familiar and unfamiliar spaces. In his constant back-and-forth movement between veiled and unveiled existence, Moses embodies and performs the memory of being an alien. This memory begins to find its place within the law—precisely, within the communal gathering around the law. In their interactions with Moses, the community is finding new ways not to eliminate one who has—upon his extended stay at the mountaintop—become like an alien. Discourse about the law is connected to its material effects on Moses' body and the communal body. A future for the mobile community is no longer fixed on a mandated extermination of others; rather that future is premised on self-determination through political, cultural, and religious revitalization held together by steadfast love—the premium command.

CAN LIBERATION HAPPEN IN THE RITUAL SPACE?

Along with its redesign of the story and the legislative infrastructure, the community facing the Mountain builds ritual spaces and enacts ritual ceremonies that simulate and resist the sacredness of the partially scalable mountain. Ritual space around the Mountain puts life and death in close proximity and theorizes modes of life lived in the wake of death (e.g., Exod. 24). Blood from sacrificed animals is smeared on the altar and on the participating community in a ritual that echoes other life-forging narrative scenes in marginalized places: Zipporah's act of circumcising Gershom (Exod. 4), the plagues (Exod. 7–11), and the Passover (Exod. 12). Exodus rituals continue to summon adherents to consider survival in vicarious terms, as if to signal a costly endeavor—a cost that survivors carry inside their social, religious, and physical bodies.

Terence Fretheim notes that about a third of the book of Exodus is devoted to instructions for, and the production of, the tabernacle. This elaborate construction dramatically slows down the narrative pace and highlights contrasts between two iconic constructions that define Israel's identity in relation to life and death: the tabernacle and golden calf. These contrasts include: (1) who initiates the construction, (2) the planning involved, (3) the duration of construction, and (4) the accessibility of the divine being.[31] And yet, the language, rituals, and conversation (between Moses and Joshua—Exod. 32:17–18) about the calf also suggest that it functions as a symbol of divine presence (and protection), a military emblem in a precarious political circumstance. The conflicting portrayals of the deity—as gracious and forgiving, yet punishing—are reflective of unresolved tensions that characterize narrative depictions of the life and death nature of the divine-human relationship (e.g., 24:1–12 and 32:1–6), and thus of the exodus-exile story. This life and death struggle is captured in notions of ritual practice.

On the backside of mountain-induced displaced existence, Moses' face undergoes veiling and unveiling (Exod. 34:28–30). Moses is barred access to face-to-face encounter with the divine because that space is filled by all-encompassing divine weightiness (Exod. 40:34–35). The face-to-face encounter between Yahweh and Moses (Exod. 34:35) is no longer possible. Moses is permanently veiled. The future folds and unfolds "through a glass,

---

31. Terence E. Fretheim, *Exodus* (Louisville, KY: John Knox Press, 1991), 263–67.

FACING AND BACKSIDING THE MOUNTAIN 183

darkly" (1 Cor. 13:12).[32] The future is uncertain, only glimpsed. To live into that future is to be a survivor, attached to the literary or material body of another. Thus, although Moses dies in the shadow of the Mountain, backside Africana hermeneutics insists that his body—not just his spirit—survives (unfolds) into the world of the honorable and honored ancestors and becomes folded into the divine-human body, protected by an angelic being (Jude v.9). In backside hermeneutics redesign of the Mountain, the community refuses to allow Moses to become a pharaoh, refuses to allow Exodus to become a conquest narrative, and refuses to give final custody of Moses' body to the empire.

That is the power and significance of the communally produced tabernacle (Exod. 35–39), which is anticipated by the ritual around the golden calf. The construction of the tabernacle begins with Moses' instructions that the people bring material gifts, echoing Aaron's invitation for material to build the calf. The work is credited to skilled laborers and those whose "heart was moved" (Exod. 35:5, 21, 29). The enthusiastic response to this invitation to innovative work produces outcomes that surpass expectations from the divine command, prompting Moses to issue another command asking the people to stop bringing gifts (Exod. 36: 3–7). There is a symbiotic relation between command and love, between law and grace, between legislation and culture. The construction of the sacred space and the tabernacle end with a blessing from Moses (Exod. 39:43). This extended work producing religious and cultural artifacts is also reminiscent of another critical moment in exodus narration—the slave labor that built cities in Egypt. This time, however, the genesis of cultural, religious, economic, and political construction is motivated by self-authenticating values.

Along with the tabernacle, a divine tent of meeting is set up in dialectical relation to each person's tent. This spatial construction of communal belonging is reminiscent of the spatial relationship defined by Moses' ascent to the mountaintop, only this time the spatial relationship between the divine and the human community is horizontal, not hierarchical. The power relations are defined not in terms of one's ability to access the top of the mountain and envision new futures but in terms of shared space on the land and the community's shared movement around insider/outsider identifiers. For this marginalized community and its leader, the future resides not in new revelations

---

32. For more on this Pauline text, see Dorota Hartman, "'Through a Glass, Darkly' (1 Cor 13,12) in Paul's Literary Imagination," *Vetera Christianorum* 54 (2017): 59–91.

but in perspectives from behind, in hindsight, in reinterpretations and visions of the narrated or mobile past, and communally internalizing the external, the proximate other (33:7–23).

CONCLUSION

Upon the completion of the construction of these sacred spaces and objects (the covenant text, the tabernacle, and the tent of meeting with its veil), Exodus concludes by narratively placing these sacred objects together (Exod. 40:1–33). These sacred objects function as "linking objects" that repeatedly bring the reader back to the beginning of the story of communal movement coordinated with divine movement and the movement of clouds and fires. For this unfolding future, the elements of creation—the clouds and the fire—become signposts, dynamic interpretive catalysts for the work of liberation (Exod. 40:34–38; cf. Exod. 17:1). The Mountain is not just the site where exodus imagination begins; the Mountain is also the site that needs to be transformed by the linking objects of liberation work. The Mountain's capacity to erase, to alienate, and to singularize is repeatedly identified and then challenged in the text. Moses resists the allure of empire—its productions of toxic singularity (strongman rule), of erasure (physical and narrative erasure), and of alienation (institutional and/or geographical)—and is ultimately veiled from the story, written out and taken by the Mountain at his death. But the community to which he belongs carries him into the future by repeatedly gathering around the covenantal text, around the tabernacle they built, and around the tent of meeting. This continuous gathering constitutes the ongoing work of exodus redesign that extends from Egypt to the Wilderness and to the Mountain.

Conclusion

Let My People Live

Oppression is by definition and function a choking mechanism. Recognizing that reality, the Exodus story is a narrative about a daring claim: that life can be created out of death, not just as a function of movement from one place to another but also as a function of processes of redesign that transform—to various degrees—the structures of oppression: nationally, globally, and imperially. The story summons political, ecological, and religious subjectivity and activity; it mobilizes multiple alliances across generations and geographical locations—from Egypt to the wilderness and the mountain area. The narrative framing and focus of Exodus interpretation largely follows these three landscapes of the story. Egypt is the place where Israel is oppressed and must fight to be free. Erasure ravages Egypt. The wilderness becomes a temporary host of an alienated people in transit. And the mountain area is the singular space of ultimate power. A triple consciousness is deeply embedded in the story's narrative structure and movement.

Of importance, however, is recognition of the narrative's depictions of recurring threats to human and non-human life, of its displacement and pollution, of its isolation from community in each of these geographical locations. Triple consciousness is invested in all three locations. Egypt not only struggles with political violence and ecological devastation but also with marginalization and isolation. The wilderness is not just a temporary host for an alienated community but also the space where Israel raises concerns about extinction (Exod. 14:11), and

Miriam is singled out for harsh treatment (Num. 12). The mountain is not just the place where the allure of empire manifests as a form of single-hero narration (God promises to begin again with Moses alone), but also the place where the community experiences massive death and is invited to contemplate the alienation of indigenous communities in the land of promise.

The story therefore is also about a clarion voice that demands release from the grip of spectacular and episodic erasure and isolation, as well as from the equally devastating grip of marginalized existence, what Rob Nixon calls "slow violence."[1] There is a substratum to exodus story-telling, an undercurrent of psychic, cultural, and political creativity and history that must be unearthed to create systems that are cultur-ally healing, not erasing; to foster the return of memories and futures that are restorative rather than alienating; and to create communities that are integrative and wholistic, not isolating or singularizing. Engag-ing that substratum means that the three geographical locations in the story also function as ideological spaces that need redesign: Egypt, Wilderness, and Mountain. Exodus' triple consciousness is narrative-exegetical and spatial-temporal, but also hermeneutical and ideologi-cal. In Africana hermeneutics, I have argued, one identifies, engages, and tries to transform that triple consciousness—its stratum, its substra-tum, and its manifestations—rather than simply explain its existence or narrate its recurrences in providential and linear terms. Hermeneutics becomes the work of making hope, of bending the traumas of erasure, marginalization, and isolation into trauma-hopes of new life forms. Accordingly, Exodus is not simply about liberation and its movements ("let my people go"); it is also about creating qualitative structures of liv-ing ("let my people live") that embody the values of these movements. Africana hermeneutics abandons a providential reading of the narrative structure of Exodus as well as a one-directional understanding of its generative movement. Instead, it takes up a more dialectical approach to the pressing questions of theodicy that the story of Exodus and its motif of liberation raise: namely, the intersectional work of survival,

---

1. Nixon's *slow violence* is developed in the context of his exploration of the violence that marginalized com-munities endure over time, at a glacial pace. Rob Nixon, *Slow Violence and the Environmentalism of the Poor* (Cam-bridge, MA: Harvard University Press, 2011). Nixon defines slow violence as "a violence of delayed destruction that is dispersed across space and time, an attritional violence that is typically not viewed as violence at all" (2). The expression "I can't breathe" is the haunting cry of Eric Garner's last words when he was placed in a chokehold by police officers in New York on July 17, 2014. For analyses of the institutional and cultural apparatus in which Garner lived and that ultimately suffocated his life, see Matt Taibbi, *I Can't Breathe: A Killing on Bay Street* (New York: Spiegel and Grau, 2017). The ecological dimension of "I can't breathe" is the fact that Garner suffered from asthma.

CONCLUSION 187

human and environmental thriving, and ultimately the creation of healthy community across time and place.

I identified Gershom—the first son to Moses and Zipporah—as a signifier of the embodied subject and narrative epistemological framework for this work. I named that work and that community *gershomite* to highlight the fact that the birth of Gershom comes at the end of a narrative in which Moses is singularly rescued from the Nile, is engaged in violence and erasure, and is alienated in Midian (Exod. 2). The birth of Gershom is both a narrative culmination and the embodiment of this hermeneutical and epistemological resistance. In postcolonial African work, I focused on changelings—*ogbanje* children—as the ideological and epistemological kin of *gershomite*. I also theorized and proposed badass womanism as a necessary antecedent to Africana epistemological and embodied hermeneutical approaches to Exodus. Badass womanism summons the courage to narrativize such work as invaluable to a full appreciation of interpretive methods and spaces and times that create and sustain holistic liberation. Such intentionality creates multiplicity that privileges non-hierarchical formulations and structures of power and knowledge production. Its unrelenting, multimodal, and multi-spatial movements and vibrancy sparks the imagination and informs the strategic expressions and actions of the story's key leaders and characters: the midwives, the Egyptian princess, Moses, Aaron, Miriam, Jochebed, Jethro, his daughters (and perhaps their unnamed mother), the earth/land, the waters, the pillars of cloud and fire, and, above all, Yahweh.

In Africana formulation, these characters are the originators of Exodus' discourse of the non-disposability of all life-forms, Exodus' discourse of return as strategic repositioning against alienation, and Exodus' discourse about futures defined by the values of multiplicity rather than singularity. As the midwives tell Pharaoh, the Hebrew women—the embodiment of badass womanism—give birth before the arrival of the ideology and infrastructure of erasure (Exod. 1:19). Badass womanism lives and produces and governs before, and thus beyond, the power of disposability, marginalization, and singularity. One ultimately understands exodus movement—departure from the places and ideologies of oppression—to exceed the trope of flight by including the trope of redesign: internally generated, recurring, purposeful journeying that seeks to transform existing oppressive structures into life-giving places and structures. Badass womanism insists that liberation can, and must, happen in Egypt, in the Wilderness, and in the Mountain, and one must recognize *how* liberation is brought to these places.

The first marker of this imagined life that infuses Exodus is that of resistance against shifting and permanent forms of erasure. Israel's narrative and epistemological journey into Egypt is *already* fraught and weighty because Joseph was *already* there, having been sold into an imperial nightmare of singularized power he dreamed about and whose traumas agonized his community (Gen. 37). The journey into Egypt is therefore also a "postcolonial" journey into the afterlives of Israel's long history of encounters with erasing empires. Dynamic departures from empire, or deconstructions of its powerful ideological underpinnings, are as much about ruptures as they are acts and processes of remembering and hope building. To engage this spatial and temporal bending of narrative history toward a liberation ethos, the exodus work initiates a major shift from Joseph to Moses and then performs that shift in political and spatial forms through the epistemological and strategic work of the story's badass women. By connecting Moses to Joseph (who is forgotten by Pharaoh), Israel's departure from Egypt is cast as departure from empire's capacity and uncanny propensity to erase bodies and retain narrative custody of those bodies.

Through the badass womanist placement of Moses in Pharaoh's court, sustained with the endangered community's capacity to nurture him and his stay in the imperial court, the story begins to transition Joseph-as-Moses from the desirer of imperial prestige to membership in the highly desired communal body that precedes Israel's enslavement in Egypt, anticipates their departure, and accompanies them on their journey out. In this way, Joseph (and his generation) is reclaimed from imperial erasure and custody. Joseph is an *ogbanje-gershomite* child, a changeling that returns in the body of the communal mother-body on the move, into the future and the wilderness. When the exodus community arrives at the mountain area and Moses is once again confronted with the allure of empire and its privileging of singularized stories and ideologies, he resists. Having been nurtured by badass womanist epistemology and modes of communal belonging, he can effectively dissuade the imperial deity from erasing an entire generation and making Moses a strongman founder of a postcolonial nation (Exod. 32:10–13).

Secondly, badass womanism counters consciousness associated with geopolitical alienation. In Egypt (the signifier of the colony/empire), the Hebrews are marginalized from political power and internally dispersed through the land to scavenge for straw as they perform enslaving

CONCLUSION 189

labor for the nation (Exod. 5:10–14). The labor and cultural achievements of the oppressed group becomes synonymous with, and symptomatic of, structural dislocation and disenfranchisement. Hebrew labor and work ethic in this colonial and imperial land is slave labor—undignified work. In the Wilderness, where Pharaoh is removed as the primary instigator of communal distress, alienation is explored in relation and correlation to the narrative, epistemological, and geographical space that immediately follows the ecological devastation of the plagues. Can Wilderness sustain the community? The bitter experience of oppression intersects with the bitter waters of the wilderness (Exod. 15:23). On or around the Mountain, alienation manifests in the form of the exodus community's position at the bottom of an imperial structure, during Moses' extended stay at the top of the mountain. Can the people rise up from their structural marginalization? How might liberation stories and events resource their afterlives, in addition to resourcing their initial existence?

Miriam emerges as a critical theorist, interpreter, and resister of this consciousness of geopolitical alienation. She observes Moses during his exposure at the Nile, and she summons the community to sing after their survival/exposure around the Red Sea. While Moses' story and song represents movement from water to land (Exod. 2:6–10; 15:4–17), Miriam's story and song represents movement from water to water (Exod. 2:6–8; 15:20–27). This ability to transform the Wilderness—as a place and as an epistemological experience—into life supporting space begins with the transformation of the bitter wilderness water into sweet water (Exod. 15:25) and extends to the transformation of wilderness rocks into water producing objects (Exod. 17:1–9). By her rhetorical and narrative proximity to water, Miriam represents the anxieties and traumas of water and its ability to sustain and renew life. But by her strategic and prophetic leadership, she is also able to transform the traumas associated with water into hopeful, renewing futures.

In a critical moment of encounter with the divine cloud (Num. 12), Miriam is alienated from the community. Her absence—also signifying ecological alienation—brings the community to a standstill. The exodus community's capacity to coordinate its movement with the movement of clouds and divine presence continues beyond the Wilderness into the Mountain area (Exod. 40:34–38) and constitutes a critical part of addressing geopolitical alienation associated with human and ecological devastation. This ecologically integrated response begins with recognizing the subjectivity of nature in Exodus. As Aliou Niang writes, "nature is . . . a subject humans meet on equal terms."[2] In my Africana reading of Exodus, that realization is most poignantly represented and embodied in the person and work of Miriam, the water-woman, the progenitor of eco-political renewal as a response to alienation and as a self-authenticating form of life giving.

A third consciousness moving through Exodus centers on the experience of singularity. In Egypt, the Hebrews are singled out for persecution and oppression under Pharaoh's ethnocentric policy. That policy becomes gendered as Pharaoh focuses on Hebrew birthing women and assigns specific outcomes to their male and female children. In the Wilderness, Miriam is singled out for punishment after she and Aaron speak against Moses, who himself is positioned as singularly exceptional (Num. 12). On or around the Mountain, an entire generation is targeted for potential erasure as an imperial deity contemplates creating a new nation with Moses as its strongman. The construction of oppressive policies targeting singularized groups, and the associated allure of privilege for a few or for the singularly exceptional individual, constitutes another perennial and traumatizing form of exodus consciousness.

Again, badass womanism provides a contrasting epistemological and methodological approach to single-hero narration and constructions of social relations. In a badass womanist reading, exodus work begins to create safe habitats for the qualitative good life—the formed futures—that Moses' mother envisioned for her newborn (Exod. 2:2) and immediately connects those futures to community initiatives for institutional reforms (Exod. 2:7–9). When Miriam's leadership is isolated in the Wilderness, in favor of Moses' singular abilities, the community comes to a standstill (Num. 12:15). And when the narrative faces the allure of imperial privilege and (potential) erasure in the Mountain, Moses argues for communal memory that secures and entrenches long-term survival (Exod. 32:11–14; 34:6–7). The gifted and marginalized migrant subject and worker, fighting and fleeing for her life, must not be coopted by the ideology and mannerisms of a conquering warrior, nor must she be compelled to understand her survival and her futures as only possible in the form of a perpetual fight to the death. The generation that is compelled and enslaved to build cities in pharaonic governance ultimately participates in building the tabernacle, activity that is spurred by internal volition and generosity (cf. Exod. 35:21–35).

---

2. Aliou Cissé Niang, *A Poetics of Postcolonial Biblical Criticism: God, Human-Nature Relationship, and Negritude* (Eugene, OR: Cascade Books, 2019), 176, 182.

CONCLUSION   191

This mode of future building, around and by the community, stands outside of, but also in contrasting relation to, the singularizing work of empire—its tendency to wrestle multiplicity into forms of toxic singularity that create privilege for a few rather than value for the many. The producers of such work are multiple, and the result of such work is a multiethnic community (cf. Exod. 12:38), a *gershomite* community.

This triple consciousness of erasure, alienation, and singularity has informed my Africana reading of Exodus and the ideologies and systems that create such triple consciousness. My proposed Africana hermeneutic of redesign away from such triple consciousness has informed my reading of Exodus not as a story of a single flow but as one of multiple flows, out of Egypt, out of the Wilderness, and out of the Mountain. This reading connects the deconstructive communal work/flow of "let my people go" to constructive work/flow of "let my people live." Like the embalmed and ultimately exhumed body of Joseph in the biblical account, the Africana self lives partly as a posthumous self and partly as a hopeful self that creates new life-forms out of, and outside of, the wreckage of colonial, colonizing, or imperializing history, literature, geography, and politics. Resourced around the portrayal of the Hebrew women in the opening pages of the Exodus story, and framed by my theorizing on badass womanism, I have argued that Africana exodus work resides in the bosom—indeed in the womb—of this triple consciousness of marginalized subjectivity and its capacity to (1) resist erasure, alienation, and singularization and (2) ultimately overwhelm necropolitics with biopolitics. Survival transforms erasure, community overcomes alienation, and multiplicity transcends singularity. The question of exodus hermeneutics connects moments of liberation and rescue to movements that address structures and revolve around institutional and programmatic changes and reforms.

To be oppressed is to be denied the right of originality, the most fundamental right of human existence and living. But to be oppressed is also to live in a patronage system of thought and existence, to struggle against that system and, faced with its entrenched character, to oscillate between dismantling or reforming the system. This is the realization that has informed postcolonial and, recently, anticolonial and decolonial subjectivities and their melancholies.

Throughout many African countries, particularly Cameroon, euphorias of postcolonial governance transitioned into postcolonial enclaves and space-times from which formerly colonized subjects continually try to escape. As it turns out—not to the surprise of liberation theologians and liberation theologies, but to their disgust—oppression can and does mutate, adapt, adjust, and grow into new, future forms. The histories of colonialism, imperialism, and racism are replete with just such manifestations of supposed invincibility, which then cause the oppressed and marginalized to either succumb to apathy or re-embark on justice work on the long roads of liberation. The possibility of liberation—its promise—is not a neutral concept; instead, the work of redesigning the future away from the triple threats of erasure, alienation, and isolation is one of the ways that oppressed communities imagine life beyond the holding cells of a brutal history and its global geopolitical logics of extraction.[3]

Because the places of exodus (anticolonial) beginning and exodus (postcolonial) residing are also the places of erasure, alienation, and isolation, the question of the afterlives of survival take mythical and symbolic form as the story moves. Can such storytelling really bend history toward justice and liberation? Yes. And might such stories also be doing something slightly different: gathering and repurposing the wreckages, the dispersals and marginalization of human, divine, and non-human life for futures that are more equitable? Yes. In its ideal form, exodus transforms exile into futures for communal bodies that are defined by their capacity to produce multiplicity: bodies that are partially riddled with the wounds of the colonial violence they have endured but yet bonded by the healing of those wounds; bodies partially plagued (disfigured) yet reimagined (transfigured) out of the plaguing assaults on their abused earthy lands. At the end of the story, the Exodus deity is wholly integrated into the community and its ecosystem. As the divine presence moves with the clouds, so too does the human community. Or, perhaps, it is the other way around: as the human community reorganizes its shifting and abbreviated affinity to land, reworks its legislative precepts about alien-native identities, and reemerges from the political and ritual ashes and fires of erased, alienated, and singularized existence, so too does the divine. Either way, the story-motif of Exodus-exodus shapes human, environmental, and divine identity and purpose, not simply through the trope of movement-demand for liberation ("let my people go") but also through a generative act that precedes and outlasts oppression in Egypt, pushing into the Wilderness and the Mountain, and beyond: Let my people live.

---

3. See, Kathryn Yusoff, *A Billion Black Anthropocenes or None* (Minneapolis: University of Minnesota Press, 2018).

Bibliography

Achebe, Chinua. *Things Fall Apart*. New York: Anchor Books, 1994. First published 1956 by Heinemann (London).

Achenbach, Reinhard. "Gêr—nåkhrî—tôshav—zâr: Legal and Sacral Distinctions regarding Foreigners in the Pentateuch." In *The Foreigner and the Law: Perspectives from the Hebrew Bible and the Ancient Near East*, edited by Reinhard Achenbach, Rainer Albertz, and Kakob Wöhrle, 29–51. Wiesbaden: Harrassowitz Verlag, 2011.

Adamo, David T. *Biblical Interpretation in African Perspective*. Lanham, MD: University Press of America, 2006.

Adéèkó, Adélékè. "Great Books Make Their Own History." *Transition* 100 (2008): 34–43.

Adibe, Jideofor, ed., *Who Is African? Identity, Citizenship and the Making of Africa-Nation*. London: Adonis and Abbey Publishers Ltd, 2009.

Amin, Samir. *Re-reading the Postwar Period: An Intellectual Itinerary*. Translated by Michael Wolfers. New York: Monthly Review, 1994.

Anderson, Cheryl B. *Ancient Laws and Contemporary Controversies: The Need for Inclusive Biblical Interpretation*. New York: Oxford University Press, 2009.

_____. *Women, Ideology, and Violence: Critical Theory and the Construction of Gender in the Book of the Covenant and the Deuteronomic Law*. New York: T & T Clark International, 2004.

Angelou, Maya. *And Still I Rise*. London: Virago Press, 1978.

Assmann, Jan. *Moses the Egyptian: The Memory of Egypt in Western Monotheism*. Cambridge, MA: Harvard University Press, 1997.

_____. *The Mind of Egypt: History and Meaning in the Time of the Pharaohs*. Translated by Andrew Jenkins. Cambridge, MA: Harvard University Press, 2002.

_____. *The Price of Monotheism*. Translated by Robert Savage. Stanford, CA: Stanford University Press, 2010.

Ayres, Barbara. "Effects of Infant Carrying Practices on Rhythm in Music." *Ethos* 1 no. 4 (1973): 387–404.

Battle, Michael. *Ubuntu: I in You and You in Me*. New York: Seabury Books, 2009.

Beal, Timothy. "Cultural-Historical Criticism of the Bible." In *New Meanings for Ancient Texts: Recent Approaches to Biblical Criticism and Their Approaches*, edited by Steven L. Mckenzie and John Kaltner, 1–20. Louisville, KY: Westminster John Knox Press, 2013.

Bergmann, Claudia D. *Childbirth as a Metaphor for Crisis: Evidence from the Ancient Near East, the Hebrew Bible, and 1QHXI, 1–18*. Berlin: Walter de Gruyter, 2009.

Blocher, Ewald. "Dammed Water: Water as a National Commodity." *RCC Perspectives* 2 (2012): 35–43.

Blount, Brian K. "The Souls of Biblical Folk and the Potential for Meaning." *Journal of Biblical Literature* 138, no. 1 (2019): 6–21.

Boer, Roland. *The Sacred Economy of Ancient Israel*. Louisville, KY: Westminster John Knox Press, 2015.

Brand, Dionne *A Map to the Door of No Return: Notes to Belonging*. Toronto: Vintage Canada, 2001.

BIBLIOGRAPHY

Brenner, Athalya. "Female Social Behaviour: Two Descriptive Patterns within the 'Birth of a Hero' Paradigm." *Vetus Testamentum* 36, no. 3 (1986): 267–69.

Brenner, Martin L. *The Song of the Sea: Ex. 15:1–21*. Berlin: De Gruyter, 2012.

Brueggemann, Walter. *The Land: Place as Gift, Promise, and Challenge in Biblical Faith*. 2nd ed. Overtures to Biblical Theology. Minneapolis: Fortress Press, 2002.

Burns, Rita J. *Has the Lord Indeed Spoken Only through Moses? A Study of the Biblical Portrait of Miriam*. Atlanta: Scholars Press, 1987.

Burnside, Jonathan P. "Exodus and Asylum: Uncovering the Relationship between Biblical Law and Narrative." *Journal for the Study of the Old Testament* 34, no. 3 (2010): 243–66.

Butler, Trent. "An Anti-Moses Tradition." *Journal for the Study of the Old Testament* 12 (1979): 9–15.

Butler, Trent. "Anti-Moses Tradition." *Lexington Theological Quarterly* 14, no. 3 (1979): 33–39.

Callahan, Allen Dwight. *The Talking Book: African Americans and the Bible*. New Haven: Yale University Press, 2006.

Chen, Cecilia Janine MacLeod, and Astrida Neimanis, "Introduction: Toward a Hydrological Turn?" In *Thinking with Water*, edited by Cecilia Chen, Janine MacLeod, and Astrida Neimanis, 3–22. London: McGill-Queen's University Press, 2013.

Childs, Brevard S. "The Birth of Moses." *Journal of Biblical Literature* 84, no. 2 (1965):109–15.

Claassens, L. Juliana M. *Mourner, Mother, Midwife: Reimagining God's Delivering Presence in the Old Testament*. Louisville, KY: Westminster John Knox Press, 2012.

Coats, George. *Moses: Heroic Man, Man of God*. Sheffield: JSOT Press, 1987.

———. *The Moses Tradition*. Sheffield: JSOT Press, 1993.

Cohen, Jonathan. *The Origins and Evolution of the Moses Nativity Story*. Leiden: E. J. Brill, 1993.

Coleman, Monica, ed. *Ain't I a Womanist, Too?: Third-Wave Womanist Religious Thought*. Minneapolis: Fortress Press, 2013.

Davies, Gordon F. *Israel in Egypt: Reading Exodus 1–2*. Sheffield: JSOT Press, 1992.

Dedji, Valentin. "The Ethical Redemption of African Imaginaire: Kä Mana's Theology of Reconstruction." *Journal of Religion in Africa* 31, no. 3 (2001): 254–74.

Diop, Cheikh Anta. *African Origin of Civilization: Myth or Reality*. Chicago: Chicago Review Press, 1989.

Douglass, Frederick *Narrative of the Life of Frederick Douglass, an American Slave, Written by Himself*. 1845. Republished in *The Oxford Frederick Douglass Reader*, edited by William L. Andrews. New York: Oxford University Press, 1996.

Dozeman, Thomas B. *Commentary on Exodus*. Eerdmans Critical Commentary. Grand Rapids: William B. Eerdmans Publishing Company, 2009.

———. *God at War: Power in the Exodus Tradition*. Oxford: Oxford University Press, 1996.

———. *God on the Mountain: A Study of Redaction, Theology, and Canon in Exodus 19–24*. SBL Monograph Series 37. Atlanta: Scholars Press, 1989.

Dozeman, Thomas B., Craig A. Evans, and Joel N. Lohr, eds. *The Book of Exodus: Composition, Reception and Interpretation*. Leiden: Brill, 2014.

Dube, Musa W. *Other Ways of Reading: African Women and the Bible*. Atlanta: Society of Biblical Literature, 2001.

———. *Postcolonial Feminist Interpretation of the Bible*. Atlanta: Society of Biblical Literature Press, 2000.

Du Bois, W. E. Burghardt. "Of the Culture of White Folk." *The Journal of Race Development* 7/4 (1917): 434–47.

———. *The Souls of Black Folk*. Atlanta: A.C. McClurg & Co., 1903.

Duchet, Michèle. *Anthropologie et Histoire au Siècle des Lumières*. Paris: Francois Maspero, 1971.

BIBLIOGRAPHY

Durham, John I. *Exodus*. World Biblical Commentary, vol. 3.Waco, TX: Wood Books, 1987.

Éla, Jean-Marc. *The African Cry*. Translated by Robert R. Barr. New York: Orbis, 1986.

Emecheta, Buchi. *The Joys of Motherhood*. London: Heinemann, 1994.

Engelmayer, Shammai. "Ivri: Naming Ourselves." *Judaism* 54, no. 1–2 (2005):13–26.

Esposito, Roberto. "Biopolitics." In *Biopolitics: A Reader*, edited by Timothy Campbell and Adam Sitze, 317–349. Durham, NC: Duke University Press, 2013.

Feldt, Laura. "Fantastic Re-Collection: Cultural vs. Autobiographical Memory in the Exodus Narrative." In *Religious Narrative, Cognition and Culture: Image and Word in the Mind of Narrative*, edited by Armin W. Geertz and Jeppe Sinding Jensen, 191–208. Sheffield: Equinox, 2011.

Fentress-Williams, Judy. "Exodus." In *The Africana Bible: Reading Israel's Scriptures from Africa and the African Diaspora*, edited by Hugh R. Page Jr., et al, 80–88. Minneapolis: Fortress Press, 2010.

Fewell, Danna Nolan. *The Children of Israel: Reading the Bible for the Sake of Our Children*. Nashville: Abingdon Press, 2003.

Fewell, Danna Nolan, and David M. Gunn. *Gender, Power, and Promise: The Subject of the Bible's First Story*. Nashville: Abingdon Press, 1993.

Foucault, Michel. "Right of Life and Power over Death." In *Biopolitics: A Reader*, edited by Timothy Campbell and Adam Sitze, 41–60. Durham, NC: Duke University Press, 2013.

Frayer-Griggs, Daniel. "Spittle, Clay, and Creation in John 9:6 and some Dead Sea Scrolls." *Journal of Biblical Literature* 132, no. 3 (2013): 659–70.

Fretheim, Terence E. "Because the Whole Earth Is Mine: Theme and Narrative in Exodus." *Interpretation* 50 (1996): 229–39.

———. *Exodus*. Interpretation: A Bible Commentary for Teaching and Preaching. Louisville, KY: John Knox Press, 1991.

Freud, Sigmund. *Moses and Monotheism*. Translated by Katherine Jones. New York: Knopf, 1939.

Gafney, Wilda C. *Womanist Midrash: A Reintroduction to the Women of the Torah and the Throne*. Louisville, KY: Westminster John Knox Press, 2017.

Gates, Henry Louis, Jr. *The Signifying Monkey: A Theory of Afro-American Literary Criticism*. New York: Oxford University Press, 1988.

Gill, LaVerne McCain. *Daughters of Dignity: African Women in the Bible and the Virtues of Black Womanhood*. Cleveland: The Pilgrim Press, 2000.

Gil-White, Francisco J. "Are Ethnic Groups Biological 'Species' to the Human Brain? Essentialism in our Cognition of Some Social Categories." *Current Anthropology* 42, no. 4 (2001): 515–53.

Ginzberg, Louis. *The Legends of the Jews: Bible Times and Characters from Joseph to the Exodus. Vol. 2*. Translated by Henrietta Szold. Champaign, IL: Project Gutenberg, 1998.

Godbey, A. H. "Ceremonial Spitting." *The Monist* 24, no. 1 (1914): 67–91.

Good, Deidre, ed. *Miriam, the Magdalen, and the Mother*. Bloomington: Indiana University Press, 2005.

Grabbe, Lester L. "Exodus and History." In *The Book of Exodus: Composition, Reception, and Interpretation*, edited by Thomas B. Dozeman, Craig A. Evans, and Joel N. Lohr, 70–77. Leiden: Brill, 2014.

Greifenhagen, F. V. *Egypt on the Pentateuch's Ideological Map: Constructing Biblical Israel's Identity*. Sheffield: Sheffield Academic Press, 2002.

Gressmann, Hugo. *Mose und Seine Zeit: Ein Kommentar zu den Mose-Sagen*. Gottingen: Vandenhoeck & Ruprecht, 1912.

Habel, Norman C. "Introducing Ecological Hermeneutics." In *Exploring Ecological Hermeneutics*, edited by Norman C. Habel and Peter Trudinger, 1–8. Atlanta: Society of Biblical Literature Press, 2008.

_____. *The Land Is Mine: Six Biblical Land Ideologies*. Overtures to Biblical Theology. Minneapolis: Fortress Press, 1995.

Hamilton, Virginia. *The People Could Fly: American Black Folktales*. Illustrations by Leo Dillon and Diane Dillon. New York: Alfred Knopf, 1985.

Harris, Melanie. *Ecowomanism: African-American Women and Earth-Honoring Faiths*. Maryknoll, NY: Orbis Books, 2017.

_____, ed. *Ecowomanism, Religion and Ecology*. Leiden: Brill, 2017.

Hartman, Dorota. "'Through a Glass, Darkly' (1 Cor 13,12) in Paul's Literary Imagination." *Vetera Christianorum* 54 (2017): 59–91.

Havea, Jione, Margaret Aymer, and Steed Davidson, eds. *Islands, Islanders, and the Bible: RumInations*. Atlanta: Society of Biblical Literature Press, 2015.

Hendel, Ronald. *Remembering Abraham: Culture, Memory, and History in the Hebrew Bible*. Oxford: Oxford University Press, 2005.

Hidalgo, Irene Díaz de Aguilar. "The Niger-Libya Migration Route: An Odyssey Shaped by Saharan Connections and European Fears, 2000–2017." *Framework Document* 1 (2018): 1–31.

Hilfrich, Carola. "Making Writing Readable Again: Sign Praxis between the Discourse on Idolatry and Cultural Criticism." *The Journal of Religion* 85, no. 2 (2005): 267–92.

Hillel, Daniel. *The Natural History of the Bible: An Environmental Exploration of the Hebrew Scriptures*. New York: Columbia University Press, 2006.

Hopkins, Dwight N. "Holistic Health and Healing: Environmental Racism and Ecological Justice." In *Faith, Health, and Healing in African American Life*, edited by Stephanie Y. Mitchem and Emilie Townes, 16–31. Westport, CT: Praeger, 2008.

Houtman, Cornelis. *Exodus*. Historical Commentary on the Old Testament. Vol. 1. Kampen: Kok Publishing House, 1993.

Hurston, Zora Neale. *Moses, Man of the Mountain*. New York: Harper Perennial, 1991.

Jacob, Sharon, and Jennifer T. Kaalund. "Flowing from Breast to Breast: An Examination of Dis/placed Motherhood in African American and Indian Wet Nurses." In *Womanist Interpretations of the Bible: Expanding the Discourse*, edited by Gay L. Byron and Vanessa Lovelace, 209–38. Atlanta: Society of Biblical Literature Press, 2016.

Jenkins, Richard. *Rethinking Ethnicity: Arguments and Explorations*. 2nd ed. London: Sage, 2008.

Jensen, Jeppe Sinding. "Framing Religions Narrative, Cognition and Culture Theoretically." In *Religious Narrative, Cognition and Culture: Image and Word in the Mind of Narrative*, edited by Armin W. Geertz and Jeppe Sinding Jensen, 31–50. Sheffield: Equinox, 2011.

Johnson, Barbara. *Moses and Multiculturalism*. Berkeley: University of California Press, 2010.

Josephus, Flavius. *Against Apion*. Translation and Commentary by M. G. Barclay. Leiden: Brill, 2007.

_____. *The Genuine Works of Flavius Josephus, the Historian*. Philadelphia: Kimber & Sharpless, 1811.

Junior, Nyasha. *Hagar Reimagined: Blackness and the Bible*. Oxford: Oxford University Press, 2019.

Kass, Leon R. *Founding God's Nation: Reading Exodus*. New Haven, CT: Yale University Press, 2021.

Katongole, Emmanuel. *The Sacrifice of Africa: A Political Theology for Africa*. Grand Rapids: William B. Eerdmans Publishing, 2011.

Keddy, Paul, Lauchlan H. Fraser, Ayzik I. Solomeshch, Wolfgang J. Junk, Daniel R. Campbell, Mary T. K. Arroyo, and Cleber J. R. Alho. "Wet and Wonderful: The World's Largest Wetlands Are Conservation Priorities." *BioScience* 59, no. 1 (2009): 39–51.

Kometa, Sunday Shende, and Jude Ndzifon Kimengsi. "Urban Development and its Implications on Wetland Ecosystem Services in Ndop, Cameroon." *Environmental Management and Sustainable Development* 7, no. 1 (2018): 21–36.

Kugel, James L. *The Bible as It Was*. Cambridge, MA: Harvard University Press, 1997.

Lacoste, Nathalie. *Waters of the Exodus: Jewish Experiences with Water in Ptolemaic and Roman Egypt*. Leiden: Brill, 2018.

Lamb, David T. "Compassion and Wrath as Motivations for Divine Warfare." In *Holy War in the Bible: Christian Morality and an Old Testament Problem*, edited by H. Thomas, J. Evans, and P. Copan, 133–52. Downers Grove, IL: InterVarsity Press, 2013.

BIBLIOGRAPHY

———. "'I Will Strike You Down and Cut Off Your Head' (1 Sam 17:46): Trash Talking, Derogatory Rhetoric, Psychological Warfare in Ancient Israel." In *Warfare, Ritual, and Symbol in Biblical and Modern Contexts*, edited by Brad E. Kelle, Frank Ritchel Ames, and Jacob L. Wright, 111–30. Ancient Israel and Its Literature. Atlanta: Society of Biblical Literature Press, 2014.

Langston, Scott M. *Exodus through the Centuries*. Malden, MA: Oxford, 2006.

Leveen, Adriane. "Inside-Out: Jethro, the Midianites and a Biblical Construction of the Outsider." *Journal for the Study of the Old Testament* 34, no. 4 (2010): 395–417.

Liew, Tat-siong Benny. "Militarism, Masculinism, and Martyrdom: Conditional Citizenship for (Asian) Americans." In *Critical Theology against US Militarism in Asia: Decolonization and Deimperialization*, edited by Nami Kim and Wonhee Anne Joh, 25–52. New Approaches to Religion and Power. New York: Palgrave Macmillan, 2016.

Lorenz, Chris. "Representations of Identity: Ethnicity, Race, Class, Gender, and Religion: An Introduction to Conceptual History." In *The Contested Nation: Ethnicity, Class, Religion, and Gender in National Histories*, edited by Stefan Berger and Chris Lorenz, 34–43. New York: Palgrave MacMillan, 2008.

Lydon, Ghislaine. "Writing Trans-Saharan History: Methods, Sources, and Interpretations across the African Divide." *The Journal of North African Studies* 10, no. 3–4 (2005): 293–324.

Maathai, Wangari. *Replenishing the Earth: Spiritual Values for Healing Ourselves and the World*. New York: Doubleday, 2010.

———. *Unbowed: A Memoir*. New York: Anchor Books, 2006.

Malul, Meir. "Adoption of Foundlings in the Bible and Mesopotamian Documents: A Study of Some Legal Metaphors in Ezekiel 16:1–7." *Journal for the Study of the Old Testament* 46 (1990): 97–126.

Mamdani, Mahmood. *When Victims Become Killers: Colonialism, Nativism, and the Genocide in Rwanda*. Princeton, NJ: Princeton University Press, 2001.

Marbury, Robinson Herbert. *Pillars of Cloud and Fire: The Politics of Exodus in African American Biblical Interpretation*. New York: New York University Press, 2015.

Marcus, David. "The Mission of the Raven (Gen. 8:7)." *Journal of Ancient Near Eastern Studies* 29 (2002): 71–80.

Marks, Herbert. "Biblical Naming and Poetic Etymology." *Journal of Biblical Literature* 114, no. 1 (1995): 21–42.

Masenya, Madipoane (Ngwan'a Mphahlele). "All from the Same Source? Deconstructing a (Male) Anthropocentric Reading of Job (3) through an Eco-*bosadi* Lens." *Journal of Theology for Southern Africa* 137 (July 2010): 46–60.

———. *How Worthy Is the Woman of Worth?: Rereading Proverbs 31:10–31 in African South-Africa*. New York: Peter Lang, 2004.

Masenya, Madipoane (Ngwan'a Mphahlele) and Kenneth Ngwa, eds., *Navigating African Biblical Hermeneutics: Themes and Trends from Our Pots and Our Calabashes*. Cambridge: Cambridge Scholars Publishing, 2018.

Matory, J. Lorand. "The Many Who Dance in Me: Afro-Atlantic Ontology and the Problem with 'Transnationalism'" in *Transnational Transcendence: Essays on Religion and Globalization*, edited by Thomas J. Csordas, 231–62. Berkeley: University of California Press, 2009.

Mbembe, Achille. *Critique of Black Reason*. Translated by Laurent Dubois. Durham, NC: Duke University Press, 2017.

———. "Necropolitics." Translated by Libby Meintjes. *Public Culture* 15, no.1 (2003): 11–40.

———. "On Politics as a Form of Expenditure." In *Law and Disorder in the Postcolony*, edited by Jean Comaroff and John Comaroff, 299–335. Chicago: University of Chicago Press, 2006.

———. "On the Postcolony: A Brief Response to Critics." *Qui Parle*. 15, no. 2 (2005): 1–49.

———. *On the Postcolony*. Berkeley: University of California Press, 2001.

———. *Out of the Dark Night: Essays on Decolonization*. New York: Columbia University Press, 2021.

BIBLIOGRAPHY

_____. "Provisional Notes on the Postcolony." *Africa: Journal of the International African Institute* 62, no. 1 (1992): 3–37.

Mbuvi, Andrew. "African Biblical Studies: An Introduction to an Emerging Discipline." *Currents in Biblical Research* 15, no. 2 (2017): 149–78.

Meyers, Carol. *Exodus.* Cambridge: Cambridge University Press, 2005.

Mosala, Itumeleng J. *Biblical Hermeneutics and Black Theology in South Africa.* Grand Rapids: Eerdmans, 1989.

Mukonyora, Isabel. "Dramatization and Embodiment of God in the Wilderness." In *Faith in African Lived Christianity: Bridging Anthropological and Theological Perspectives,* edited by Karen Lauterbach and Mika Vähäkangas, 271–90. Leiden: Brill, 2020.

Nelson, Louis P. "Architectures of West African Enslavement." *Buildings & Landscapes: Journal of the Vernacular Architecture Forum* 21, no. 1 (2014): 88–125.

Ngong, David. "African Political Theology and Post-Nationalist Nationalism: The Case of the Cameroon Anglophone Conflict." *Political Theology* 10 (2021): 1–15.

Ngwa, Kenneth. "The Exodus Story and Its Literary Kinships." In *The Oxford Handbook of Biblical Narrative,* edited by Danna Nolan Fewell, 125–36. Oxford: Oxford University Press, 2016.

Niang, Aliou Cissé. *A Poetics of Postcolonial Biblical Criticism: God, Human-Nature Relationship, and Negritude.* Eugene, OR: Cascade Books, 2019.

Nixon, Rob. *Slow Violence and the Environmentalism of the Poor.* Cambridge, MA: Harvard University Press, 2011.

Nyabongo, Akiki. *The Story of an African Chief.* New York: C. Scribner, 1935.

Nyambod, Emmanuel M. "Environmental Consequences of Rapid Urbanisation: Bamenda City, Cameroon." *Journal of Environmental Protection* 1, no. 1 (2010): 15–23.

Nyamnjoh, Francis B. "Blinded by Sight: Divining the Future of Anthropology in Africa." *Africa Spectrum* 47, no. 2–3 (2012): 63–92.

Oduyoye, Mercy Amba. *Daughters of Anowa: African Women and Patriarchy.* New York: Orbis Books, 1995.

_____. *Talitha Qumi!: Proceedings of the Convocation of African Women Theologians, Trinity College Legon-Accra, September 24–October 2, 1989.* Accra, Ghana: Daystar Press, 1990.

Oduyoye, Mercy Amba, and Musimbi R. A. Kanyoro, eds., *The Will to Arise: Women, Tradition, and the Church in Africa.* Maryknoll, NY: Orbis Books, 1992.

Okure, Teresa. "First Was the Life, Not the Book." In *To Cast Fire upon the Earth: Bible and Mission Collaborating in Today's Multicultural Global Context: A Project of BISAM, and Interest Group of IAMS,* edited by Teresa Okure, 194–214. Pietermaritzburg: Cluster Publications, 2000.

Olojede, Funlola. "Miriam and Moses's Cushite Wife: Sisterhood in Jeopardy?" In *Feminist Frameworks and the Bible: Power, Ambiguity, and Intersectionality,* edited by L. Juliana Claassens and Carolyn J. Sharp, 133–45. New York: Bloomsbury T&T Clark, 2017.

Olson, Dennis T. "The Jagged Cliffs of Mount Sinai: A Theological Reading of the Book of the Covenant (Exod 20:22–23:19)." *Interpretation* 50, no. 3 (1996): 251–63.

_____. "Violence for the Sake of Social Justice? Narrative, Ethics, and Indeterminacy in Exodus 2:11–15." In *The Meanings We Choose: Hermeneutical Ethics, Indeterminacy and the Conflict of Interpretations,* edited by Charles H. Cosgrove, Andrew Mein, and Claudia V. Camp, 138–48. Harrisburg, PA: Bloomsbury Academic, 2004.

Oyono, Ferdinand. *Houseboy.* Translated by John Reed. Long Grove, IL: Graveland, 1966.

Page, Hugh R., Jr. *Israel's Poetry of Resistance: Africana Perspectives on Early Hebrew Verse.* Minneapolis: Fortress Press, 2013.

Page, Hugh R., Jr., et al., eds., *The Africana Bible: Reading Israel's Scriptures from Africa and the African Diaspora.* Minneapolis: Fortress Press, 2010.

BIBLIOGRAPHY

Paton, Alan. *Cry, the Beloved Country*. New York: C. Scribner's Sons, 1948.

Pearce, Sarah J. K. *Land of the Body: Studies in Philo's Representation of Egypt*. Tübingen: Mohr Siebeck, 2007.

Porten, Bezalel. *The Elephantine Papyri in English: Three Millennia of Cross-Cultural Continuity and Change*. Leiden: Brill, 1996.

Potkay, Adam, and Sandra Burr, eds., *Black Atlantic Writers of the Eighteenth Century: Living the New Exodus in England and the Americas*. New York: St. Martin's Press, 1995.

Powery, Emerson B., and Rodney S. Sadler Jr., *The Genesis of Liberation: Biblical Interpretation in the Antebellum Narratives of the Enslaved*. Louisville, KY: Westminster John Knox Press, 2016.

Propp, William H. C. *Exodus 1–18: A New Translation with Introduction and Commentary*. The Anchor Bible. New York: Doubleday, 1999.

Ramantswana, Hulisani. "'I Shavha i sia muinga i ya fhi?' Decolonial Reflections on African Biblical Hermeneutics." *Stellenbosch Theological Journal* 2, no. 4 (2016): 401–29.

Rees, Anthony. *Voices of the Wilderness: An Ecological Reading of the Book of Numbers*. Sheffield: Sheffield Phoenix Press, 2015.

Reis, Moshe. "Miriam Rediscovered." *Jewish Bible Quarterly* 38, no. 3 (2010): 183–90.

Rendtorff, Rolf. "The Gēr in the Priestly Laws of the Pentateuch." In *Ethnicity and the Bible*, edited by Mark G. Brett, 77–87. Boston: Brill, 2002.

Russell, Brian D. *The Song of the Sea: The Date of Composition and Influence of Exodus 15:1–21*. New York: Peter Lang, 2007.

Schmid, Konrad. *Genesis and the Moses Story: Israel's Dual Origins in the Hebrew Bible*. Translated by James D. Nogalski. Winona Lake, IN: Eisenbrauns, 2010.

Scholz, Susanne. *Introducing the Women's Hebrew Bible: Feminist, Gender Justice, and the Study of the Old Testament*. London: Bloomsbury T&T Clark, 2017.

Seters, John Van. *The Life of Moses: The Yahwist as Historian in Exodus–Numbers*. Louisville, KY: Westminster John Knox Press, 1994.

Shahan, Sarah. "Alice Walker and Her Badass Women: How Womanism Is Stronger than Feminism and Why It Pertains to the African American Woman Experience." Odyssey. https://www.theodysseyonline.com/alice-walker-badass-women.

Sharpe, Christina. *In the Wake: On Blackness and Being*. Durham, NC: Duke University Press, 2016.

Shinan, Avidgor, and Yair Zakovitch. *From Gods to God: How the Bible Debunked, Suppressed, or Changed Ancient Myths and Legends*. Translated by Valerie Zakovitch. Philadelphia: The Jewish Publication Society, 2012.

Siebert-Hommes, Jopie. *Let the Daughters Live! The Literary Architecture of Exodus 1–2 as a Key for Interpretation*. Leiden: Brill, 1998.

Smith, Mitzi J. *Womanist Sass and Talk Back: Social (In)Justice, Intersectionality, and Biblical Interpretation*. Eugene, OR: Cascade Books, 2018.

Smith, Shanell. *The Woman Babylon and the Marks of Empire: Reading Revelation with a Postcolonial Womanist Hermeneutic of Ambiveilence*. Minneapolis: Fortress Press, 2014.

Taibbi, Matt. *I Can't Breathe: A Killing on Bay Street*. New York: Spiegel and Grau, 2017.

Tangwa, Godfrey B. *Elements of Africa Bioethics in a Western Frame*. Mankon, Bamenda: Langaa Research & Publishing CIG, 2010.

Taylor, Keeanga-Yamahtta. *From #BlackLivesMatter to Black Liberation*. Chicago: Haymarket Books, 2016.

Thomas, Natalie, and Sumant Nigam. "Twentieth-Century Climate Change over Africa: Seasonal Hydroclimate Trends and Sahara Desert Expansion." *Journal of Climate* 33 (2018): 3349–72.

Thomas, Rhondda Robinson. *Claiming Exodus: A Cultural History of Afro-Atlantic Identity, 1774–1903*. Waco, TX: Baylor University Press, 2013.

Trevett, Christine. "Wilderness Woman: The Taming of Miriam." In *Wilderness: Essays in Honour of Frances Young*, edited by R. S. Sugirtharajah, 26–44. New York: T&T Clark, 2005.

Trible, Phyllis, and Letty M. Russell, eds., *Hagar, Sarah, and Their Children: Jewish, Christian, and Muslim Perspectives*. Louisville, KY: Westminster John Knox Press, 2006.

Tutu, Desmond. *No Future without Forgiveness*. New York: Image Books, 1999.

Volkan, Vamik. *Killing in the Name of Identity: A Study of Bloody Conflicts*. Charlottesville, VA: Pitchstone Publishing, 2006.

Walker, Alice. *In Search of Our Mothers' Gardens: Womanist Prose*. San Diego: Harcourt Brace Jovanovich, 1983.

Walker-Jones, Arthur. *The Green Psalter: Resources for an Ecological Spirituality*. Minneapolis: Fortress Press, 2009.

Walzer, Michael. *In God's Shadow: Politics in the Hebrew Bible*. New Haven, CT: Yale University Press, 2012.

Warrior, Robert. "Canaanites, Cowboys, and Indians," *Union Seminary Quarterly* 59, nos. 1–2 (2005): 1–8.

Watts, James W. "Aaron and the Golden Calf in the Rhetoric of the Pentateuch." *Journal of Biblical Literature* 130, no. 3 (2011): 417–30.

Weems, Renita J. *Just a Sister Away: A Womanist Vision of Women's Relationships in the Bible*. San Diego: LuraMedia, 1988.

Wellhausen, Julius. *Israelitische und Jüdische Geschichte*. Berlin: Walter de Gruyter, 1958.

Wenham, Gordon J. "The Golden Calf in the Psalms." In *A God of Faithfulness: Essays in Honour of J. Gordon McConville on his 60th Birthday*, edited by Jamie A. Grant, Alison Lo, and Gordon J. Wenham, 169–81. New York: T&T Clark, 2011.

West, Gerald O. "African Biblical Scholarship as Post-Colonial, Tri-Polar and a Site-of-Struggle." In *Present and Future of Biblical Studies: Celebrating 25 Years of Brill's Biblical Interpretation*, edited by Tat-siong Benny Liew, 240–73. Leiden: Brill, 2018.

———. "Do Two Walk Together? Walking with the Other through Contextual Bible Study." *Anglican Theological Review* 93, no. 3 (2011): 431–49.

———. *The Stolen Bible: From Tool of Imperialism to African Icon*. Leiden: Brill, 2016.

Williams, Delores. *Sisters in the Wilderness: The Challenge of Womanist God-Talk*. New York: Orbis Books, 1993.

Williams, Joseph J. *Hebrewisms of West Africa: From the Nile to Niger with the Jews*. Baltimore: Black Classic Press, 1931, 1999.

Wilson, Douglas Ian. "The Song of the Sea and Isaiah: Exodus 15 in Post-Monarchic Prophetic Discourse." In *Thinking of Water in the Early Second Temple Period*, edited by Ehud Ben Zvi and Christopher Levin, 123–47. Berlin: De Gruyter, 2014.

Wimbush, Vincent L. "Interpreters—Enslaving/Enslaved/Runagate." *Journal of Biblical Literature* 130, no. 1 (2011): 5–24.

———. "It's Scripturalization, Colleagues!" *Journal of Africana Religions* 3, no. 2 (2015): 193–200.

———. *White Men's Magic: Scripturalization as Slavery*. Oxford: Oxford University Press, 2012.

Wimmer, Andreas. "The Making and Unmaking of Ethnic Boundaries: A Multilevel Process Theory." *American Journal of Sociology* 113, no. 4 (2008): 970–1022.

Winters, Joseph R. *Hope Draped in Black: Race, Melancholy, and the Agony of Progress*. Durham, NC: Duke University Press, 2016.

Wright, Benjamin G., III. *The Letter of Aristeas: 'Aristeas to Philocrates' or 'On the Translation of the Law of the Jews.'* Berlin: Walter de Gruyter, 2015.

Yafeh, Alice. *Paul's Sexual and Marital Ethics in 1 Corinthians 7: An African-Cameroonian Perspective*. New York: Peter Lang, 2015.

Yusoff, Kathryn. *A Billion Black Anthropocenes or None*. Minneapolis: University of Minnesota Press, 2018.

Zlotnick-Sivan, H. "Moses the Persian? Exodus 2, the 'Other' and Biblical 'Mnemohistory.'" *Zeitschrift für die Alttestamentliche Wissenschaft* 116 (2004): 189–205.

Index of Scripture

Old Testament		1:1–6	52	2:7–10	101
		1:5	18, 37	2:7–11	129
Genesis		1:7	15, 38	2:10	86, 97, 97n21,
1	38, 146	1:8	37, 56		101, 103, 106, 140
1:2	50	1:9	15, 104	2:11	16n5, 97,
1:3	50	1:10	14, 58, 96, 102,		97n21, 99n26,
4:9	87		129, 178		102n31, 103, 105
8:7	128n39	1:11	102n31, 104	2:11–12	101–4
8:7–8	128	1:12	57	2:11–13	103
14:13	16n5	1:13	3	2:11–15	92, 96–99,
15–16	85n4	1:14	118, 120		99–101, 140
16	85	1:15	16, 178	2:12	103
16:7	93	1:15–16	16n5	2:13	16n5, 99n26,
17:12	107n39	1:15–22	55, 56		104, 105
17:27	107n39	1:16	16, 85, 102	2:13–14	57, 104–5
21:8	97n21	1:19	16, 16n5, 38,	2:14	97, 100, 103,
21:8–21	85		48, 187		104
21:9	163	1:22	178	2:14–15	100, 101
21:15	93	2	84, 108, 129, 130,	2:15	105–6
21:15–21	28		140, 150, 152, 187	2:16–22	92, 98n24,
21:16	102	2–3	157		106–8
21:20	97n21	2:1–10	56, 85, 92,	2:17	107
22:1–19	161, 165		92–96, 99, 100, 130,	2:18	156, 177
31:15	107n39		131, 139–43	2:19	26, 85, 107, 176
37	188	2:1–15	175	2:20	87
37–50	37	2:2	87, 101, 103,	2:22	83, 84, 85, 107,
39:14	16n5		106, 190		107n39
39:17	16n5	2:3	130	2:23–24	110
40:15	16n5	2:4	102	2:24	51
41:12	16n5	2:5	103, 130	2:25	101n30
43:32	16n5	2:5–10	176	3:1–12	27
44:34	102	2:6	26, 99n26, 101,	3:6	144n18
			102n32, 103, 104, 151	3:7	101n30
Exodus		2:6–7	16n5, 101	3:7–8	110
1	84, 129	2:6–8	189	3:8	18, 26, 27, 136
1–2	27, 38	2:6–10	136, 189	3:9	101n30
1–15	87	2:7	102, 139	3:12	156
1:1	157	2:7–9	102, 190	3:13	177

INDEX OF SCRIPTURE

Exodus (*cont.*)

Reference	Page
3:13–16	155
3:13–18	28
3:17	26, 27
3:18	16n5
4	182
4–5	56
4:1–17	28
4:2	29
4:6	143
4:6–7	144
4:10–12	143
4:13	101n30
4:15–16	21
4:19	161
4:20	118–19
4:21	161
4:21–26	55
4:22	85
4:24–26	85, 98n24, 165
5–6	129
5:1–6:12	140
5:2	166
5:3	16n5
5:3–5	129
5:4	28
5:5	101
5:5–9	56
5:6–18	51, 57, 118
5:10–14	189
5:19	101n30
6:1	162
6:2	28
6:5	51
6:6–8	27
6:9	57, 69
7–11	51, 121, 129, 182
7–23	184
7:15	131, 140
7:15–18	123
7:16	16n5
7:17–24	140
7:18	120
7:21	120
8:22 [8:18 MT]	141
8:27	125
9–24	156
9:1	16n5
9:8	126
9:13	16n5
9:16–21	141
9:27	99n28
9:29	141
10:3	16n5
10:13–15	126
10:15	145
10:19	130
11:1	162
12	51, 182
12–13	141
12:8	120
12:26	2, 55
12:26–27	6
12:28	155
12:36	161, 176
12:38	15, 26, 157, 191
12:40–41	155
12:43	107n39
13–15	140
13:8	6, 55
13:14	6
13:14–15	2, 55
13:15	12
13:17–22	120
13:18	151
13:21	50
14–15	27, 51, 55, 56, 121, 122, 130, 131
14:2–3	141
14:11	185
14:16	143, 151
14:30	124, 131, 160
15	120, 121, 141n13, 142, 149, 150, 152, 160
15:1	138, 141, 142
15:1–12	124, 125, 142
15:4–17	189
15:13–17	142
15:17–19	125
15:18	142
15:19	138, 142, 151
15:20	135, 138, 150, 152
15:20–21	142, 150
15:20–27	150–52, 189
15:21	138, 142, 150, 151
15:22	126, 151
15:22–25	150
15:22–27	142, 150
15:23	120, 151, 189
15:24	149
15:24–25	152
15:25	131, 136, 151, 152, 189
15:25–26	150, 152
15:25–27	132
15:26	136
15:27	126, 138, 142, 143, 150, 151, 152
16	50, 51, 120, 121, 122, 131
16:10	50
16:40	50
17	120, 121, 131
17:1	53, 184
17:1–9	189
18:1–12	98n24
18:2	143n16
18:3	107n39
18:3–4	107n40
18:14–23	98n24
18:18	178
19	157
19–24	156
19–34	156
19:1	157
19:2	160
19:4	50, 127, 128, 160
19:18	120
20–23	179
20–24	157
20:1	149
20:3–4	155
20:5–6	180
20:22	161
20:22–23:19	161
20:23	161
20:24	161

INDEX OF SCRIPTURE

21:2	16n5	33:21–23	172	12:10	143
21:8	107n39	34	167	12:12	144, 145
21:21	179	34–35	52	12:14	144–45
22:9	179	34–38	50	12:15	146, 190
22:21	83, 86, 162	34–40	157, 169	13:17–20	148
23:9	83, 86	34:1	180	13:25–33	148
24	182	34:6	181	13:32	27
24:1–12	182	34:6–7	180, 190	14	120, 121, 131
24:7	161	34:8	181	14:18	180
24:12	175	34:11	162, 180	14:25	130, 148, 149
25–31	169	34:11–28	181	16	120, 121
25:21	175	34:11–36	162	16:2	102n32
25:22	120	34:28–30	182	16:13	119
25:23	120	34:30	162	16:14	119
32	26, 157, 161, 163,	34:30–31	181	16:14–17:12	
	164, 165, 168, 175,	34:35	182	[17:6–21 MT]	149
	177	35–39	183	16:32	120
32–33	52, 55, 122, 169	35–40	169	17	120, 121, 131
32:1	163, 166, 169	35:5	183	20:1	137, 148
32:1–6	165, 182	35:20–29	161	20:1–13	149
32:6	163, 178	35:21	183	20:5	149
32:7–18	166	35:21–35	190	25:6	102n32
32:8	167	35:29	183	26:10	120
32:10	166, 175, 181	36:3–7	183	26:59	137
32:10–13	188	39:43	183		
32:10–14	17	40	50, 52, 169	**Deuteronomy**	
32:11	169, 176	40:1–33	184	1:6	155
32:11–13	167	40:34–35	182	5:9–10	180
32:11–14	163, 190	40:34–38	53, 120, 184,	6:4	28
32:12	23, 166, 176		189	9	167–68, 169
32:13	176			9:18	168
32:15	163	**Leviticus**		9:21	168
32:17–18	175, 182	13–14	144	9:27–28	168
32:18	163	13:49	145	12–26	179
32:19–35	167	14:37	145	15:12	16n5
32:20	120, 167	19:34	162	25:1	99n28
32:21	120, 163, 164	23:42–43	155	25:9	145
32:24	163, 169	34:11–36	162	27–28	28
32:25–29	163			30:19	122
32:32	163	**Numbers**		33–34	157
32:35	120, 172	2–3	169	34:1	162
33	169	9:21	155	43:4–6	162
33:1	157	10:10	178		
33:2	163	11:15	102	**Joshua**	
33:3	173	12	137, 143–48, 145,	2:2	102n32
33:4–6	163, 173		186, 189, 190	**1 Samuel**	
33:7	155	12:1	143	2:21	97n21
		12:8	143		

INDEX OF SCRIPTURE

1 Samuel (*cont.*)
3:19 — 97n21
4:6 — 16n5
4:9 — 16n5
13:3 — 16n5
13:7 — 16n5
13:19 — 16n5
14:11 — 16n5
14:21 — 16n5
24:28 — 102n32
29:3 — 16n5

2 Samuel
7:14 — 96

1 Kings
8:23 — 99n28
12:26–30 — 164
17:1–6 — 129

2 Kings
10:16 — 102
17:16 — 164
22:20 — 102

1 Chronicles
5:29 — 137

Ezra
10:2 — 107n39
10:10 — 107n39
10:11 — 107n39
10:14 — 107n39
10:17 — 107n39
10:18 — 107n39
10:44 — 107n39

Nehemiah
9:2 — 107n39

Esther
8:6 — 102

Job
3:12 — 139–40

Psalms
2:7 — 96
22:2 — 87
106:19–23 — 168

Proverbs
23:27 — 107n39
24:24 — 99n28
27:2 — 107n39

Isaiah
15:6 — 145
19:6 — 130
35:1 — 121, 125n30
40:31 — 128
41:18 — 126
43:18–19 — 2
43:19 — 126
46:9 — 2
52:8 — 102
54:10 — 161
55:12 — 161
65:17 — 2

Jeremiah
20:9 — 167
29:32 — 102
34:9 — 16n5
34:14 — 16n5

Ezekiel
3:3 — 167
30:24 — 51n40

Hosea
11:1 — 24

Amos
9:7 — 23

Jonah
1:9 — 16n5

Micah
6:1–2 — 136

6:4 — 47–48, 134, 135, 136
6:6–8 — 136
7:9 — 102

New Testament

Matthew
4:8–10 — 165
17:4 — 163
17:20 — 160
21:21 — 160

Mark
5:21–43 — 40
8:22–24 — 146

Luke
9:33 — 163

John
4:12 — 147
4:15 — 147

Acts
2 — 131
7:23 — 97n21

1 Corinthians
13:12 — 183

Jude
1:9 — 163, 183

Revelation
21:5 — 2

Apocrypha

Jubilees
47:1 — 97n21
48:1 — 97n21

Index of Subjects

Aaron
  cluster narration and, 21
  golden calf and, 164, 167, 169–70, 183
  Miriam's leprosy and, 145
  Moses critique by, 143, 143n16, 144, 190
  resistance and, 47
  role in Exodus, 134
Abraham, 15, 161, 165
Achebe, Chinua, 83, 90, 171
adjunctive memory, 91–92
adoption, divine, 160
adoption story, 17, 92–96, 96n17, 97n21, 102n32, 103, 108. *See also* counter-adoption, of Moses; re-adoption story
Africa
  Bible in, 64–67
  death and decay, as place of, 29
  European relationship, 60–61
  future creation of, 158
  geography of, 123, 125–27
  liberation of, and Mountain, 157–60
  postcolonial liberation of, 157
African American women, 40, 45. *See also* women
Africana scholars, 29–30
Africana Bible, The (Page), 13
Afroecology, 111–12. *See also* environmental oppression
Afropolitanism, 157–60
AgroEcology Fund, 111
Akedah, 161
Albert, James. *See* Gronniosaw, Ukawsaw
alienation
  about, 2

by colonial governance, 83
  departure and, 82
  ecological, 153
  economies and, 56
  geopolitical, 188
  machine body and, 58–59
  of Miriam, 143–48, 153
  of Moses, 100, 105–7
  motherhood rescue from, 85
  Mountain and, 165–66, 189
  Pharaoh and, 16
  resistance to, 114, 151–52
  social, 162
  Ubuntu and, 33
  womanism on, 44–45
  See also triple consciousness *when referred to with* erasure *and* singularity
amnesia, 37–38, 56–57, 95
Amos, 23–25
anatomo-politics, 58–59
Ancient Laws and Contemporary Controversies (Anderson), 179
Anderson, Cheryl, 179
androcentrism. *See* patriarchy/androcentrism
anger, Yahweh as slow to, 181
Anglophones, African, 158
anticolonial movements, 35–36, 159. *See also* colonialism
anticolonial nationalism, 157–58
apartheid, 5, 8, 77–78
architectures, of slavery, 69, 78
arrivals, 157
autocratic regimes, womanism on, 51

baby carrying, 170–71

INDEX OF SUBJECTS

badass womanism, 187–88, 190–91
  about, 38–39, 42
  on alienation, 44–45
  androcentrism and, 47–48
  Circle of Concerned African Women Theologians, 40–45
  disposability and, 49–50
  on erasure, 45–46
  on midwives, 48–49
  Miriam as, 139, 142
  patriarchy and, 41–43
  redesigned futures and, 50–53
  on singularity, 43–44
  storytelling of, 43–44
  wilderness experience and, 39–40
  See also womanism; women
Balu, 25
beginnings, 36
belonging, 29. *See also* communal/communities
Bible
  African displacement and, 67
  Blackness absence in, 72–74
  in colonial Africa, 64–67
  scripturalization, 60–61
  theft of, 64–65
biblical interpretation
  Africana, about, 1n1, 29–30
  badass womanism and, 39, 43
  Black, 61, 74
  divination and, 44
  interpreter categories and, 61–62
  self-reflexive approach to, 60–61
biopolitics, 16, 58–61
birds, 127–29, 160
birth stools, 14–16, 52, 139
bitterness, 120–21
Black Lives Matter (BLM), 11, 128
Blackness, as solitary, 7–8
Blackness absence, in Bible, 72–74
blessings, African, 146
Blocher, Ewald, 124
Blount, Brian, 19, 33
bodies, carrying of, 170–74
body
  anatomo-politics of, 58–59
  missing, 165–66

Book of the Covenant, 161–62, 169, 179–80. *See also* law
bosadi, 117, 137
breath, 127–29
burning bush, 20, 29, 144, 144n18

Callahan, Allen Dwight, 30
Cameroon, 5n10, 31, 74–75, 127, 158–59, 191
Canaan, 26–27, 118, 130
castle, slave. *See* slave castle
changelings, 83–84, 90–92, 160, 187
childbearing, 41, 48–49, 90, 144, 190. *See also* motherhood
Circle of Concerned African Women Theologians (the Circle), 40–45
civil rights movement, 5
climate change, 115, 122–23
clothing, 173
clouds, 47, 121–22, 130–31, 141, 143–44, 146, 189
cluster hermeneutics, 48
cluster narration, 20–21
cohabitation, 76
colonialism
  adoption, 102
  Bible and, 64–67
  decolonial work and, 158
  desires as unmet and, 81–82
  by Europe, interwar period, 35
  geographic, 65–67, 77
  hope within, 49
  memory, 82
  movement against, 35–36
  patriarchy/androcentrism, 160
  Red Sea and, 141
  resistance, 100
  sovereignty, 75
  triple consciousness and, 73, 83
  violence, 82, 89
  water and, 147
Commentary on Exodus (Dozeman), 96–97
communal/communities
  belonging, 91
  bonding, 170–71
  ethnicity in, 99–101
  forced, 76

INDEX OF SUBJECTS

fragmented, 147
and hero relationships, 92 (*see also*
single-hero narration)
identities, 55–56, 84–85, 91–101,
108, 142, 147, 161 (*see also* Moses'
identity)
isolation, 185 (*see also* alienation)
loss of, 70–74
Moses and, 104
Mountain bottom (*see under* Mountain)
production of, 12
rebellion, 148
redesign of, 166
regeneration, 140
singularity and, 167
storytelling and, 43–44
survival of, 28, 82–84, 86, 88, 94, 122,
129, 131, 150
Tent of Meeting and, 183
and triple consciousness challenge,
83–84
wilderness experience and, 40
work, 116
Congo Basin, 126–27
conjunctive memory, 90
consciousness, forms of, 61–62
consciousness, triple. *See* triple
consciousness
consulting readers, 44
"The Contested Bible" (West), 67
coroners, ecological, 124, 124n25, 130
counter-adoption, of Moses, 99–101, 106,
108
Covenant, Book of the. *See* Book of the
Covenant
creation, Miriam's alienation and, 144,
146
creativity, 44–46, 55, 76–79. *See also*
futures, creation of
cries, 17, 51, 72, 94, 110, 129, 152
Critique of Black Reason (Mbembe), 81
cultural belonging, 113. *See also*
communal/communities
culture, popular, 36

Daughters of Anowa (Oduyoye), 41
Daughters of Dignity (Gill), 44–45

daughters of Jethro, 87, 107–8, 155–56
Day of Atonement, 164
death
life within, 56
of male children, by Pharaoh (*see* infant
death decree, Pharaoh's)
of Miriam, 137, 148–50
of Moses, 162–63
motherhood rescue from, 85
at Mountain bottom, 165, 169, 182,
186
politics and (*see* biopolitics;
necropolitics)
refusal of, 82, 91 (*see also* survival)
rituals and, 182
spiritual/social, 71
water and, 123–24, 124n25, 140–42,
149, 189 (*see also* infant death
decree, Pharaoh's; Red Sea; Nile,
River)
debts, colonial, 82
decolonial work, 82–83
deforestation, African, 112
deity, exodus. *See* Yahweh
departures, 6n13, 15, 33, 71, 82, 89, 152,
156–57, 175, 188. *See also* liberation
desert, 125–26. *See also* earth/land;
Wilderness
desires, unmet, 81–82, 84, 108
Deuteronomic Code, 179
diaspora, 5–6, 15, 62–63, 72, 88, 114–16,
119, 130. *See also* displacement
dictatorships, 76
disjunctive memory, 91
displacement, 15, 56–57, 62–68. *See also*
diaspora
disposability, women's response to, 48–50
Diversity Lottery (DV), 5
divination, 43–44
divine adoption, 160
diviner-healers, 44
doors of no return, 6, 6n13, 63–64, 68,
79, 133, 165–66
Douglass, Frederick, 61–62
dove, 128–29
Dozeman, Thomas, 96–97, 156
dreams/nightmares, 81–82, 84, 108

INDEX OF SUBJECTS

Du Bois, W. E. B, 18–20
Dube, Musa, 29, 43–44

eagles' wings, 50, 127–28, 160
Earth, kinship with, 135
earth/land, 28, 47, 118–19, 121–22, 125, 142, 151, 189
ecoautobiography, 118
eco-bio-communication theory, 117
ecology/ecological
  bodies, impact on, 133
  cloud and fire pillars as, 131
  coroners, 124, 124n25, 130
  crises, 115–16
  death, 139–43, 149
  destruction, 27–28, 51, 123–25, 129, 140
  Exodus, reading of (*see* environmental oppression)
  hermeneutics, 117
  identity, 130
  liberation, 15, 125, 148
  Miriam and, 143–45, 149–52
  oppression, 172
  plagues and, 119–22, 189 (*see also* plagues)
  postcolonialism and, 116
  regeneration and, 145
  survival, 116–17, 119, 122, 128–29, 141
  traumas of, 116
  trees and (*see* trees)
  Wilderness and, 58, 128, 132
  See also afroecology; environment/environmental
ecomemory, 118
economic hardships, 99, 99n27, 101–2
ecowomanism, 116, 138
Egypt
  about, 58, 185
  ethnicity in, 26
  in Exodus, 87
  Jewish reworking of, 24
  liberation and, 118–19, 175–78, 187
  loss of, 79
  as uninhabitable, 130
  Yahweh against, 177

Egyptian princess, 17, 27, 47, 94, 99n26, 102, 106, 109, 139
Ekwefi, 90
Éla, Jean-Marc, 31
Elmina Castle, 133
enlightenment, 70
enslavement, 49, 51, 56, 61–62, 69, 71–72, 78, 189
environmental oppression
  Exodus story, implications on, 115–19
  Green Belt Movement and, 112–14
  Moses' song and, 141–42
  plagues, 119–22
  survival of, 116–17, 119, 122
  water and, 120–21, 123–25, 140–41
environment/environmental
  conservation, 127
  environmentalists, 116
  ethics, 116–17
  Miriam's leprous body and, 145
  oppression (*see* environmental oppression)
  Red Sea and River Nile, importance of, 123–24, 130
  survival, 122
  trauma, 120
Equiano, Olaudah, 60–61
erasure, 187–89
  about, 2
  by colonial governance, 83
  communal response to, 94
  creative responses to, 55–56
  cultural, fig trees and, 113
  decolonial work of, 82
  of enslaved, 62
  generational, 167, 181, 190
  Miriam and, 144, 148–50, 153
  Mountain and, 167
  Pharaoh and, 16
  of Promised Land inhabitants, 181
  redesign and, 161
  Red Sea and, 151
  resistance to, 32, 82, 93, 188
  slave castle and, 68–69
  species body and, 58–59
  violence of, 76
  womanism on, 45–46

INDEX OF SUBJECTS

by Yahweh, 175
See also infant death decree, Pharaoh's;
triple consciousness when referred to
with alienation and singularity
Esposito, Roberto, 59
ethics, environmental, 116–17
ethnic profiling, 51
ethnicities, 26, 99–101. See also under
Moses' identity
ethnocentric oppression, 120, 139. See also
genocide
ethno-nationalism, 143
Europe, African relationship and, 60–61
exodus
as circular, slave ships and, 62–63
deity (see Yahweh)
environments, 120
paused, during Miriam's alienation, 144
poetics of, 150–52 (see also songs)
redesign (see redesign)
stories, 24
survival, 146–48
exodus-Exodus (motif-story), 24, 32–33,
37–38, 52, 83, 192
Exodus-exodus motif, 22–23, 27–30,
32–33
extraction politics, 126
Ezekiel, 167
Ezinma, 90–91

family structure, 40
farming, diverse, 111–12
feminism, 41. See also badass womanism;
womanism; women
fig trees, 113
fire, 42
fire, pillars of. See pillars of cloud and fire
First World War, 35–36
flow, river, 127
food insecurity, 51, 112, 121, 149
foreignness, 109
forgiveness, 168
Foucault, Michel, 58
founding violence, 75–76
free choice, 165
freedom, 26, 73. See also liberation
Fretheim, Terence, 178, 182

futures, creation of
African, 158
bodies carried into, 171
communal, 190
habitability of, 177–78
Miriam and, 145, 147, 153
Moses' song and, 142
Mountain and, 157
political vs ecological, 149
postcolonial communities and, 172
redesign and, 174 (see also under redesign)
scripturalization and, 61
in Wilderness, 137–38
futures, redesign of, 35, 50–53, 90, 93,
160–69, 175

GBM (Green Belt Movement), 112–14
gender, 26, 40, 48, 112, 117. See also
badass womanism; womanism;
women
genealogical narratives, 12, 84, 137, 167,
180–81, 190
genocide, 77–78, 95, 163. See also infant
death decree, Pharaoh's
geocultural insiders, 95
geography/geographic
of Africa, 123–27
alienation, 162, 184 (see also alienation)
colonialism and, 66–67, 77
gendered language and, 27
identities, 81, 105–7
memory and, intergenerational, 78
motherhood as, 89–90
rupture of, 63
song of Moses and, 141
See also diaspora; Egypt; Mountain;
Wilderness
geopolitics
communal work of, 32, 56–58, 188–89
Gershom and, 85, 88
as identifier, 27
imperialism and, 179
insiders, 95
Pharaoh and, 14, 130
of Red Sea and River Nile, 123
triple consciousness and, 29
of Yahweh and Pharaoh, 55

Gershom, 83–88, 98n24, 107, 187
gershomites
  about, 83–84
  community, 187, 191
  identity, in Exodus, 84–88
  identity construction, 92–96
  identity deconstruction, 96–99
  identity reconstruction, 99–101
  Mountain community and, 162
  subjectivity, 107
Ghana, 133
ghost towns, 75
gifts, Tabernacle and, 183
God. *See* Yahweh
God on the Mountain (Dozeman), 156
gods, 161, 177
gold, 161
golden calf
  Aaron and, 164, 169–70
  construction of, 182
  in Deuteronomy, 167–68
  idolatry and, 163–64
  as linking object, 174
  Moses' negotiations for survival and, 166–67
  narrative purpose of, 164–65
  narrative redesign and, 175
  political failure and, 120
  in Psalm, 168
  punishment for, from Moses, 167
Goshen, 141
"The Great Green Wall," 114
Green Belt Movement (GBM), 112–14
greening, of Miriam, 145–48
groaning, 51, 51n40
Gronniosaw, Ukawsaw, 70–74
guilt, colonial, 82
guns, 66

Hagar, 15, 85, 93, 93n16
Harare, 138
Harris, Kamala, 9n14
Harris, Melanie, 116, 118
Hebrews, vs Israelites, 16n5
heroes, 25. *See also* single-hero narration
Hilfrich, Carola, 164
holism, 90

homelands, 81
homeopathy, 30, 32, 73, 118
hope, 33, 49, 129, 186
Hosea, 23–24
human and non-human connection, 118, 135
Hurston, Zora Neale, 35–36, 38, 41

"I Can't Breathe" protests, 128, 186n1
identities
  African, 4, 158
  communal, 55, 108, 147, 153, 161
  construction, 92–96
  cultural, 113, 168
  deconstruction, 96–99
  diaspora and, 63, 115–16
  as disposable (*see* erasure)
  erasure resistance and, 56
  ethnicity and, 99–101
  formation, 13–14, 87, 90, 101
  geographical, 81, 108
  gershomite, 84–88
  law and, 179
  literature and, 69–70
  loss and, 173
  markers of, 101, 108
  political, 27
  reconstruction, 99–101
  social, 91
  See also Moses' identity
idolatry, 163–67, 177
illiteracy, 65
imaginaire, 78
imagination, 11–12, 122. *See also* futures, creation of; redesign
immigration, 5
imperialism
  communities and, 71
  decolonial work and, 158
  government failures and, 63
  law and, 179–80
  patronage, 72
  redesign of, 172
  singularity and, 57
inclusivity, in law, 179
infant death decree, Pharaoh's, 14–15, 17, 57, 79, 93–94, 96, 108, 139, 187

INDEX OF SUBJECTS

In Search of Our Mothers (Walker), 38
interwar period, 35
In the Wake (Sharpe), 49, 135
Isaiah, 145, 161
Ishmael, 15
isolation, Blackness as, 7–8
Israelites, vs Hebrews, 16n5
Israel's Poetry of Resistance: Africana Perspectives (Page, Jr.), 115

Jeremiah, 167
Jeroboam, 164
Jesus Christ, 146, 146n21, 147, 165
Jethro, 47, 87, 109, 155–56
Jethro's daughters, 87, 107–8, 155–56. *See also* Zipporah
Jochebed, 47, 86, 93–94, 139
Joseph, 18, 37, 188, 191
Joshua, 163, 175
Judah, 141
Judaism, 24, 86, 164
judicial authority, 104–5
justice work, 24–25, 45

Kadesh, 148–49
kanju, 46
Kanyoro, Musimbi R. A., 42–43
Kass, Leon, 165, 176
Kenya, 112–14
Killing in the Name of Identity (Volkan), 173
kin, of Moses, 99, 99n26, 101–2

land. *See* earth/land; Wilderness
law, 150, 152, 161, 168–69, 178–82. *See also* tablets, stone
Legends of the Jews, The (Ginzberg), 86
legitimizing violence, 75–76
leprosy, 143, 145
let my people go vs let my people live, 3, 32, 78–80, 186, 191–92
Levites, 169
liberation
　about, 3
　African, 64–67, 157–60
　afterlives of, 180
　communal work for, 86

ecological, 15, 125, 148
Egyptian, 118–19, 175–78, 187
as exodus work, 47
golden calf and, 170
Israel's, as generational, 155
law and, 178–82
Mountain and, 156–61, 174–78, 184, 187
oppression and, 192
pillars of cloud and fire and, 130–31
political, 11, 15, 56, 113, 125, 131, 148
power of, 33, 187
privilege and, 162
ritual space and, 182–84
singularizing, 33, 177
trauma and, 77–78
triple consciousness and, 15–16
from within, 95
Wilderness end, 39, 187
linking objects, 172–74, 184
literacy, 65
literature, identity and, 69–70
locusts, 126, 145
loss, 82, 173
love, 180–81

Maathai, Wangari, 112–14
machine body, 58–59
Mamdani, Mahmood, 77–78
man of power, 71
manna, 51, 121. *See also* food insecurity
Map to the Door of No Return, A (Brand), 63
marginalization
　Blacks and, 10–11
　Hurston on, 35
　inclusion and, 162
　law and, 179
　Miriam as, 140
　Moses and, 17
　nationalism and, 159
　paradoxically majority of, 179
　See also alienation
marriage, 143n16, 146n22, 147
Martin, Trayvon, 9–11
Mary/Miriam link, 134–35

INDEX OF SUBJECTS

Masenya, Madipoane, 44, 116–17, 137
Masowe Apostles, 138
Mbembe, Achille, 49, 55, 74–76, 81, 157–58, 174
McCain, LaVerne Gill, 44–45
meaning line, 19, 21, 33, 44, 56
Mecca pilgrimage, 26n22
memory/memories
  accountable, 77–78
  colonial, 82
  communal, 113–14
  earthy, 122
  ecological, 118
  Exodus and, 12
  future and, 38, 171–72
  history and literature and, 37
  "Mother is Supreme" and, 90
  narrative, 97–98, 102
  postcolonial, 90–91
  violent, 97–98
Midian, 26, 45n27, 84, 100, 106, 109, 118, 161
midwives, 16, 48–49, 55–56, 140
migration, 122–23, 138, 146–47
Miriam
  about, 133–35
  alienation of, 143–48, 153, 189–90
  androcentrism and, 47–48
  death and burial of, 137, 148–50
  erasure of, 144, 148–50, 153
  greening of, 145–48
  as marginalized, 140
  and Mary link, 134–35
  Moses and, 143, 143n16, 145, 153, 190
  as prophet, 138, 143
  resistance by, 47, 139–43
  roles of, 135, 152–53
  song of, 138, 142, 150–52, 175
  water and, 135–38, 140, 142, 189–90
  water rescue of Moses and, 17, 93–94, 96, 108
  as womanist leader, 138
miriamic secret, 134
Miriamic talkback, 48–49
missionaries, 66. *See also* colonialism
Moab, 145, 162

Mosala, Itumeleng, 31, 64
Moses
  adoption of, 92–96, 103
  age of, 97n21
  alienation of, 100, 105–7
  androcentrism and, 48
  authority of, 98n24, 104–5
  burning bush and, 20, 29, 144, 144n18
  children of, 107n40 (*see also* Gershom)
  counter-adoption of, 99–101
  death and burial of, 162–63, 183
  Egypt, return to, 175
  foreignness of, 109
  identity of (*see* Moses' identity)
  infant death decree and (*see* infant death decree, Pharaoh's)
  Israel relationship and, 97–99
  kin of, 99, 99n26, 101–2
  marginalization and, 17
  in Midian, 45n27
  Miriam and, 143, 143n16, 145, 153, 190
  Mountain and, 52, 157, 162, 165–66, 175, 177–78, 181, 189
  negotiation for survival by, 23, 163, 166–68, 188, 190
  privilege of, 94, 96, 102, 106
  prophetic authority of, 143
  re-adoption of, 106–8
  resistance and, 47
  seeing of, 101–4
  single-hero narration and, 25, 186
  survival of/triple placement of, 94
  tablets and (*see* tablets, stone)
  Tent of Meeting and, 52
  tradition, 98
  as veiled/unveiled, 162, 181–82
  violence by, 96–101, 103, 105–6, 163, 167
  water rescue of (*see* infant death decree, Pharaoh's)
  wives of, 143, 143n16 (*see also* Zipporah)
  Yahweh and, 20–21, 143–44, 148–49, 161, 163–67, 172, 176, 180–81
Moses, Man of the Mountain (Hurston), 35
Moses and Monotheism (Assmann), 164

INDEX OF SUBJECTS

Moses' identity
  as displaced, 84
  ethnic, 29, 84–85, 87, 94–95, 100–102, 105–9
  as fragmented, 105–6
  geographical, 107
  Gershom and, 83–85, 87
  names of, 86–87
  as ruler and judge, 98n24, 100
  as sojourner, 84, 107
"Mother is Supreme," 88–92
motherhood, 26–27, 41, 85, 89, 93, 93n16, 101, 170–71. *See also* childbearing
motherland, 89–90
Mountain
  African liberation and, 157–60
  alienation and, 165–66, 189
  bottom community of, 122, 156, 165, 169, 179–80, 182–84, 186, 192 (*see also* golden calf)
  death at bottom of, 165, 169, 182, 186
  erasure and, 167
  futures, creation of, 157
  liberation and, 156–61, 174–78, 184, 187
  Moses and (*see under* Moses)
  power and, 121–22, 162
  redesign/rupture of, 161–67, 171, 177
  "seeing" and, 160
  singularity of, 166–67
  as structure and sovereignty, 122
  survival, 167
  triple consciousness and, 52
  Yahweh and (*see under* Yahweh)
mourning, 173
Munmorah, Isabel, 138
multiplicity
  in Africana hermeneutics, 21–22
  colonialism and, 83, 158
  community and, 9, 15, 158, 161, 175
  of exodus lands, 119, 176
  future and, 187
  Hebrew life and, 16
  liberation, holistic and, 187
  matriarchal, 26–27
  Miriam story and, 140

redesign/rupture and, 167
tree planting and, 114
murmuring, 131–32, 152

names, 134–35
narration, cluster, 20–21
narrative cosmology, 26, 26n22
narrative memory, 97–98, 102
nationalism, 81, 120, 157–59
necroecology, 16, 139–43
necropolitics, 16, 31, 43, 49, 51, 55, 75, 174
Negritude movement, 8
Never Stop Breathing, 128
Ngong, David, 158
Niang, Aliou, 29, 115, 189–90
nightmares/dreams, 81–82, 84, 108
Nile, River, 57, 57n2, 123–24, 130, 136, 139. *See also* infant death decree, Pharaoh's
Noah's ark, 128–29
North America, African American women in, 40, 45

Obama, Barack, 9–11
Oduyoye, Mercy Amba, 40–42, 45
offerings/sacrifices, 161, 178, 182
ogbanje, 83–84, 90–92, 160, 187
Okonkwo, 88–92, 171
olive tree, 129
Olson, Dennis, 91, 105, 179–80
oppression
  Black Lives Matter and, 23, 128
  earth and, 121–22
  environmental (*see* environmental oppression)
  ethnocentric, 77–78, 95, 163
  human-earth/land relationship, 118–19
  law and, 179
  liberation and, 192
  Moses' song and, 141–42
  plagues and, 120
  redesign and, 124
  resistance to, 18, 105
  River Nile and, 130
  systems of, redesign, 176
  transformation from, 185

214   INDEX OF SUBJECTS

oppression (*cont.*)
  trauma and, 116
  water and, 121
  womanism and, 116–17
organic farming, 111
Other Ways of Reading (Dube), 43–44
Out of the Dark Night (Mbembe), 157–58
oxygen, production of, 127–28

Page, Hugh R., Jr., 13, 115
Passover, 2, 51, 93, 141
patriarchy/androcentrism
  biblical and textual readings, 117
  the Circle on, 42–43
  colonial, 160
  decolonial work on, 158
  hope within, 49
  matriarchy and, 89
  Miriam and, 47–48
  Moses and, 48
  of Okonkwo, 88
  patronage, 72
  singularity and, 57
  womanism on, 41–43, 47–48
People Could Fly, The (Hamilton), 128
Pharaoh
  amnesia of, 37–38, 56–57, 95
  groaning of, 51n40
  infant death decree of (*see* infant death
    decree, Pharaoh's)
  on Israelites, 14
  Moses' violent act and, 106
  necropolitics and (*see* necropolitics)
  negotiation with Moses, 99n27
  plagues and, 118 (*see also* plagues)
  political behavior of, 121
  power of, as old, 178–79
  as singularizing, 101
  war and, 129
  Yahweh and, 118, 123
pillars of cloud and fire, 47, 121–22,
  130–31, 141
Pillars of Cloud and Fire (Marbury), 130
plagues, 27, 119–23, 126, 140, 145, 172
Poetics of Postcolonial Biblical Criticism, A
  (Niang), 30, 115
politics/political

authority, of Moses, 104–5
biopolitics (*see* biopolitics)
creative vs destructive, 77–78
futures, 149
identities, 27
liberation, 11, 15, 56, 113, 125, 131,
  148
outcry, 47
Pharaoh and, 121
power, Bible as cypher for, 64–65
power, guns and, 66
power, literacy as legitimization of, 65
singularity and, 103
See also necropolitics
pollution, 140–42, 147
polyphony, 30, 65, 178
pop culture, 36
postapartheid, in South Africa, 77–78
Postcolonial Feminist Interpretation (Dube),
  29
postcolonialism
  African liberation and, 157–60
  Cameroon and, 74–75
  communal redesign of, 166, 172
  as ecological and political, 116
  Egypt, journey to, 188
  memory, African, 90–91
  in Rwanda, 77–78
  South Africa and, 77–78
  violence manifestations and, 75–76
post-nationalist nationalism, 158–59
power
  Africana infrastructures of, 60
  Bible as cypher for political, 64–65
  biblical interpretation and, 60–61
  divine, 152
  gender and, 48
  guns and, 66
  liberation and, 33, 187
  literacy as legitimization of, 65
  man of, 71
  Mountain and, 121–22, 162
  Pharaoh's vs Yahweh's, 178–79
  postcolonial, 74–78
  singularizing, 167
privilege, 81–82, 94, 96, 102, 106, 161–
  62, 190

INDEX OF SUBJECTS

promised land, 79, 119, 136, 148–49,
 156–57, 181
prophet, Miriam as, 138
Propp, William, 25, 97
public identity, Moses, 17, 93–95, 100,
 108, 139

racism, 8, 19, 68–70, 126, 143n16, 158,
 160
Ramsar Convention, 127
raven, 128–29
re-adoption story, 106–8
redesign
 communal, 166, 172
 erasure and, 161
 exodus, 160, 175
 futures, 35, 50–53, 90, 93, 160–69,
  175
 of imperialism, 172
 of Mountain, 161–67, 171, 177
 of oppression, 185, 187
 and rupture, of Mountain, 162–69
 triple consciousness and, 191–92
 womanism and, 50–53
Red Sea
 battle at, 140–41
 crises in Kadesh and, 149
 as ecological coroner, 123
 erasure and, 151
 importance of, 57, 123–24, 130
 Miriam and, 136
 oppression and, 124
 return to, 148–50, 153
 Yahweh at, 141
refugee camps, 173
regeneration, 140
relocation. *See* diaspora
rememory, 37
reproduction, 57
rescue, 56, 85. *See also under* water
residence time, 50, 136, 140
residency, around water, 142, 151
resilience, 138
resistance
 from within, 95
 of alienation, 114, 151–52
 Black Lives Matter protests, 128

of colonial ideologies/systems, 100
of erasure, 32, 82, 93, 188
Exodus characters and, 48
imperialism, 172
of infant death decree, Pharaoh's,
 55–56, 93
kinships and, 48
literature as, 70
of oppression, 18, 105
pillars of clouds and fire, 47
privilege, 161–62
racism, systemic, 128
of singularity, 57, 152
tree planting as, 113–14
wilderness experience and, 40
wind and, 127–28
by womanists, 41
restoration, communal, 65
rising of, 40, 49, 52, 127, 156, 166, 175.
 See also resistance
rituals/ritual spaces, 25, 182–84
rocks, water from, 148–49, 189
runagates, as interpreters, 62
Rwanda, 77–78

sacrifices/offerings, 161, 178, 182
Sahara Dessert, 125–26
Samaritan woman at the well, 146–47
Sarah (wife of Abraham), 15
sass, womanist, 46
satellite states, 158, 160
scholars, Africana, 29–30
scripturalization, 60–61
secret, miriamic, 134
seeing
 language, 101–4, 101n30
 at Mountain, 160–62
 of Yahweh, 172
shame, 145
Sharpe, Christina, 49, 67–68, 135
shawls, 170–71
Shembe, Isaiah, 64–65
ship, slave, 62–68, 135
shootings, of Blacks, 9–11, 128
sign usage, cultural, 164–65
Sinai, Mount. *See* Mountain
Sinai Complex, 156

216 INDEX OF SUBJECTS

single-hero narration
  communities and, 15, 52, 94
  Gershom and, 87–88
  Gressmann on, 92
  Miriam and, 152–53
  Moses as, 17, 25, 58, 100–101, 177,
    186
  Okonkwo as, 89, 91
  womanism and, 190
singularity, 190
  about, 2
  of author/author's son, 6
  body as, 59
  colonial, 73, 83
  community and, 167
  as consciousness, 57
  liberation and, 33, 177
  marginalization and, 17
  Miriam and, 140, 144
  Mountain and, 166–67, 175–76
  political, 103
  resistance of, 57–58, 152
  violence, 76
  womanism on, 41, 43–44
  See also triple consciousness when
    referred to with erasure and alienation
sister, Miriam as, 152
Sisters in the Wilderness (Williams), 39
slave castle, 8, 68–74, 133–34
slave labor. See enslavement
slave ships, 62–68, 135
slave trade, 6, 62–68
slavery. See enslavement
slow violence, 186, 186n1
Smith, Mitzi, 46, 146–47
social identity, 91
songs, 138, 140–42, 150–52, 175, 189
souls, 19–20, 61
Souls of Black Folk (Du Bois), 19
South Africa, 77–78
sovereignty, 49–50, 57, 68, 73, 75–76,
    122, 159, 174
spaces
  meanings of, 69
  sacred, 183–84
species body, 58–59
spit, 145–46, 146n21

staff, of Moses, 121, 123, 126, 140, 143,
    144n18, 149, 151
statutes. See law
stillborn baby, Miriam as, 144
Stolen Bible, The (West), 64
stone tablets. See tablets, stone
storytelling, 43–44, 70
strongmen, 76, 82, 103–4, 166, 172, 190
survival
  communal (see under communal/
    communities)
  cultural, 146
  ecological, 116–17, 119, 122, 128–29,
    141
  of environmental destruction, 122
  exodus, 146–48
  Green Belt Movement and, 112–13
  infant death decree and, 104n36
  Moses and, 94, 190
  Moses' negotiations for, 23, 163, 166–
    68, 188, 190
  through motherhood, 85, 89
  Mountain, 167
  Noah's ark and, 128–29
  of oppression (see oppression)
  religion and, 28
  of self, 82

Tabernacle, 52, 161, 169, 174, 182–83,
    190
tablets, stone, 167–68, 174–75, 178–81.
    See also law
Talitha Cum ("Little girl, I say wake up"),
    40–41
Talking Book, The (Callahan), 30, 70,
    72–73
Tangwa, Godfrey, 117
Ten Commandments, 169, 180. See also
    law
Tent of Meeting, 52, 183
theft, of Bible, 64–65
Things Fall Apart (Achebe), 83, 88, 171
time-space, African, 66–67
tradition, loss of, 113
trauma, 28, 33, 37, 116, 120, 173–74,
    178, 186. See also environmental
    oppression

INDEX OF SUBJECTS

trees, 112–14, 129, 145–46, 151–52
triple consciousness
  about, 2–3
  Africana hermeneutics and, 186
  badass womanism and, 38, 43
  biblical absence of Blackness and, 72–73
  biopolitics and, 58–59
  colonial memory and, 82
  forms of, 61–62
  geography of, 185
  as governance survival techniques, 83
  law and, 178–79
  layers of, 55–58
  liberation and, 15–16
  Miriam and, 144
  Mountain and, 52
  political outcry against, 47
  redesign and, 191–92
  resistance of (*see under* resistance)
  slave castle and (*see* slave castle)
  slave ship and (*see* slave ships)
  tasks of, 59
  See also alienation; erasure; singularity
Trump, Donald, 29
Truth and Reconciliation Commission, 32
Tutu, Desmond, 32

Ubuntu, 8, 32–33
un/inhabitability, 130, 177–78
unknown, 165–66
urban development, 127

veiling/unveiling of Moses, 162, 181–82
violence
  colonial, 82, 89
  deconstruction by, 103
  escape from, 160
  ethnic, 99, 102–3, 108
  forms of, 75–76
  identity and, 58
  justification of, 25
  memory and, 97–98
  by Moses, 96–101, 103, 105–6, 163, 167
  "Mother is Supreme" and, 88
  necropolitics and, 174

patriarchal, 89
political authority and, 103
postcolonial, 75
of slave trade, 69
slow, 186, 186n1
See also genocide
voice, Black literary, 70
Volkan, Vamik, 173

Walker, Alice, 38, 41
war, 14, 18–19, 35, 58, 75, 121, 129
water
  absence of, 112, 148–49
  as character, 47, 120–21
  colonialism and, 147
  communal survival and, 150
  death and, 123–24, 124n25, 140–42, 149, 189 (*see also* infant death decree, Pharaoh's)
  devastation surrounding, 140
  environmental distress of, 120–21, 123–25
  ethnic and racial vs of the Nile and Red Sea, 57
  as flow, 147
  importance of, in Exodus, 129–30
  life-giving, 147, 151
  Miriam and, 135–38, 140, 142, 189–90
  as residence for Black bodies, 135–36
  residency around, 142, 151
  River Nile (*see* Nile, River)
  from rocks, 148–49, 189
  transition from, to land, 125, 142, 151, 189
Watts, James, 169
waves metaphor, 39
Well of Miriam, 134
West, Gerald, 3, 64, 66–67
wetlands, 127
White Men's Magic (Wimbush), 60
Wilderness
  ecology and, 58, 128, 132
  future creation and, 137–38
  liberation and, 39, 187
  Miriam and, 137, 146
  patriarchy/autocracy in, 51

INDEX OF SUBJECTS

Wilderness (*cont.*)
 political/environmental trauma and,
  120–21
 Red Sea and, 151
 transition to, from water, 125
 womanism and, 39–40
 Yahweh in, 142
Williams, Delores, 39–40
Wimbush, Vincent, 60–62, 66
wind, 127–28
womanism, 38–39, 116–17, 138, 152. *See
 also* badass womanism; women
women
 African American, in North America,
  40, 45
 biblical, Miriam and, 134, 150, 152
 creativity of, 39
 as cultural identity custodians, 113
 Egyptian, 48, 50
 empowerment of, 114
 Hebrew, 38, 48–51
 Kenyan, 112–14
 Miriam (*see* Miriam)
 "Mother is Supreme," 88–92
 necropolitics and, 43, 51
 theologians, 40–45
 wilderness experience and, 40
work, decolonial, 82–83
World War I, 35–36
writers, Black, 69–70

Yahweh
 anger, as slow to, 181
 breath and, 127
 Egypt and, 177
 exodus community and, 162
 geopolitics and, 55
 as heroic character, 25
 Israelites and, 178
 Judah and, 141
 on Miriam, 137
 Moses and (*see under* Moses)
 Mountain and, 156, 171
 Mountain bottom community and, 192
 non-gendered care of, 117
 Pharaoh and, 118, 123
 pillars of clouds and fires and, 122
 power of, vs Pharaoh's, 178–79
 on prophets, 143
 at Red Sea, 141
 seeing of, 172
 threat of, to destroy exodus community,
  148
 in wilderness, 142
 wrath of, 164, 172–73
yaraq, 145

Zakovitch, Yair, 164
Zipporah, 83, 98n24, 119, 143n16, 156,
  165, 176

Printed in the USA
CPSIA information can be obtained
at www.ICGtesting.com
JSHW020139300124
56070JS00004B/24